STUDY GUIDE TO ACCOMPANY
LIBERTY, EQUALITY, POWER
A HISTORY OF THE AMERICAN PEOPLE
THIRD EDITION

VOLUME I: TO 1877

John M. Murrin
Paul E. Johnson
James M. McPherson
Gary Gerstle
Emily S. Rosenberg
Norman L. Rosenberg

Prepared by
Mary Jane McDaniel
University of North Alabama

WADSWORTH

THOMSON LEARNING ™

Australia   Canada   Mexico   Singapore   Spain   United Kingdom   United States

0-15-506050-3

Cover Credit: *North American Medicine Pipe Stem Dance* by Paul Kane (1810–71). Bridgeman Art Library/SuperStock.

For more information about our products, contact us at:
Thomson Learning Academic Resource Center
1-800-423-0563

For permission to use material from this text, contact us by:
Phone: 1-800-730-2214
Fax: 1-800-730-2215
Web: www.thomsonrights.com

Asia
Thomson Learning
60 Albert Complex, #15-01
Albert Complex
Singapore 189969

Australia
Nelson Thomson Learning
102 Dodds Street
South Melbourne, Victoria 3205
Australia

Canada
Nelson Thomson Learning
1120 Birchmount Road
Toronto, Ontario M1K 5G4
Canada

Europe/Middle East/South Africa
Thomson Learning
Berkshire House
168-173 High Holborn
London WC1 V7AA
United Kingdom

Latin America
Thomson Learning
Seneca, 53
Colonia Polanco
11560 Mexico D.F.
Mexico

Spain
Paraninfo Thomson Learning
Calle/Magallanes, 25
28015 Madrid, Spain

PREFACE

Liberty, equality, and power are themes that have been interwoven throughout the events in American history The relative position of these concepts varies considerably over the centuries, with many ups and downs and forward and backward steps. If, however, a student follows American history from the earliest times to the present, he or she should be able to see a growth of liberty, equality, and empowerment for both individuals and groups of people. Despite the fact that American society still has a way to go in these matters, students should realize that this transformation is an ongoing process that they can carry forward during their lifetime.

This Study Guide is designed to help students in their study of American history and to complement, but not replace, the basic textbook. The chapters correspond with those in the text regarding material covered and the basic emphasis. Each chapter relates to the overall theme of liberty, equality, and power. It is followed by a basic chronology of the important events covered in each chapter, which gives the student a better sense of the span of time involved. A number of very different activities could have happened at the same time in history.

The glossary of important terms permits the student an opportunity to master key terms and concepts covered by the text chapter. The basic definitions deal with the terms as they were used in the period covered, but some attempt was made to develop definitions that also could be useful to the student today.

The Who? What? Where? Sections should help students develop a sense of the important people, places, and events of the period. The multiple-choice questions test basic knowledge gained by a thorough study of the chapter. Students should also learn to evaluate maps, charts, and illustrations. Many of the questions dealing with these seem minor, but they are designed to encourage careful study of the visual material offered in the text.

Essay question responses develop writing, organizational, and analytical ability. They also encourage a broad overall view of events of the American past. Most of all, they are designed to encourage students to think, compare, and understand the significant events of each time period. Hopefully, some comparison can be made with modern times and the reality of life today. The What If? section, added to each chapter, encourages students to identify with groups and individuals in American history. It should help them to understand important decisions of the past.

Many people supported me in this work, especially my friends in the Department of History and Political Science at the University of North Alabama. Students in some of my classes were exposed to many of the questions and ideas developed in this Study Guide. Special thanks to Amy Calvert and Laura Watson, who typed the revisions for the third edition. I appreciate their work and encouragement very much.

Mary Jane McDaniel
University of North Alabama

CONTENTS

CHAPTER 1

WHEN OLD WORLDS COLLIDE: CONTACT, CONQUEST, CATASTROPHE

All of North and South America was settled by immigrants. Before Christopher Columbus sailed in 1492, five waves of immigrants swept over the Americas. Three came from Asia; the fourth, the Polynesians from the Pacific islands, may have just brushed the Americas; and the fifth, the Norse from northern Europe, decided not to stay. The three from Asia drifted in over Beringia as small bands during the ice ages. Gradually they spread over both North and South America as primitive hunters. With the extinction of the game animals, most of these people gradually evolved into agricultural societies. Over thousands of years these people that Europeans called Indians developed increasingly complex and distinctive cultures.

By the fifteenth century, Europe was recovering from the traumatic late Middle Ages. Although population continued to decline, people were more prosperous. Technology and interest in learning were revived with the Renaissance. Contacts with the Mediterranean and Arab worlds were multiplying. Portugal, at the crossroads of the Atlantic and Mediterranean, concentrated primarily on Africa, the slave trade, and Asia. Spain expanded westward across the Atlantic Ocean, first with the voyages of Columbus and then by other explorers.

In less than a century, navigators representing Portugal and Spain joined together societies that had lived in isolation for thousands of years. Europe, Asia, Africa, and many parts of the Americas came into violent contact with one another. Europeans conquered the Americans with military technology, aggressiveness, and diseases. By 1600, the first global economy in the history of mankind had been created. Also, the greatest known catastrophe that human societies had ever known had taken place. The Indian population was decimated and African regions seriously damaged with the export of slaves to the New World.

LIBERTY, EQUALITY, POWER

The stratified, complex cultures of the Indians were not noted for equality or liberty. Ruling classes had tremendous power over the people. In some cases, this structure led to human sacrifice by such groups as the Aztecs. When the Portuguese and Spanish expanded overseas, they had no respect for nor understanding of the new cultures they found. They used their power to introduce slavery, both of Indians and Africans. Improved military and maritime technology allowed them to conquer major portions of the world. Their plants, animals, and diseases continued the destruction. This was one of the rawest demonstrations of power in the history of mankind.

OBJECTIVES

After studying this chapter, a student should be able to

1. Trace the pre-Columbian civilizations in North and South America.

2. Describe the advantages of Europe for exploration and colonization.

3. Trace the early use of slavery and the origins of the African slave trade.

4. Compare Portugal and Spain in their basic techniques and motives in exploration and colonization.

5. Describe the role of agriculture in the development of Indian civilization.

6. Discuss the cultural differences between the Europeans and Indians and why they created misunderstandings.

7. Analyze the motives and success of the early Spanish missionaries.

8. Explore the biological and technological effects of long-term isolation on the Americas.

CHRONOLOGY

50,000 B.C.	A land bridge emerged across the Bering Strait between Siberia and Alaska. The exposed area, referred to as Beringia, was dry land on which plants, animals, and humans could live.
23,000 B.C.	This was the second time the sea level dropped enough to expose Beringia and to allow small bands of people to migrate from Asia to North America.
9000 B.C.	The superior Clovis spear point appeared in the New Mexico-Texas area. Within a thousand years it was in use nearly everywhere in North and South America.
8000 B.C.	Migrating bands of people reached all the way to Tierra del Fuego off the southern tip of South America.
7000 B.C.	The last of the Asian migrations took place.
5000 B.C.	The Red Paint People, or Maritime Archaic, emerged along the northeast coast of North America. They were noted for sword fishing and, probably, whaling. Their burial mounds are the oldest found in America.
4000 B.C.	Agriculture transformed Indian life in most parts of North and South America.
3400–700 B.C.	The oldest mound-building cultures appeared among preagricultural people in Louisiana at Watson Break. Early mound builders also flourished at Poverty Point, Louisiana.
3000–2100 B.C.	Monumental architecture and urbanization began in the Andes, and organized communities appeared along the Peruvian coast and in the interior.

1600 B.C.	Polynesians from near the coast of Southeast Asia moved out into the Pacific and, over the next 2000 years, settled hundreds of islands scattered across more than thirty million square miles of ocean.
1500 B.C.	The first of three "mound-building" societies emerged near the Ohio and Mississippi Rivers. Named for the distinctive earthen mounds they constructed, these cultures flourished until A.D. 1700.
1200 B.C.	The Olmecs, parent culture of Mesoamerica, appeared along the Gulf Coast.
1200–900 B.C.	The oldest culture of Mesoamerica, San Lorenzo, flourished until it was conquered by invaders.
1100 B.C.	Olmec influence prospered during the domination of La Venta, which became an urban center around 1100 B.C., reached its peak three hundred years later, and then declined between 500 and 400 B.C.
50 B.C.	The earliest Mayan writings date to 50 B.C. However, beginning around A.D. 300, Mayans began recording their history in considerable detail.
A.D. 300	Polynesians colonized Easter Island.
	The Mochica culture emerged on the northwest coast of Peru. This culture produced finely detailed pottery and built pyramids as centers of worship.
A.D. 874	The Vikings occupied Iceland. In 982–983, Erik the Red led his Norse followers to a permanent settlement in Greenland.
900–1250	The city of Cahokia flourished near present-day St. Louis. At its peak it may have had a population of 30,000, making it the largest city north of Mexico.
900	The postclassic era of Mayan culture witnessed a kind of renaissance in the northern lowlands of the Yucatán.
1000	The final pre-Columbian phase of Inuit culture extended for the next 700 years.
1001	Leif, son of Erik the Red, sailed west from Greenland and began to explore the coast of North America. In 1014, he made his last voyage and established the colony of Vinland on the northern coast of Newfoundland.
1200	The Toltecs, a fierce warrior people, controlled the Valley of Mexico for almost three centuries before they declined in 1200.
1271	Marco Polo, a Venetian merchant, reached the Chinese court and served emperor Kublai Khan for the next 20 years. His journals were later published in Europe and created much interest in Asia.
1300	Europe's population grew to 100 million. However, after 1300, Europe's farms could not sustain further growth and years of famine resulted. In the

1340s, the Black Death (bubonic plague) struck the people of Europe, who were already struggling with a famine, and reduced the population by more than a third. Recurring bouts of the plague kept European populations low until about 1500, when vigorous growth resumed.

1400	The Incas emerged as the dominant power in the Andes. In the next hundred years, the Inca empire came to rule approximately eight to twelve million people. No other nonliterate culture has come close to matching that accomplishment.
1405–1434	Cheng Ho, a Chinese explorer and trader, led six large fleets from China to the East Indies and the coast of Africa. After his death, China turned inward and became a totally self-contained economic and political system.
1418	As the fifteenth century advanced, Portuguese vessels sailed farther along the African coast. By 1418, the Portuguese began to settle the Madeira Islands and explored the Azores between 1427 and 1450, the Cape Verde group in the 1450s, and São Tomé in 1470.
1420	Prince Henry of Portugal became head of the Order of Christ and used its revenues to sponsor voyages along the African coast.
1430s	Johann Gutenberg invented the printing press and movable type. This revolution in communications allowed information to be circulated more rapidly and efficiently.
1434	One of Prince Henry's captains, Gil Eannes, sailed west into the Atlantic, beyond the sight of land, and successfully returned to Europe.
1448	The Portuguese built their first African fort on Arguin Island near Cape Blanco. After this the slave trade assumed its classical form as the Portuguese established small posts, or "factories," along the coast or on small offshore islands.
1453	Constantinople was conquered by Ottoman Turks, who proceeded to take over the Balkans.
1469	Prince Ferdinand of Aragon married Princess Isabella of Castile and, after they inherited their respective thrones, they formed the modern kingdom of Spain.
1487	Bartolomeu Días succeeded in reaching the southern tip of Africa and headed east toward the Indian Ocean, but his crew rebelled and forced him to turn back.
1492	Christopher Columbus sailed west from Spain and crossed the Atlantic Ocean, landing in San Salvador, now Watling Island. He returned in 1493 and made three other voyages in search of China. He was a poor administrator and was never really trusted by the Spanish. Returned to Spain in chains in 1500, he died in 1506, a bitter and disappointed man.

1497   Vasco da Gama of Portugal succeeded in leading a small fleet around the Cape of Good Hope and on to the Malibar Coast of southwestern India. In a voyage that lasted more than two years (1497–1499), da Gama bargained and fought for spices that brought profits of 20 to 1.

1500   Portuguese sailor Pedro Alvares Cabral accidentally located Brazil when he was blown off course.

1513   Vasco Núñez de Balboa became the first European to reach the Pacific Ocean after crossing the Isthmus of Panama.

1514   Spaniards introduced European livestock in the Caribbean, where the beasts ate everything in sight. This led to increasing malnutrition for the Indians. Nevertheless, the Spaniards forced the malnourished Indians to work for them and, even before the onset of contagious diseases, the Indian population declined throughout the Caribbean. By 1514 only 22,000 (out of approximately one million) able-bodied adults remained on Hispaniola. This scenario was soon repeated in Cuba, Jamaica, and other islands.

1519   Hernán Cortés landed at a place he named Vera Cruz and succeeded in finding the Aztec capital of Tenochtitlán in the Valley of Mexico. Although driven out, the Spaniards left behind the smallpox virus that soon killed thousands of Aztecs. The next year, with the aid of the Tlaxcalan Indians, Cortés destroyed the Aztec capital.

1519–1522   Ferdinand Magellan, a Portuguese captain serving the king of Spain, sailed around the world between 1519 and 1522. Magellan never completed the voyage, as he was killed in the Philippines.

1531–1532   Francisco Pizarro located the Inca Empire high in the Andes Mountains.

1536   Alvar Núñez Cabeza de Vaca journeyed from Florida through Texas and into northern Mexico and arrived in what is now Mexico City. In a published brief of his adventures, Cabeza de Vaca made a single reference to Indian tales of great and populous cities, and this claim soon became magnified into stories about "golden cities."

1539   Hernando de Soto landed in Florida and traveled through the southeastern United States in search of "cities of gold."

1542   Francisco Vasquez de Coronado returned to Mexico after exploring the Southwest in a search for cities of gold.

1550   In the fifteenth century, as the Portuguese advanced steadily southward along the coast, their factories began to pull trade away from the Sahara caravans. This change further weakened the West African empire of Mali and other interior states, and the empire fell apart by 1550.

1556–1598   The reign of Spain's King Phillip II stretched over four decades. During this time, he commanded the largest army in Europe, held the Ottoman Turks in check in the Mediterranean, and tried to suppress the Protestant Reformation.

| 1573 | Phillip II of Spain issued the Royal Orders for New Discoveries, which made it illegal to attack or enslave Indians. |
| 1630 | There were 86,000 Indians in New Mexico who had accepted baptism. By mid-century there were 26,000 baptized Indians in Florida. |

GLOSSARY OF IMPORTANT TERMS

Amerind	The forerunner of the vast majority of Indian languages in the Americas.
astrolabe	A device that permitted accurate calculation of latitude or distances north and south.
bandeirantes	Brazilian frontiersmen who traveled deep into South America to enslave Indians. The slaves then were worked to death on the sugar plantations.
Beringia	A land bridge across the Bering Strait between Siberia and Alaska. It was once an area where plants, animals, and humans could live.
caravel	A new type of oceangoing vessel that could travel from three to twelve knots per hour.
chinampas	The highly productive gardens built on Lake Taxcoco by the Aztecs.
Clovis tip	A superior spear point developed before 9000 B.C. It was in use nearly everywhere in North and South America and produced such an improvement in hunting ability that it contributed to overhunting.
conquistadores	The Spanish word for conquerors.
encomienda	A system of labor introduced into the Western Hemisphere by the Spanish. This permitted the holder, or *encomendero*, to claim labor from Indians in a district for a stated period of time.
factories	A term used to describe small posts established for the early slave trade along the coast of Africa or on the small offshore islands.
hacienda	Large estate established by the Spanish.
hidalgos	The minor nobility of Spain. Often they possessed little wealth and were interested in improving their position through the overseas empire.
lateen	A triangular sail borrowed from the Arabs by the Portuguese.
maritime	Of or relating to the sea.
matrilineal	A society that determines inheritance and roles in life based on the female or maternal line.
Mesoamerica	An area embracing Central and South America.
millennium	The period at the end of history when Christ is expected to return and rule with his saints for a thousand years.

monotheistic   The belief that there is only one God or deity.

neolithic   The period known also as the late Stone Age. Agriculture developed, and stone, rather than metal, tools were used.

prehistoric   A civilization that has no written past. Study of such societies is based on the investigation of their artifacts rather than on written documents. Historic cultures can be examined through their written records.

sedentary   Societies that are rooted locally or are nonmigratory. Semisedentary societies are migratory for part of the year.

serfdom   Early medieval Europe's predominant labor system that tied peasants to their lords and the land. They were not slaves because they could not be sold from the land.

slash and burn   A system of agriculture in which trees were cut down, girded, or in some way destroyed. The underbrush then was burned and a crop was planted. This method helped develop separate gender roles among Indians. Men created the farms and women managed the farming. The system eventually depleted the fertility of the soil, and the entire tribe would move to a new area in a few years.

staple crop   A crop grown for commercial sale. It usually was produced in a colonial area and was sold in Europe. The first staple crop was sugar.

stratified societies   Societies divided into separate social classes or different levels of status.

Tierra del Fuego   The region at the southern tip of South America.

WHO? WHAT? WHERE?

WHO WERE THEY?

Complete each statement below (questions 1–13) by writing the letter preceding the appropriate name in the space provided. Use each answer only once.

    a. Christopher Columbus
    b. Ferdinand Magellan
    c. Francisco Pizarro
    d. Freydis
    e. Inuits
    f. Johann Gutenberg
    g. Juan Ponce de León
    h. Olmecs
    i. Pedro Alvares Cabral
    j. Prester John
    k. Phillip II
    l. Prince Henry
    m. Vasco da Gama

_____ 1. First European woman known to North American history.

_____ 2. Inventor of the printing press and movable type.

_____ 3. Last Indian group to arrive in America and the first to encounter Europeans.

_____ 4. Mythical Christian king who lived somewhere in Africa.

_____ 5. Head of the Order of Christ, who used its revenues to sponsor voyages along the African coast.

_____ 6. Commander of the first Portuguese fleet to reach India.

_____ 7. Accidental discoverer of Brazil for Portugal.

_____ 8. Sea captain who underestimated the circumference of the earth by 10,000 miles.

_____ 9. Spanish commander who tramped through Florida in quest of a legendary fountain of youth.

_____ 10. Leader of the first fleet to sail around the world, he died before the voyage was completed.

_____ 11. Builders of the first pyramids and ball parks in Mesoamerica.

_____ 12. Spanish officer who located the Inca Empire in the Andes Mountains.

_____ 13. Head of the greatest empire the world had ever seen and the person who provided the framework for the first truly global economy.

WHAT WAS IT?

Complete each statement below (questions 1–11) by writing the letter preceding the appropriate response in the space provided. Use each answer only once.

a. Astrolabe
b. caravel
c. _chinampas_
d. Clovis tip
e. dog
f. factories
g. _hacienda_
h. maize
i. smallpox
j. sugar
k. syphilis

_____ 1. Superior spear point in use in North and South America that contributed to overhunting and helped bring about the decline in the number of game animals.

_____ 2. Only animal domesticated by Indians in both Americas.

_____ 3. Most important native crop produced in both North and South America.

_____ 4. First crop grown using plantation-style agriculture.

_____ 5. New oceangoing vessel used by the Portuguese that was superior to those used by other Europeans at the time.

_____ 6. Device that permitted accurate calculation of latitude.

_____ 7. Term used to describe small posts established by the Portuguese for the African slave trade.

_____ 8. Highly productive gardens built by the Aztecs.

_____ 9. Large Spanish estate with its own crops and herds.

_____ 10. Most deadly disease introduced to the Indians by the Spanish.

_____ 11. Disease carried back to Europe by the earliest Spanish explorers.

WHERE WAS IT?

Complete each statement below (questions 1–11) by writing the letter preceding the appropriate response in the space provided. Use each answer only once.

a. Brazil
b. Cuzco
c. Fiji
d. Mesoamerica
e. Portugal
f. San Salvador
g. Spain
h. Tenochtitlán
i. Vera Cruz
j. Vinland
k. Yucatán

_____ 1. Cultural and linguistic center for Polynesians.

_____ 2. First permanent settlement of Europeans in the Western Hemisphere.

_____ 3. Country located at the intersection of the Mediterranean and Atlantic worlds.

_____ 4. Only colony of settlement in the Portuguese empire.

_____ 5. Center of Europe's most fiercely Catholic society.

_____ 6. First place the Spanish landed in the Western Hemisphere.

_____ 7. Place where the Spanish first landed in Mexico.

_____ 8. Aztec capital that was larger than any city in western Europe at the time it was conquered.

_____ 9. Area embracing Central and South America.

_____ 10. Center of Mayan culture.

_____ 11. Capital of the Inca Empire in the Andes Mountains.

CHARTS, MAPS, AND ILLUSTRATIONS

1. The device used by the Incas to keep accounts based on the decimal system was

   _____.

2. The glowering statue used as a huge receptacle for the hearts of sacrificial victims was

   _____.

3. According to the map on p. 31, the Anasazi culture spread over portions of five present-day states in the Southwest. Name two of them:

   _____ and _____.

4. The major silver mines of South America were found at

   _____.

MULTIPLE CHOICE

Circle the letter that best completes each statement.

1. Five distinct pre-Columbian waves of immigrants swept over the Americas. Three groups came from Asia; one from the Pacific islands or may have just brushed America; and one group came from
   a. northern Europe.
   b. South America.
   c. Antarctica.
   d. southern Europe.

2. The most recent ice age ended about
   a. 1,000 years ago.
   b. 12,000 years ago.
   c. 90,000 years ago.
   d. 400,000 years ago.

3. The temporary land bridge across the Bering Strait between Siberia and Alaska is referred to as
   a. Tierra del Fuego.
   b. Yukon.
   c. Brazil.
   d. Beringia.

4. What was the forerunner of the vast majority of Indian languages on both continents?
   a. Amerind
   b. Na-Déné
   c. Algonquian
   d. Mayan

5. The oldest burial grounds yet found in America belong to the Maritime Archaic Indians, also known as the
   a. Muskogean.
   b. Siouan.

    c. Apache.
    d. Red Paint People.

6. Norsemen descended from a Germanic people who had occupied Scandinavia and were known as
    a. Vikings.
    b. Hawaiians.
    c. Polynesians.
    d. Indians.

7. Which of the following statements incorrectly characterizes Erik the Red?
    a. He led his Norse followers to Greenland and established a permanent settlement.
    b. He was outlawed from Iceland for committing mayhem.
    c. He was accused of manslaughter in Norway.
    d. He was an Irish monk.

8. China under the Ming dynasty was the world's most complex culture. The Chinese invented the compass, gunpowder, and early forms of printing. However, most foreigners were interested in their teas, silks, and other fine products. Most of what Europe knew about China came from a Venetian merchant named
    a. Cheng Ho.
    b. Kublai Khan.
    c. Christopher Columbus.
    d. Marco Polo.

9. By the fifteenth century, who controlled overland trade to Asia and the existing seaborne route through the Persian Gulf?
    a. Norsemen
    b. China
    c. the Islamic world
    d. Christian Europe

10. In 1348, Europe was devasted by the Black Death, which is also known as
    a. bubonic plague.
    b. measles.
    c. yellow fever.
    d. smallpox.

11. Which of the following statements was not an advantage in Portugal's overseas exploration?
    a. Its merchant class was tiny and it had accumulated little capital.
    b. It had a reasonably efficient government at a time when its neighbors were beset by war.
    c. It enjoyed internal peace.
    d. It was located at the intersection of the Mediterranean and Atlantic worlds.

12. During the long history of the Atlantic slave trade, nearly every African shipped overseas had first been enslaved by other Africans. The enslavement of Africans by Euro-

peans differed from the enslavement of Africans by Africans in all of the following ways except that
a. in Africa, slaves were allowed to buy their freedom.
b. in Africa, slaves were not forced to toil endlessly to produce staple crops.
c. in Africa, the descendents of slaves often became fully assimilated into the captor's society.
d. in Africa, slaves were not isolated as a separate caste.

13. Which explorer opened the way for Portugal's empire in the East by sailing his fleet around the Cape of Good Hope and on to the Malibar Coast of southwestern India?
a. Christopher Columbus
b. Prince Henry
c. Vasco de Gama
d. Bartolomeu Días

14. Cristoforo Columbo (Christopher Columbus in Latin) sailed for King Ferdinand and Queen Isabella in 1492 as a representative of
a. China.
b. France.
c. Spain.
d. England.

15. Who was the first European to reach the Pacific Ocean after crossing the Isthmus of Panama in 1513?
a. Hernán Cortés
b. Juan Ponce de León
c. Bartolomeu Días
d. Vasco Núñez de Balboa

16. The "slash and burn" system of agriculture
a. eventually depleted the soil.
b. was used in long-term farming of the land.
c. never was used by Indians.
d. replenished the nutrients in the soil.

17. Which of the following cultures emerged in 1400 as the dominant power in the Andes and, by 1500, ruled approximately eight to twelve million people—the only nonliterate culture ever to accomplish such a feat?
a. Mochica
b. Inca
c. Aztec
d. Chavin

18. Choose the incorrect statement from the following:
a. The Aztecs gained power in the Valley of Mexico during the eleventh century.
b. The Aztecs were a warrior people who had migrated from the north.
c. The Aztecs built the city of Tenochtitlán and raised agricultural productivity.
d. The Aztecs waged perpetual war to gain captives for their religious ceremonies.

19. Located near the Ohio and Mississippi Rivers, three distinct "mound-building" societies succeeded one another. The inhabitants constructed distinctive earthen mounds that were used for
    a. food storage.
    b. housing.
    c. burial sites.
    d. farming.

20. All of the following statements correctly represent the Anasazi Indians of the Southwest except
    a. They were a cliff-dwelling people.
    b. They studied astronomy and created a calendar.
    c. They built a network of roads that ran for miles in several directions.
    d. The name Anasazi comes from the Cheyenne word meaning "the traveling ones."

21. Which of the following Spanish terms refers to a system of labor?
    a. *conquistador*
    b. *audencia*
    c. *hacienda*
    d. *encomienda*

22. In 1573, Phillip II issued the Royal Order for New Discoveries. This decree
    a. required Indians to become slaves of Spain.
    b. outlawed further exploration and expansion.
    c. created Protestant missions to convert Indians.
    d. made it illegal to enslave or attack Indians.

23. The nun who claimed that angels carried her across the Atlantic where she preached to Indians in their own language was
    a. Isabella Castile.
    b. Maria de Cortez.
    c. Maria de Jesus de Agreda.
    d. Esther Marie de Jesus.

ESSAY

Description and Explanation (one- to two-paragraph essay)

1. Describe why China and the Norse had little impact on North America or Europe.

2. Describe the early use of slave labor in the Mediterranean and Africa and the differences between the African practice of slavery and the way it developed among Europeans.

3. Describe the requirements of a successful European overseas expansion.

4. Describe the Mayan civilization at its height and during its decline.

5. Describe the religious practices of Aztecs and the role of religion in their fall.

6. Did civilization triumph over savagery? Explain your answer with specific information.

7. Describe the role of missionaries in the building of the Spanish Empire.

Discussion and Analysis (class discussion or one- to two-paragraph essay)

1. Discuss the role of agriculture in the development of Indian life and the importance of the decline of agriculture in the fall of Indian cultures.

2. Discuss the advantages and disadvantages of western Europe on the eve of exploration.

3. Discuss the misunderstandings between Europeans and Indians; place special emphasis on religion and social organizations.

4. Discuss the effects of the long-term isolation of the Americas, especially the biological and technological effects of this isolation.

What If (Include an explanation of your position)

1. If you were a young Spanish sailor, would you sail with Columbus?

2. If you were a member of an Indian group conquered by the Aztecs, would you support them or Cortez?

Crossword Puzzle: When Old Worlds Collide: Contact, Conquest, Catastrophe

DOWN

1. Aztec floating gardens
2. The ___ revolution in agriculture was much slower among Indians than Europeans
3. Strength of Prince Henry of Portugal
4. First Portuguese explorer to reach India by going around Africa
5. ___ against Spanish rule continued for most of sixteenth century in Peru
7. Eucharist activity
11. Number of golden cities Coronado searched for in vain
12. Ferdinand's kingdom
13. Inca's beasts of burden
15. Europe in 1400s had little to offer ___ , the Celestial Kingdom
16. The Anasazi calendar tracked 19 1/2 ___ moon cycles
17. When Isabella ___ Ferdinand, the basis for modern Spain was formed
18. The world compared to Columbus's estimate

ACROSS

1. Cortes, Pizarro, etc.
6. Europeans were able to conquer Indians because of the ___ nature of life in the Americas
8. A literate person, such as an Aztec
9. Descent was determined ____ among Indian families
10. Beringia neighbor
14. Word describing location of Prester John's kingdom
15. That a ___ should produce staples was an idea that preceded Columbus in European thinking
17. First word of preamble
19. People of Tikal
20. Spanish system for requisitioning labor
21. Part of Columbus's title

ANSWER KEY

WHO? WHAT? WHERE?

Who Were They?

1. d. Freydis, p. 6
2. f. Johannes Gutenberg, p. 8
3. e. Inuits, p. 3
4. j. Prester John, p. 9
5. l. Prince Henry, p. 10
6. m. Vasco da Gama, p. 13
7. i. Pedro Alvares Cabral, p. 14
8. a. Christopher Columbus, p. 15
9. g. Juan Ponce de León, p. 17
10. b. Ferdinand Magellan, p. 17
11. h. Olmecs, p. 24
12. c. Francisco Pizarro, p. 34
13. k. Phillip II, p. 41

What Was It?

1. d. Clovis tip, p. 3
2. e. dog, p. 5
3. h. maize, p. 5
4. j. sugar, p. 8
5. b. caravel, p. 10
6. a. Astrolabe, p. 10
7. f. factories, p. 11
8. c. *chinampas*, p. 27
9. g. *hacienda*, p. 40
10. i. smallpox, p. 40
11. k. syphilis, p. 43

Where Was It?

1. c. Fiji, p. 5
2. j. Vinland, p. 6
3. e. Portugal, p. 10
4. a. Brazil, p. 14
5. g. Spain, p. 15
6. f. San Salvador, p. 15
7. i. Vera Cruz, p. 17
8. h. Tenochtitlán, p. 17
9. d. Mesoamerica, p. 20
10. k. Yucatán, p. 26
11. b. Cuzco, p. 35

CHARTS, MAPS, AND ILLUSTRATIONS

1. *quipu*, p. 23
2. *chacmool*, p. 28
3. Nevada, New Mexico, Arizona, Utah, and Colorado, p. 31
4. Potosí, p. 35

MULTIPLE CHOICE

1. a. (p. 2)
2. b. (p. 3)
3. d. (p. 3)
4. a. (p. 3)
5. d. (p. 5)
6. a. (p. 6)
7. d. (p. 6)
8. d. (p. 7)
9. c. (p. 7)
10. a. (p. 8)
11. a. (p. 10)
12. a. (pp. 12–13)
13. c. (p. 13)
14. c. (p. 15)
15. d. (p. 17)

16. a. (p. 19)

17. b. (p. 22)

18. a. (p. 27)

19. c. (p. 28)

20. d. (pp. 30–31)

21. d. (p. 40)

22. d. (pp. 37–39)

23. c. (p. 39)

ESSAY

Description and Explanation

1. pp. 6–7

2. pp. 11–13

3. p. 14

4. pp. 25–26

5. pp. 27–28

6. Chapter 1 *passim*

7. pp. 35–39

Discussion and Analysis

1. pp. 3–5

2. pp. 8–9

3. pp. 32–34

4. pp. 42–43

What If

1. p. 15

2. pp. 27–28

Crossword Puzzle

CHAPTER 2

THE CHALLENGE TO SPAIN AND THE SETTLEMENT OF NORTH AMERICA

After 1600, the French, Dutch, and English all established colonies in the new areas. The societies created by Europeans varied as much as their parent cultures did. They ranged from the lifestyle and economy that accompanied the fur trade of New France and New Netherland to the family farms of Puritan New England, to the tobacco-producing areas of Virginia and Maryland, to the very wealthy, slave-dependent sugar islands of the Caribbean, and to the mixed economies of the Restoration colonies.

The Protestant Reformation, which began with Martin Luther and John Calvin, increased differences among the peoples and added a powerful religious factor. The early French empire experimented very briefly with religious toleration. The Dutch introduced religious pluralism to North America. There was some toleration also in early Maryland and indifference in Virginia and the Caribbean. Religion played an especially important role in the settlement and development of early New England. Theological concerns were urgent matters to Puritans. These concerns colored their way of life and helped produce several new colonies in the area.

Six colonies were founded after the Restoration of the monarchy in 1660. Extending from New York to Carolina, all were deliberately planned and proprietary in form. There acquisition of land was made easy, and each colony of the six new colonies competed for settlers by offering strong guarantees of civil and political liberties as well as some religious toleration. These colonies tended to have more ethnic and religious diversity than the earlier colonies had. By 1700, England controlled the Atlantic coastline from Maine to South Carolina.

LIBERTY, EQUALITY, POWER

Life in seventeenth-century colonies demonstrated more about the power of government and church over people than the vague, mostly nonexistent concepts of liberty and equality. The English acceptance of slavery, first in the sugar islands and then in the tobacco areas, demonstrated the power of wealthy whites over Africans. It was also one of the first instances of inequality based on race, which has been a major issue for Americans for centuries.

However, principles of liberty and equality were beginning to emerge. There was some freedom of worship available in various French, Dutch, and English colonies. This could be considered a form of liberty. Most of the early white settlers in English colonies outside of New England arrived as poor indentured servants. The availability of free land gave them a chance to achieve upward social mobility. With the increase in economic power came increased equality. Most Puritans wanted the freedom to form their own type of community, and they were successful at this. The Restoration colonies offered either toleration or religious freedom and strong guarantees of civil and political liberties. They often became the forerunners of other American areas.

OBJECTIVES

After studying this chapter, a student should be able to

1. Describe French colonization in North America.

2. Discuss the factors in Dutch colonization.

3. Trace the problems of early Jamestown, Virginia.

4. Discuss the role of religion in early New England.

5. Compare and contrast family life in the Chesapeake colonies, New England, and the Restoration colonies.

6. Characterize the general features of Restoration colonies.

CHRONOLOGY

1497	Henry VII sent Giovanni Cabot (John Cabot), an Italian mariner who had moved to Bristol, to search for a northwest passage to Asia. Cabot reached Newfoundland but was lost at sea in **1498**. His voyages gave England a vague claim to portions of the North American coast.
1517	Martin Luther launched the Protestant Reformation and systematically shattered the religious unity of Europe by nailing his Ninety-Five Theses to the cathedral door at Wittenberg.
1524	King Francis I of France sent Giovanni da Verrazzano, an Italian, to America in search of a northwest passage to Asia. Between **1534** and **1543** Jacques Cartier completed three voyages to North America. He suffered through the severity of a Canadian winter and gave up.
1536	John Calvin, a French Protestant, published *The Institutes of the Christian Religion*. Calvin's followers, known as Calvinists, rejected papal supremacy and clerical celibacy and embraced the principle of predestination.
1560–1640	England attempted to impose its agriculture, language, local government, legal system, aristocracy, and religion on a clan-based, mostly pastoral and Gaelic-speaking people. Ireland attracted more English settlers than all American and Caribbean colonies combined. The Irish responded by becoming more fiercely Roman Catholic.
1580–1587	During these years Francis Drake plundered Spanish possessions along the Pacific coast and continued west to circumnavigate the world to England.
1585	An expedition landed on Roanoke Island, but the colony subsequently established lasted only a short time. In 1587, Walter Raleigh sent a second expedition, including women. This was to be a permanent settlement, but the colonists disappeared some time in the next few years.

1602	The States General chartered the Dutch East India Company, the wealthiest corporation the world had seen yet.
1604–1606	Samuel Champlain established a French settlement on Acadia. In 1608, he founded Quebec.
1606	King James I of England (1603–1625) chartered the Virginia Company, granting it power to colonize North America between the 34th and 45th parallels. The company was headquartered in Plymouth and London.
1607	The Plymouth part of the Virginia Company tried to establish a colony on the coast of Maine but gave up quickly. The London group sent out three ships to the Chesapeake Bay area and established the colony at Jamestown.
1607–1609	The Pilgrims, who were Separatists, left England for the Netherlands, convinced that the Church of England was no true daughter of the Reformation. They hoped to worship freely in Holland.
1609	Henry Hudson, an Englishman in Dutch service, sailed to North America and claimed the Hudson Valley for the Netherlands.
	Of a total of 325 English settlers who came to Jamestown before **1609**, fewer than one hundred were still alive in the spring of that year.
	The colony's first Indian war began. Powhatan's warriors picked off any settlers who strayed far from Jamestown. The English retaliated by slaughtering whole villages and destroying crops, even though the settlers still were dependent on Indians for their food supply. This war lasted five years.
1613	John Rolfe imported a type of tobacco from the West Indies that was milder than the native Virginia species. The new variety sold well in England. Soon tobacco was being grown in the streets of Jamestown.
1619	Africans reached Virginia, but their status in early Virginia and Maryland remained ambiguous for decades.
1620	The Pilgrims arrived on the *Mayflower* and established Plymouth. They planted a crop the next year and, after the 1621 harvest, they celebrated the first Thanksgiving feast.
1621	War between Spain and the Netherlands was renewed, and interest in the Americas increased significantly.
	The Dutch West India Company was chartered. In North America it put most of its effort into the Hudson River valley. In 1626, the port of New Amsterdam was founded.
1624	The king of England declared the London Company bankrupt and assumed direct control of Virginia. This made it the first royal colony.
	The first permanent settlers arrived in the Dutch colony in the Hudson Valley. Two years later the town of New Amsterdam was established.

1629–1640	King Charles I governed without Parliament, but when he tried to impose the Anglican *Book of Common Prayer*, his Scottish subjects rebelled and invaded England. In 1640, Charles I summoned a new Parliament to gain revenue, but many of its members, especially the Puritans, sympathized with the Scots.
1629	An advance party of Puritans took over a small fishing village on the coast of New England and renamed it Salem.
1630	A major group led by John Winthrop arrived and established the colony of Massachusetts Bay.
1632	The Maryland Charter made Lord Baltimore, a Catholic, proprietor of the Maryland colony. This colony became the model for other proprietary projects.
1634	The Virginia colony was divided into counties. Each county had its own justices of the peace who sat together as the county court and, by filling their own vacancies, soon became a self-perpetuating oligarchy.
Mid-1630s	Alarmed by John Cotton's preaching in Boston, Reverend Thomas Hooker led his people west to the Connecticut River, where they founded Hartford.
1636	Roger Williams fled Massachusetts and settled in what later became the colony of Rhode Island.
1637	The Puritans massacred the Pequot Indians in a war of annihilation that was part of a quest for more land.
1638	Financed by private Dutch capital, Pierre (Peter) Minuit returned to America with Flemish and Swedish settlers to found New Sweden with its capital at Fort Christina near the mouth of the Delaware River.
	Anne Hutchinson was banished from the Massachusetts Bay colony and moved with her followers to the Narragansett Bay area.
1641	Massachusetts defined its legal system in the "Body of Liberties," which has a strong claim to be regarded as history's first bill of rights.
1642	The English Civil War broke out in the aftermath of a massive revolt of Irish Catholics in 1641 against the Protestant colonizers of their land. King Charles I and Parliament agreed that the Irish must be defeated, but neither trusted the other, and fighting soon broke out between them.
1643	Governor Willem Kieft slaughtered the men, women, and children of a tribe of Indian refugees to whom he had granted asylum. The Pavonia Massacre set off a war with neighboring Indians and almost destroyed the colony of New Netherland.
1648	Spain's long war with the Swedes and Dutch finally ended.
1649	The Toleration Act granted freedom of religion to Christians in Maryland.

Parliament beheaded Charles, abolished the House of Lords, proclaimed a commonwealth, or republican form of government, in England, eventually headed by Oliver Cromwell.

1650   Upheaval in England filtered down to the rest of the emerging empire. As royal power collapsed, England's West Indian colonies demanded and received elective assemblies, and the Dutch seized control of trade in and out of the West Indian and Chesapeake colonies. By 1650, most of the sugar and tobacco trade went to Amsterdam, not to London.

Parliament banned foreign ships from English colonies. The following year, it passed the comprehensive Navigation Act, aimed at Dutch competition.

1651–1652   An English naval force in America compelled Barbados and Virginia to submit to Parliament. In return, Virginia was allowed to elect its own governor, a privilege revoked in 1660. Trade with the Dutch continued in the absence of resident officials who were supposed to enforce English policy.

1656   James Harrington, England's most prominent republican thinker, published *Oceana*. He had a major impact on colonial governments.

1658   Cromwell's experimental government collapsed with his death.

1660   The Restoration Era began with the restoration of Charles II to the throne of England in 1660. During this period six colonies were founded in North America, and new English trade regulations were instituted.

The Navigation Acts of 1651 were extended to require that all colonial trade be carried on English ships and that the master and three fourths of the crew had to be English. Enumerated commodities, such as sugar and tobacco, were to be shipped from the colony of origin only to England or to another English colony.

Europeans outnumbered slaves in the islands of the West Indies by 33,000 to 22,000. For the rest of the century, the European population stagnated while the slave population increased sixfold. By 1775, it tripled again.

1662   Puritan clergy worked out the Half-Way Covenant. Parents who had been baptized but had not yet experienced conversion could bring their children before the church, "own the covenant," and have them baptized. By the 1680s, this had led to something like universal baptism.

1663   Royal intervention transformed New France when Louis XIV and his minister, Jean-Baptiste Colbert, took direct charge of the colony. The two men tried to turn it into a model absolutist society—peaceful, orderly, and deferential. Over the next few years, agriculture was encouraged and women were shipped over to marry the men.

A charter was granted to eight men for the colony they named Carolina. During the first decade, they had little success with the colony.

1664	James, duke of York, obtained a charter for a colony between the Delaware and Connecticut Rivers. The Dutch in the area surrendered without resistance. The English renamed the colony New York.
1665	New Jersey was made a separate colony from New York under two proprietors, George Carteret and John, lord Berkeley.
1669	Anthony Ashley-Cooper and the proprietors of Carolina drafted a complex plan for organizing the colony known as the Fundamental Constitutions of Carolina. It was meant to establish a properly designed aristocratic society.
1674	New Jersey proprietors split the colony into West and East New Jersey. West New Jersey was sold to Quaker investors.
1680	Charleston, the first city in the South, was founded.
1681	William Penn launched a "Holy Experiment" in brotherly love with a charter for the colony of Pennsylvania.
1682	William Penn's constitution, or First Frame of Government, revealed that more thought went into the launching of Pennsylvania than into the organization of any other colony. The next year, a simpler form of government, known as the Second Frame, or the Pennsylvania Charter of Liberties, was devised. Penn also laid out the city of Philadelphia.
1683	New York's experiment with absolutism was interrupted when the Charter of Liberties proclaimed government by consent and other basic rights.
1690s	South Carolina planters learned how to grow rice from slaves who had cultivated it in Africa. Rice quickly became the staple export of South Carolina and triggered a massive growth of slavery to provide labor for the plantations.

GLOSSARY OF IMPORTANT TERMS

Anglican	A member of the Church of England. Also used to refer to the Church of England.
Arminianism	A belief named for Jacobus Arminus, a Dutch theologian who challenged the strict Calvinist position on predestination.
bicameral legislature	A legislature with two houses or chambers.
cavaliers	Supporters of the Stuart family of Charles I during the civil wars.
circumnavigate	A term meaning to "sail around the world."
coureur de bois	A French phrase interpreted as "a roamer of the woods," referring to French colonials who participated in the fur trade with the Indians and lived part of the year with them.

covenant theology	The belief that God made two personal covenants with humans: the covenant of works and the covenant of grace.
elect	Those selected by God for salvation.
established church	The church in an area that was officially recognized and was supported by the government.
fall line	The geographical region defined by the first waterfall encountered on a river. These waterfalls usually prevented oceangoing vessels from traveling farther inland and made the fall line a significant early barrier.
governor general	The French official responsible for military and diplomatic affairs and for appointment of all militia officers in a colony.
Half-Way Covenant	The Puritan practice whereby parents who had been baptized but had not yet experienced conversion could bring their children before the church and have them baptized.
headright	A colonist received fifty acres of land for every person whose passage to America he financed. This was the most popular reform in Virginia.
House of Burgesses	The assembly of early Virginia that settlers were allowed to elect. Members met with the governor and his council and enacted local laws. It first met in 1619.
Huguenots	French Protestants who followed the beliefs of John Calvin.
indentured servants	People who had their passage to America paid by a master or ship captain. They agreed to work for their master for a term of years in exchange for cost of passage, bed and board, and small freedom dues when their terms were up. The number of years served depended on the terms of the contract. Most early settlers in the English colonies outside of New England were indentured servants.
Inn of Courts	England's law schools.
intendant	The office that administered the system of justice in New France.
joint stock company	A form of business organization that resembled a modern corporation. Individuals invested in the company through the purchase of shares. One major difference between then and today was that each stockholder had one vote regardless of how many shares he owned. The first permanent English colonies in North America were established by joint stock companies.
magistrate	An official who enforced the law. In colonial America, this person was often also a justice of the peace.
militia	A community's armed force, made up primarily of ordinary citizens rather than professional soldiers.
oligarchy	A society dominated by a few persons or families.

open-field agriculture	A medieval system of land distribution used only in New England. Farmers owned scattered strips of land within a common field, and the town as a whole decided what crops to produce.
pacifist	A person opposed to war or violence. The religious group that was most commited to pacifism was the Quakers.
parish	Originally, a term used to describe an area served by one church. Gradually, the word was used to describe a political area that was the same as that served by the church. The term was used primarily in regions settled by members of the Church of England.
patroonships	Vast estates along the Hudson River that were established by the Dutch. They had difficulty attracting peasant labor, and most were not very successful.
piedmont	A term referring to the land above the waterfalls but below the Appalachian Mountains.
politique	A man who believed that the survival of the state took precedence over religious differences.
predestination	A theory that states that God has decreed, even before he created the world, who will be saved and who will be damned.
primogeniture	The English practice requiring that the eldest son inherited all the land of his father's estate.
proprietary colony	A colony owned by an individual(s) who had vast discretionary powers over the colony. Maryland was the first proprietary colony, but others were founded later.
public friends	The men and women who spoke most frequently and effectively for the Society of Friends. They were as close as the Quakers came to having a clergy. They occupied special elevated seats in the meeting house.
Puritans	An English religious group that followed the teachings of John Calvin. They wanted a fuller reformation of the Church of England and hoped to replace the *Book of Common Prayer* with sermons. They wanted to purify the Church of England.
quitrent	A relic of the feudalism, a quitrent was a small required annual fee attached to a piece of land.
Restoration Era	The period when the Stuart dynasty under Charles II was restored to the throne of England. It ended with the overthrow of James II in 1688–1689.
royal colony	A colony controlled directly by the English king. The governor and council were appointed by the Crown.
seigneurs	The landed gentry who claimed most of the land between Quebec and Montreal. They were never as powerful as the aristocrats in France.

separatists	One of the most extreme English Protestant groups that were followers of John Calvin. They denied that the Church of England was a true church and began to separate and form their own congregations.
States General	The legislative assembly of the Netherlands.
tithe	A portion of one's income that is owed to the church. In most places, it was one tenth.
tidewater	The area between the ocean and the fall line. In the southern coastal areas, the tidewater was fairly wide and was open to oceangoing transportation. The coastal area around the Chesapeake Bay region of Virginia and Maryland was known especially as the tidewater. This became the leading tobacco-producing area.
vestry	A group of prominent men who managed the lay affairs of the local Anglican church, including the choice of minister.
yankee	A Dutch word that originally meant something like "land pirate."

WHO? WHAT? WHERE?

WHO WERE THEY?

Complete each statement below (questions 1–12) by writing the letter preceding the appropriate name in the space provided. Use each answer only once.

  a. Francis Drake
  b. George Calvert
  c. George Fox
  d. Humphrey Gilbert
  e. Jacques Cartier
  f. James Harrington
  g. Jean-Baptiste Colbert
  h. John Rolfe
  i. Oliver Cromwell
  j. Peter Minuit
  k. Richard Hakluyt
  l. Squanto

_____ 1. French explorer who made three voyages to North America and sailed up the St. Lawrence River.

_____ 2. The French minister under Louis XIV who took the direct charge of the French colony in North America and encouraged it to develop agriculturally.

_____ 3. The Dutch colonizer who bought Manhattan Island from the Indians.

_____ 4. Commander of the first English ship to circumnavigate the world.

_____ 5. One of the brutal English captains in Ireland who unsuccessfully tried to establish a colony on Newfoundland.

_____ 6. One of two cousins who systematically collected accounts of English adventures overseas and offered advice on how to make future colonization.

_____ 7. Early settler who imported a new species of tobacco into Virginia and helped make it a successful cash crop.

_____ 8. Founder of Maryland whose family believed that Catholics and Protestants could live together peacefully.

_____ 9. Indian who taught the Pilgrims to fish and raise corn.

_____ 10. Parliament's most successful general and later Lord Protector of England.

_____ 11. Author of *Oceana* and England's most prominent republican thinker of the seventeenth century.

_____ 12. The founder of the Society of Friends.

WHAT WAS IT?

Complete each statement below (questions 1–11) by writing the letter preceding the appropriate response in the space provided. Use each answer only once.

  a. Bank of Amsterdam
  b. Baptist
  c. cavaliers
  d. *coureur de bois*
  e. Huguenots
  f. open field
  g. ownership of land
  h. proprietary colony
  i. Quakers
  j. Restoration Era
  k. royal colony

_____ 1. French Calvinists.

_____ 2. French colonial in the fur trade.

_____ 3. Europe's most important financial institution for 100 years.

_____ 4. Most popular reform in early Virginia.

_____ 5. Colony controlled directly by the English king.

_____ 6. Colony controlled by an individual.

_____ 7. Medieval form of land distribution used only in early New England.

_____ 8. Religious group that believed the rite of baptism should be received by converted adults only.

_____ 9. Period when the Stuart dynasty under Charles II was restored to the throne of England.

_____ 10. Supporters of the Stuart family of Charles I during the English civil wars.

_____ 11. First Christian group to limit family size in order to give more attention to the children they did have.

WHERE WAS IT?

Complete each statement below (questions 1–9) by writing the letter preceding the appropriate response in the space provided. Use each answer only once.

   a. Carolina
   b. Charleston
   c. Fort Christina
   d. New Netherland
   e. Pennsylvania
   f. Roanoke
   g. St. Domingue
   h. Spain
   i. tidewater

_____ 1. Most militant Catholic country in Europe.

_____ 2. Sugar colony belonging to France that became the world's richest colony at one time.

_____ 3. North America's first experiment in ethnic and religious pluralism.

_____ 4. Capital of New Sweden that was located near the mouth of the Delaware River.

_____ 5. Area between the ocean and the fall line.

_____ 6. First area in which English women settled in North America.

_____ 7. Colony chosen to be a laboratory for a properly designed aristocratic society.

_____ 8. First city in the American South.

_____ 9. Colony that seemed to have more thought put into its launching than any other colony.

CHARTS, MAPS, AND ILLUSTRATIONS

1. The city that was the center of world commerce in the seventeenth century was _____.

2. The English surname for Pocahontas was _____.

3. According to the table on the pattern of settlement (p. 58), the area with the highest percentage of settlers from Africa was _____.

4. The location of the Puritan massacre of the Pequot Indians was _____.

5. According to the map on p. 67, one island owned by the Dutch in the Caribbean area was _____.

6. The largest manor in early New York was _____.

MULTIPLE CHOICE

Circle the letter that best completes each statement.

1. Who launched the Protestant Reformation in 1517?
   a. Martin Luther
   b. María de Jesús de Agreda
   c. the bishop of Havana
   d. Phillip II

2. Who published *The Institutes of the Christian Religion* in 1536?
   a. Phillip II
   b. John Calvin
   c. Martin Luther
   d. María de Jesús de Agreda

3. All of the following statements are correctly associated with Samuel de Champlain, except
   a. He revived French colonization efforts after 1600.
   b. He was successful in his effort to bring Catholics and Protestants together in harmony.
   c. He made eleven voyages to Canada before his death in 1635.
   d. He planted a predominantly Huguenot settlement in Acadia from 1604 to 1606.

4. All of the following statements about the Society of Jesus are accurate except
   a. They were known as Jesuits.
   b. They emerged in the sixteenth century as the best-educated and the most militant religious order in the Catholic Church.
   c. They saw nothing contradictory about a nation of Christians retaining Indian customs, provided the practices could be brought into conformity with Catholic morality.
   d. They were uncompromising and inflexible in dealing with non-Christian peoples from China to North America.

5. In the colony of New France (Canada) under Louis XIV
   a. taxes were high.
   b. there were no import duties.
   c. couples were penalized for producing more than one child.
   d. the governor appointed all militia officers who earned promotions through merit.

6. The most important motive for Dutch expansion overseas was to obtain
   a. quality land.
   b. religious freedom.

    c. profit.

    d. glory.

7. The Dutch West India Company had jurisdiction over the African slave trade in all of the following except

    a. Brazil.

    b. the Caribbean.

    c. North America.

    d. England.

8. The Dutch claimed three major river systems—

    a. the Mississippi, the Connecticut, and the Hudson.

    b. the Hudson, the Delaware, and the Tennessee.

    c. the Delaware, the Hudson, and the Connecticut.

    d. the Ohio, the Tennessee, and the Mississippi.

9. The governor of New Netherland slaughtered a tribe of Indian refugees to whom he had granted asylum from other Indians. The incident set off a war with neighboring Algonquian tribes that nearly destroyed the colony. The governor responsible for the Pavonia Massacre was

    a. Peter Stuyvesant.

    b. Willem Kieft.

    c. Pierre (Peter) Minuit.

    d. Jean de Brebeuf.

10. All of the following statements correctly depict Jamestown except

    a. They expected the local Indians to work for them.

    b. The settlement was a death trap, with only thirty-eight of 104 settlers surviving the first year.

    c. The settlement was established by the French.

    d. Every summer the James River near the settlement became contaminated with dysentery, typhoid fever, and malaria.

11. The soldier and adventurer who took charge of Jamestown, tried to maintain friendly relations with the Indians, and was associated with Pocahontas was

    a. Sir Humphrey Gilbert.

    b. Captain John Smith.

    c. Richard Hakluyt.

    d. Lt. Governor Thomas Gates.

12. The Toleration Act of 1649, which granted freedom of religion to Christians but not to the tiny Jewish minority in the province, was approved under Lord Baltimore in the colony of

    a. Massachusetts.

    b. Georgia.

    c. Maryland.

    d. Virginia.

13. All of the following statements are true of family life in the Chesapeake colonies except
    a. In a typical marriage, the groom was in his twenties and the bride was five to nine years younger.
    b. Chesapeake-area immigrants had survived childhood diseases in Europe, but life expectancy for men at age twenty hovered around forty-five, with 70 percent dead by age fifty.
    c. About 70 percent of the men never married.
    d. Orphans were a major community problem, and stepparents were common because surviving spouses with property usually remarried.

14. The production of sugar required a heavy investment in
    a. slaves, mills, and other equipment.
    b. land, seeds, and other equipment.
    c. paid labor, fertilizer, and other equipment.
    d. machinery, mules, and other equipment.

15. In the generation after 1680, the caste structure of the Chesapeake colonies became firmly set. Fewer indentured servants reached the Chesapeake from England, and slaves took their place for all of the following reasons except
    a. Slaves cost more to buy but also served for life.
    b. In 1705, the Virginia legislature forbade the whipping of a white servant without the court's permission, a restriction that did not apply to slaves.
    c. Slaves were cheaper to buy and less expensive to maintain.
    d. Virginia promised every ex-servant fifty acres of land, which further widened the gap between a white indentured servant and an African slave.

16. The Pilgrims were
    a. atheists.
    b. Catholics.
    c. Jesuits.
    d. Separatists.

17. All passengers of the *Mayflower* signed an agreement to obey the decisions of the majority. It was known as the
    a. Edict of Nantes.
    b. Constitution of the United States.
    c. Mayflower Compact.
    d. Treaty of Paris.

18. In his famous sermon, the idea of erecting a model "city upon a hill" was proposed by
    a. John Winthrop.
    b. William Laud.
    c. Jacobus Arminius.
    d. John Smith.

19. The economy of early New England was based primarily on
    a. tobacco and cotton.
    b. lumber products, grain, and shipbuilding.
    c. sugar and indigo.
    d. rubber and glassware.

20. Who was the Separatist who briefly served as Salem's minister and eventually was one of the founders of Rhode Island?
    a. Thomas Hooker
    b. Anne Hutchinson
    c. John Cotton
    d. Roger Williams

21. All of the following were Restoration colonies except
    a. Carolina.
    b. Pennsylvania.
    c. New Jersey.
    d. Georgia.

22. All of the following statements correctly apply to the Restoration colonies, except
    a. They were proprietary in form.
    b. They were founded by men with big ideas and small purses, excluding Pennsylvania.
    c. They promised religious toleration, at least for Christians, so there was a mix of religious and ethnic groups.
    d. They made it difficult to acquire land.

23. Commonwealth England's most important republican thinker, James Harrington,
    a. argued that the distribution of money ought to be the key factor in deciding whether government should be entrusted to a monarchy, aristocracy, or republic.
    b. was against frequent rotation of officeholders and term limits.
    c. suggested an open ballot as opposed to a secret ballot.
    d. proposed a bicameral legislature.

24. The Fundamental Constitutions of Carolina proposed all of the following except
    a. a simple form of government.
    b. eight supreme courts and a lower tribunal in every county, precinct, and barony.
    c. the aristocracy always controlled 40 percent of the land.
    d. religious toleration was afforded to all who believed in God, but everyone had to join some church or lose his citizenship.

25. New York's experiment with absolutism was interrupted in 1683 with the
    a. Charter of Liberties.
    b. Declaration of Independence.
    c. Bill of Rights.
    d. Duke's Laws.

26. All of the statements correctly correspond to the religious group known as the Society of Friends, or Quakers, except
    a. They became pacifists.
    b. They denounced all oaths.
    c. They practiced polygamy.
    d. They refused to accept or confer titles.

27. Quakers transformed the structure of the family in all of the following ways except
    a. Women enjoyed almost complete equality and participated in making community decisions.

    b. They saw children as tiny sinners whose wills had to be broken by severe discipline.

    c. They began to limit family size in order to give more love to the children they did have.

    d. After the missionary impulse declined, they seldom associated with non-Quakers.

28. The Quakers founded two colonies in America. They were
    a. West New Jersey and Maryland.
    b. Georgia and Virginia.
    c. Pennsylvania and Virginia.
    d. West New Jersey and Pennsylvania.

ESSAY

Description and Explanation (one- to two-paragraph essay)

1. Describe French colonial administration.

2. Describe the differences between the Church of England and the Puritan and Separatist religious groups.

3. Describe the early problems of Jamestown and why the settlement finally succeeded.

4. Compare family life in Puritan and Chesapeake colonies.

5. Describe the similarities and differences among the Restoration colonies.

6. Describe Quaker religious views and how these affected Quaker family life.

Discussion and Analysis (class discussion or one- to two-paragraph essay)

1. Discuss the economic factors in Dutch expansion and the wealth of the Dutch economy.

2. Discuss the covenant theology of the Puritans, including the individual, communal, and national covenants and what they meant as the Puritans tried to put them into effect.

3. Discuss the ideas of James Harrington and the effects of these ideas on early Carolina, West Jersey, and Pennsylvania. Do his ideas have any validity in the present-day world?

4. Compare life expectancy, sex ratios, family structure, racial and ethic mixture, and intensity of religion in the areas from the Caribbean islands to New France and the colonies in between.

What If (Include an explanation of your position)

1. If you were a young Frenchman moving to Canada, would you be interested in becoming a *coureur de bois*?

2. If you were moving to colonial America, which colony would you prefer? Would it make a difference if you were traveling as a family, or belonged to certain religious group, or had some capital to invest?

Crossword Puzzle: The Challenge to Spain and the Settlement of North America

DOWN

1. Extreme English Protestants
2. Huge majority of immigrants from 1492–1810 were of ___ ancestry
3. Jamestown problem in winter of 1609–1610
4. Calvin's concern
5. Archbishop Laud's heresy
8. According to Puritans, first to learn of the covenant of grace
11. Thomas West, the Baron ___ , saved the Jamestown colony
13. Form of verb "to be"
15. Dutch dynasty
18. Mideast nation
19. Source of fuel, building material for colonists
20. Emotion evoked by Sir Francis Drake in Spain
23. Utilize

ACROSS

1. The ___ ___ kept Governor John White from returning to the Roanoke colony until 1590
6. Massachusetts Bay Protestant
7. Citrus fruit
9. English company and colony
10. Nova Scotia to Huguenots
12. Short for Cape Cod's region
13. Likely victim of malaria
14. Dutch home of Pilgrims
16. Long narrative story
17. Fifty percent of Pilgrims didn't survive their first ___ in America
21. Virginia boundary
22. Leeward island staple
24. Founder of Roanoke colony (variant spelling)
25. What Pilgrims were able to do from Squanto
26. Tool of choice in Indian agriculture

ANSWER KEY

WHO? WHAT? WHERE?

Who Were They?

1. e. Jacques Cartier, p. 47
2. g. Jean-Baptiste Colbert, p. 51
3. j. Peter Minuit, p. 53
4. a. Francis Drake, p. 55
5. d. Humphrey Gilbert, pp. 55–56
6. k. Richard Hakluyt, p. 58
7. h. John Rolfe, p. 62
8. b. George Calvert, p. 64
9. l. Squanto, p. 69
10. i. Oliver Cromwell, p. 78
11. f. James Harrington, p. 79
12. c. George Fox, p. 83

What Was It?

1. e. Huguenots, p. 46
2. d. *coureur de bois*, p. 51
3. a. Bank of Amsterdam, p. 52
4. g. ownership of land, p. 62
5. k. royal colony, p. 63
6. h. proprietary colony, p. 65
7. f. open field, p. 74
8. b. Baptist, p. 75
9. j. Restoration Era, p. 78–79
10. c. cavaliers, p. 78
11. i. Quakers, p. 83–84

Where Was It?

1. h. Spain, p. 45
2. g. St. Dominigue, p. 52
3. d. New Netherland, p. 53
4. c. Fort Christina, p. 54
5. i. tidewater, p. 59
6. f. Roanoke, p. 56–58
7. a. Carolina, p. 79
8. b. Charleston, p. 80
9. e. Pennsylvania, p. 85–88

CHARTS, MAPS, AND ILLUSTRATIONS

1. Aruba or Curacao, p. 67
2. Rolfe, p. 62
3. West Indies, p. 58
4. Mystic, Connecticut, p. 73

MULTIPLE CHOICE

1. a. (p. 46)
2. b. (p. 46)
3. b. (pp. 48–49)
4. d. (p. 51)
5. d. (p. 51)
6. c. (p. 52)
7. d. (p. 53)
8. c. (p. 53)
9. b. (p. 53)
10. c. (p. 59)
11. b. (p. 59)
12. c. (p. 65)
13. a. (p. 65)
14. a. (p. 66)
15. c. (p. 68)
16. d. (p. 69)

17. c. (p. 69)

18. a. (p. 70)

19. b. (p. 71)

20. d. (p. 73)

21. d. (p. 78)

22. d. (p. 78)

23. d. (p. 79)

24. a. (p. 79)

25. a. (p. 83)

26. c. (p. 83)

27. b. (p. 84)

28. d. (p. 84)

3. pp. 59–62

4. pp. 65–66, 72

5. p. 78

6. pp. 83–84

Discussion and Analysis

1. pp. 52–54

2. pp. 69–71

3. pp. 79–80

4. Chapter 2 *passim*

What If

1. pp. 50–52

2. Chapter 2 *passim*

ESSAY

Description and Explanation

1. pp. 51–52

2. pp. 54–55

Crossword Puzzle

CHAPTER 3

ENGLAND DISCOVERS ITS COLONIES: EMPIRE, LIBERTY, AND EXPANSION

At the beginning of the seventeenth century, England was a weak power with no American colonies. By 1700 it was a global giant with twenty colonies in North America and the West Indies and important overseas trade routes. This change happened during a century of civil wars, political and religious upheaval, and long struggles between various kings and Parliament over power. The result was a distinctive form of constitutionalism resting on parliamentary supremacy and responsible government in both. Representative government was taken for granted in England and the colonies. It was assumed that English colonies would elect an assembly that voted on all taxes and consented to all local laws. Parliament claimed full power over them, but, in practice, it seldom regulated anything except overseas trade. To the English government, this was a convenience, but in America it was beginning to acquire overtones of actual rights.

England's upheavals rocked the emerging empire, politically and economically. The disruption of trade cut off some of the settlements from their regular trade sources. Increasingly, the Dutch were active in trade with the English colonies. This fact contradicted the developing theory of mercantilism. Under this system, colonial commerce was an important source of a country's wealth. Areas that produced valuable commodities unavailable at home were considered essential, and colonial expansion in those areas was encouraged. Parliament passed a series of navigation acts to regulate overseas trade on the assumption that colonies existed only to enrich the mother country.

For most of the seventeenth century, the Spanish, French, and English empires remained isolated from one another and developed in different ways. Spain concentrated zealously on missionary pursuits among the Indians in North America. After a period of exploring and some missionary activity, the French engaged in the fur trade in the Great Lakes region and expanded into the Gulf Coast. The English emphasized settlement and expansion and, hence, greatly increased the number of inhabitants in their colonies. The population of British North America doubled every twenty-five years, profoundly affecting provincial America. Life in the colonies was also affected by the wars among European countries that subsequently spread to their overseas colonies.

LIBERTY, EQUALITY, POWER

The seventeenth century saw major shifts in power that eventually would increase liberty for many Americans. Ideas adopted later, during the American Revolution and its struggles with the division of power and growth in liberty, first developed during seventeenth-century upheavals in England. Increasingly, political philosophers dealt with the ideas of liberty, equality, and power.

By 1700, all of the colonies had some form of representative government, and power was shared within the colonial governments. Increasingly, Americans felt that it was their right to enact their own local laws. Toleration for Protestants was common. Some version of liberty as a counterpoint to power was becoming an accepted matter for some Americans. At the end of the century, England and the colonies all affirmed liberty under law. At the same time, it was believed that power had to be controlled, or liberty lost.

Liberty under law, however, was a concept for English Protestant males. Religious toleration under the English did not, generally, include non-Christians or even Catholics. The Spanish, French, and English demonstrated clearly their power over Native Americans.

OBJECTIVES

After studying this chapter a student should be able to

1. Discuss the Atlantic prism and spectrum of settlement.

2. Compare the relationship problems between Indians and whites in the 1640s and 1670s and the differences in the ways the colonies handled them.

3. Describe the ideas of mercantilism and the way the English government put them into effect.

4. Trace the rise of political parties in England.

5. Outline the transition to royal government in colonial America.

6. Describe the techniques Spain and France used in dealing with the Indians.

7. Review the role of the English colonies in the first three colonial wars.

CHRONOLOGY

1636	Massachusetts founded Harvard College and, six years later, required every town to have a writing school and larger towns to support a Latin grammar school.
1650	Upheaval in England filtered down to the rest of the emerging empire. As royal power collapsed, England's West Indian colonies demanded and received elective assemblies, and the Dutch seized control of trade in and out of the West Indian and Chesapeake colonies. By 1650, most of the sugar and tobacco trade went to Amsterdam, not to London.
	Parliament banned foreign ships from English colonies. The following year, it passed the comprehensive Navigation Act, aimed at Dutch competition.
1651–1652	An English naval force in America compelled Barbados and Virginia to submit to Parliament. In return, Virginia was allowed to elect its own governor, a privilege revoked in 1660. Trade with the Dutch continued in the absence of resident officials, who were supposed to enforce English policy.
1660	The Navigation Acts of 1651 were extended to require that all colonial trade be carried on English ships and the master and three fourths of the crew had to be English. Enumerated commodities, such as sugar and

tobacco, were to be shipped from the colony of origin only to England or to another English colony.

1662–1663   Charles II granted royal charters to Rhode Island in 1662 and to Connecticut in 1663. Both colonies were allowed to elect their governors and both houses of their legislature.

1663   With the Staple Act, Parliament regulated goods going to the colonies. With few exceptions, products from Europe, Asia, or Africa could not be delivered to the settlements unless they first landed in England.

1672–1674   In the third Anglo-Dutch war, a Dutch naval force again mauled the Chesapeake tobacco fleet and then headed north toward Manhattan in 1673. As the Dutch had done nine years earlier, the English garrison gave up without resistance. When the war was over, the colony was returned to the English.

1673   The Plantation Duty Act required captains of colonial ships to post bond in the colonies that they would deliver all enumerated commodities to England, or else pay on the spot the duties that would be owed in England. This act was designed to eliminate the incentives to smuggle. The act also established customs officials in all English colonies.

In quest of a passage to Asia, Father Jacques Marquette and trader Louis Joliet paddled down the Mississippi to its juncture with the Arkansas River. They turned back after becoming convinced that the Mississippi flowed into the Gulf of Mexico and not into the Pacific Ocean.

1675–1676   Metacom's (or King Phillip's) War began in June 1675 after Plymouth executed three Wampanoags for the murder of a Harvard-educated Indian preacher who may have been spying on Metacom. The following year the settlers won a decisive military victory.

Also in 1675, what began as a dispute along the frontier between Indians and whites escalated into a clash over control of the Indian trade and the Virginia government. It became known as Bacon's Rebellion, the largest upheaval in the American colonies before 1775. It ended with the death of Nathaniel Bacon in 1676 and the execution of some of his followers in early 1677 by Governor Sir William Berkeley.

1680   Popé, a San Juan Pueblo medicine man, organized an Indian revolt against the Spanish. It was the most successful Indian uprising in American history.

1682   The sieur de La Salle traveled down to the mouth of the Mississippi, claimed the entire area for France, and named it Louisiana in honor of King Louis XIV. Five years later, La Salle became lost in Texas and was murdered by his own men.

1685   James II, duke of York, became king following the death of Charles II.

Louis XIV of France revoked the Edict of Nantes and began to persecute the Huguenots. About 160,000 fled the kingdom, the largest forced migration in the history of early modern Europe. Some of them eventually settled in English North America.

1686

King James II sent Sir Edmund Andros to Massachusetts to establish a new government with no elective assembly, called the Dominion of New England. Later, New Hampshire, Plymouth, Rhode Island, Connecticut, New York, and both Jerseys were added to the Dominion.

1688

William of Orange, the husband of James's oldest daughter, Mary, landed in England and most of the English army supported him during the first weeks. James fled to France, and Parliament declared that James had abdicated the throne. William III and Mary II were named as joint sovereigns. This event became known as the Glorious Revolution.

1689–1697

King William's War broke out between England and France and, within a year, French-allied Indians had devastated most of coastal Maine, attacked the Mohawk Valley town of Schenectady, and forced most of its inhabitants into captivity. Sir William Phips of Massachusetts sailed up the St. Lawrence River but was bluffed into retreating by the French governor. Ultimately, Phips's forces collapsed under intercolonial bickering, so the French and Indians continued to dominate the frontier.

1690–1691

Competition from France in the Gulf of Mexico prompted the Spanish to move into Texas, where they established missions. Unfortunately, they brought smallpox to the Indians and, three years later, the Indians forced them to choose between leaving or facing a treacherous uprising.

In response to a military emergency, Massachusetts invented fiat money—paper money backed only by a government promise to accept it in payment of taxes.

1691

Massachusetts's new charter gave the king the right to appoint governors and other officers and to veto laws. The charter also granted toleration to all Protestants and based voting rights on property qualifications, not church membership. It also merged Plymouth and Maine with Massachusetts.

Jacob Leisler, leader of the mostly Dutch rebels in New York, was tried for treason and then hanged and drawn and quartered.

1692

Massachusetts became involved in the hysteria of the Salem Village trials. The new charter and the witch trials brought the Puritan era to a close.

1693

The first real commitment to education by Chesapeake settlers was the founding of the College of William and Mary and a Latin grammar school in Annapolis at about the same time.

1699

During a brief lull in the wars between France and England, the French returned to the Gulf of Mexico. Pierre le Moyne d'Iberville, a Canadian, built a fort at Biloxi. Three years later, he moved to Mobile to get closer to the more populous Indian nations of the interior, especially the Choctaws, who were looking for allies against the English.

1700	By this time, England possessed about twenty colonies in North America and the West Indies. Colonial and Asian commerce accounted for 30 to 40 percent of England's overseas trade, and London was the largest city in western Europe.
1701	The Five Nations of Iroquois negotiated a peace treaty with the French and the western Indians by which they agreed to remain neutral in any war between France and England. France's Indian allies, supported by a new French fort at Detroit, began returning to the fertile lands around Lakes Erie and Huron. The region became known as the "Middle Ground" over which New France exercised considerable influence, but only by respecting Indian customs and goals.
1702–1713	During Queen Anne's War, the French and Indians destroyed Deerfield, Massachusetts, while New England and the British tried to capture Acadia. In 1710, they succeeded and renamed the colony Nova Scotia. Carolina slavers invaded Spanish Florida between 1702 and 1704 with a large force of Indian allies, dragged off four thousand women and children as slaves, drove nine thousand Indians from their homes, and wrecked the missions of Florida.
1707	With the Act of Union, England and Scotland agreed to merge their separate parliaments and become the single kingdom of Great Britain.
1732	The Hat Act prohibited the export of hats made in the colonies and limited the number of apprentices a colonial hatter could maintain. Nobody enforced the second provision.
1750	The Iron Act prohibited the erection of certain types of iron mills. It was designed to protect industries in England.

GLOSSARY OF IMPORTANT TERMS

balance of trade	The relationship between imports and exports. The difference between exports and imports is the balance between the two. A healthy nation should export more than it imports. This is known as a favorable balance of trade.
entail	A system of inheritance that prohibited a landowner, or his heir, from dividing up a landed estate.
enumerated commodities	A group of colonial products that had to be shipped from the colony of origin to England or another colony. The most important products were sugar and tobacco.
funded national debt	The state agreed to pay the interest due to its creditors before all other obligations.
Glorious Revolution	The overthrow of James II by Parliament, which invited William and Mary to ascend the throne of England. This marked the end of political upheaval in England.

heathen	A term used sometimes by Christians to refer to anyone who was not a Christian or a Jew.
Iroquois League	A group of five tribes centered around the Mohawk Valley who were very active in the fur trade. They first worked with the Dutch and then the English. They were especially successful in using adoption as a means of remaining strong.
Middle Ground	The area of French and Indian cooperation around the Great Lakes that was controlled by New France. It was the basis of their extensive fur trade.
Mourning War	An Indian war often initiated by a widow or bereaved relative who insisted that her male relatives repair the loss.
Onontio	The term used by the Algonquian Indians to designate the governor of New France.
powwow	Originally, a word used to identify tribal prophets or medicine men. Later it was used also to describe the ceremonies held by them.
praying Indians	The Christian Indians of New England.
primogeniture	The English practice requiring that the eldest son inherited all the land of his father's estate.
sachem	A word in the Iroquoian Indian language meaning chief.
Tories	A term for Irish Catholic peasants who murdered Protestant landlords. It was used to describe the followers of Charles II and became one of the names of the two major political parties in England.
Whigs	The name of an obscure sect of Scottish religious extremists who favored the assassination of Charles and James of England. The term was used to denote one of the two leading political parties of late seventeenth-century England.

WHO? WHAT? WHERE?

WHO WERE THEY?

Complete each statement below (questions 1–12) by writing the letter preceding the appropriate name in the space provided. Use each answer only once.

    a. Esther Wheelwright
    b. Increase Mather
    c. Jacob Leisler
    d. Jacques Marquette
    e. John Eliot
    f. John Sassamon
    g. Lord Shaftesbury

    h. Robert Carter
    i. Sir Edmund Andros
    j. Sir Robert Walpole
    k. Sir William Berkeley
    l. William of Orange

_____ 1. Missionary who translated the entire Bible into the Wampanoag Indian language.

_____ 2. Harvard-educated Indian minister who may have been spying on Indian leaders and was murdered by some of the Indians.

_____ 3. Prominent Boston minister who saw the conflict with the Indians in Metacom's War as God's judgment on a sinful people.

_____ 4. Governor of Virginia during the dispute with Nathaniel Bacon over power in the colonial government and the fur trade.

_____ 5. Main organizer of the opposition to James II and also the founder of one of the first English political parties.

_____ 6. Leader of the Whig government in Britain for twenty years.

_____ 7. Autocratic governor of New York who tried to establish the Dominion of New England.

_____ 8. Leader of the Netherlands and husband of the eldest daughter of James II.

_____ 9. Leader of the mostly Dutch rebels in New York City who was arrested and then hanged.

_____ 10. One of the early French explorers of the Mississippi.

_____ 11. First American planter to acquire a thousand slaves and several hundred thousand acres of land.

_____ 12. New England settler captured by the Indians and taken to Canada. She later became the mother superior of the Ursuline nuns in New France.

WHAT WAS IT?

Complete each statement below (questions 1–11) by writing the letter preceding the appropriate response in the space provided. Use each answer only once.

    a. Act of Union
    b. Board of Trade
    c. brandy
    d. Choctaws
    e. enumerated commodities
    f. Glorious Revolution
    g. hats
    h. Iron Act
    i. Iroquois
    j. Mourning War
    k. praying Indians
    l. Tories

_____ 1. Group of colonial products that had to be shipped from the colony of origin to England or another colony.

_____ 2. Five tribes centered around the Mohawk River Valley who were involved in the fur trade, first with the Dutch and later with the English.

_____ 3. Type of Indian war often initiated by a widow or bereaved relative who insisted that her male relatives repair her loss.

_____ 4. Christian Indians in New England.

_____ 5. Term for Irish Catholic peasants who murdered Protestant landlords. It later was applied as a term to describe an English political party.

_____ 6. Period when the Stuarts were overthrown and replaced by William and Mary.

_____ 7. Almost purely advisory agency that replaced the Lords of Trade in 1696. It made recommendations and collected information.

_____ 8. Measure by which England and Scotland agreed to merge their parliaments and become the kingdom of Great Britain.

_____ 9. This act prohibited the erection of certain types of iron mills in the colonies.

_____ 10. Lubricant of the French fur trade.

_____ 11. Southern Indian tribe used by the French as the anchor of their trading system out of Mobile.

WHERE WAS IT?

Complete each statement below (questions 1–9) by writing the letter preceding the appropriate response in the space provided. Use each answer only once.

    a. Acadia
    b. Deerfield, Massachusetts
    c. Glasgow
    d. Great Swamp
    e. London
    f. Natick
    g. New England
    h. Sugar Islands
    i. Salem Village

_____ 1. Most English of the colonial areas.

_____ 2. Colonial area with the greatest wealth and fewest clergymen.

_____ 3. Largest city in western Europe.

_____ 4. Missionary town among the Indians that was founded by John Eliot.

_____ 5. Place where a Puritan army, with the aid of Indian guides, attacked a fort being constructed by the Narragansett Indians. Hundreds of Indians were massacred.

_____ 6. Location of the witch-trial hysteria.

_____ 7. Scottish city built on the colonial tobacco trade.

_____ 8. Town attacked by Indians during Queen Anne's War. As a result, most of its settlers were marched off to captivity.

_____ 9. French colony captured by the British and renamed Nova Scotia.

CHARTS, MAPS, AND ILLUSTRATIONS

1. The early settler who painted many Indian scenes on Roanoke Island was

   _____ .

2. The home of Governor Berkeley at the time of Bacon's Rebellion was called

   _____ .

   Was there any similarity with the one belonging to the small planter of the same time?

   _____ .

3. According to the map on government and religion in the British colonies (p. 115), the colony with a Dutch Reformed preponderence was

   _____ .

4. The fort at the southernmost tip of the French Middle Ground was

   _____ .

5. Much of the war with the Southeast theater centered around the Spanish town of

   _____ .

MULTIPLE CHOICE

Circle the letter that best completes each statement.

1. By the last half of the seventeenth century, life expectancy was lowest in
   a. French Canada.
   b. South Carolina.
   c. Maryland.
   d. Massachusetts.

2. The colony in which the English were the minority of the white settlers by 1750 was
   a. Virginia.
   b. South Carolina.
   c. Pennsylvania.
   d. Maryland.

3. The colony on the mainland of North America with the highest percentage of slaves was
   a. South Carolina.
   b. New Jersey.

    c. Virginia.
    d. Maryland.

4. During the seventeenth century, most European powers followed a set of policies loosely described as mercantilistic. All of the following were part of these policies except
    a. Power was derived ultimately from the wealth of the country.
    b. Colonies were designed to benefit the mother country.
    c. The creation of wealth required vigorous trade.
    d. All European countries believed in free and unlimited trade.

5. According to seventeenth-century philosophers, the major passions were the following, except for
    a. glory.
    b. greed.
    c. nationalism.
    d. love.

6. In 1650, Parliament banned foreign ships from English colonies. One year later, it passed the first comprehensive Navigation Act, aimed at competition from the
    a. Dutch.
    b. French.
    c. Spanish.
    d. Portuguese.

7. In 1660, Parliament extended the Navigation Acts of 1651 to require all of the following except
    a. All colonial trade was to be carried on English ships.
    b. The master and three fourths of the crew had to be English.
    c. Captains of colonial ships would no longer post bond in the colonies to ensure that they would deliver all enumerated commodities to England.
    d. Enumerated commodities, such as sugar and tobacco, had to be shipped from the colony of origin only to England or to another English colony.

8. In the Staple Act of 1663, Parliament regulated goods going to
    a. France.
    b. the colonies.
    c. Italy.
    d. Spain.

9. The most desired and devastating commodity Europeans brought to the Indians was
    a. pots.
    b. hatchets.
    c. alcohol.
    d. European cloth.

10. Thomas Mayhew, Sr., and Thomas Mayhew, Jr., of Plymouth
    a. attacked the authority of the sachems as well as the powwows.
    b. tried to destroy the traditional tribal structure.

    c. insisted on turning Indian men into farmers, which was a female role in Indian society.

    d. encouraged Indian men to teach the settlers of Martha's Vineyard and Nantucket how to catch whales, which made them a vital part of the settler's economy without challenging their identity as males.

11. In June 1675, fighting between Indians and settlers escalated into war. The Indians had all of the following advantages except

    a. The settlers were overconfident, due to their easy triumph over the Pequots a generation earlier.

    b. Since the 1630s, the Indians had acquired firearms.

    c. The settlers were expert marksmen and hunters.

    d. The Indians had built forges to make musket balls and to repair their muskets.

12. The largest upheaval in the American colonies before 1775 occurred in Virginia. The rebellion was named after

    a. Nathaniel Bacon.

    b. John Washington.

    c. William Berkeley.

    d. John Sassamon.

13. After inheriting the throne in 1685, King James II did all of the following except

    a. disallow the New York Charter of Liberties of 1683.

    b. abolish the colonial assembly in the Dominion of New England.

    c. send Sir Edmund Andros to Massachusetts to establish a new government called the Dominion of New England.

    d. abolish all revenue acts.

14. Sir Edmund Andros

    a. governed through an appointive council and a Superior Court that rode circuit, dispensing justice throughout the Dominion.

    b. supported an elective assembly.

    c. disallowed religious toleration for the Puritans.

    d. was disliked by the merchants whom he excluded from politics.

15. Parliament's Toleration Act of the late 1680s gave the right to worship publicly only to

    a. Protestants.

    b. Catholics.

    c. Muslims.

    d. Jews.

16. Salem Village in Massachusetts was plagued in the early 1690s by

    a. witch hunts.

    b. Indian attacks.

    c. locusts.

    d. smallpox.

17. In 1696, William III replaced the Lords of Trade with the Board of Trade. All of the following statements correctly characterized the new agency except
    a. Its powers were almost purely advisory.
    b. It made policy recommendations to appropriate governmental bodies in England.
    c. Its main purpose was to collect reliable information on complex questions and offer helpful advice.
    d. Its power was comprehensive and unlimited.

18. When Massachusetts received its new charter in 1691, all of the following were included in it except
    a. The colonies of Plymouth and Maine became part of Massachusetts.
    b. Voting rights were based on a combination of property qualifications and church membership.
    c. The general court of Massachusetts retained control over the distribution of land.
    d. The English Crown would appoint the governor of the colony.

19. The most successful Indian revolt in American history was organized by a San Juan Pueblo medicine man named
    a. Jacques Marquette.
    b. Popé.
    c. James Franklin.
    d. Louis Joliet.

20. The leaders of New France were eager to erect an Algonquian shield against the Iroquois (and, in later decades, against the British), so they began supplying the Algonquians with
    a. firearms and brandy.
    b. furs and corn.
    c. bows and arrows.
    d. wives and fishhooks.

21. In 1701, France's Indian allies, supported by a new French fort erected at Detroit, began returning to the fertile lands around Lakes Erie and Huron. The region became a Middle Ground over which New France exercised considerable influence, but only by
    a. respecting Indian customs and goals.
    b. incessant warfare with the Indians.
    c. seizing Indians and holding them captive.
    d. bribing Indian leaders.

22. In 1682, the entire area surrounding the mouth of the Mississippi (Louisiana) was claimed for France by
    a. Pierre le Moyne d'Iberville.
    b. Father Jacques Marquette.
    c. the sieur de La Salle.
    d. Louis Joliet.

23. Alarmed at any challenge to its monopoly on the Gulf of Mexico, Pensacola was founded in 1698 by
   a. China.
   b. France.
   c. England.
   d. Spain.

24. All of the following statements relating to colonial military service and war are correct except
   a. Most men would serve under any officer for multiple campaigns, and many reenlisted to become soldiers (in the European sense).
   b. Military service, for those who survived it, could lead to the ownership of land and to an earlier marriage.
   c. For New England women, war increased the median age of marriage by about two years, which usually meant one less pregnancy per marriage.
   d. Provincials disapproved of blind obedience to commands.

25. In each of the colonial wars between Britain and France, New Englanders called for the conquest of
   a. Italy.
   b. New York.
   c. New France.
   d. Mexico.

ESSAY

Description and Explanation (one- to two-paragraph essay)

1. Describe the provisions of the Navigation Acts. Were they successful in accomplishing what the English government wanted?

2. Describe the Indian strategies for survival.

3. Describe the concept of a mixed and balanced constitution.

4. Describe French colonization and the fur trade.

5. Describe the role of New England in the early colonial wars.

Discussion and Analysis (class discussion or one- to two-paragraph essay)

1. Discuss the Atlantic prism and spectrum of settlement, and compare life expectancy, sex ratios, family structure, racial and ethnic mixture, and intensity of religion in the areas from the Caribbean islands to New France and the colonies in between.

2. Compare the Whigs and Tories in the origin of their names, their positions on the issues in England, shifts in their positions, and ways they retained their power.

What If (include an explanation of your position)

1. If you were a woman, which area of colonial America do you think would offer you the best chance to acquire property?

2. If you were a small planter in Virginia, how would you regard the depute between Governor Berkeley and Nathaniel Bacon?

3. If you were an Indian in New England in the 1600s, how would you regard the Puritans?

Crossword Puzzle: England Discovers Its Colonies: Empire, Liberty, and Expansion

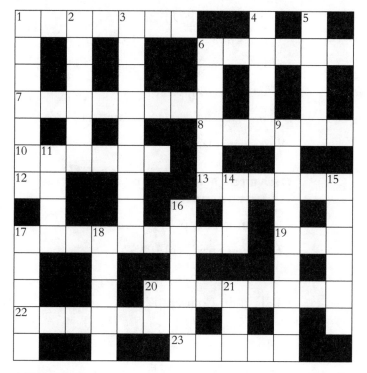

DOWN

1. Dutch rebel Jacob of New York
2. Surname for Charles and James
3. Mississippi Valley to the French
4. Jamestown firebug of 1676
5. Translation text for John Eliot
6. He was jobless in Boston after the Glorious Revolution
9. Sir William Berkeley and others
11. One of Columbus's three
14. Colonial building material
15. Sidearms for settlers
16. Tribe and valley of New York
17. Walpole's supporters
18. If England represents the source of white light, the Atlantic served as a refracting ___
20. Santa sound
21. Number of years between start of Metacom's War and the Edict of Nantes

ACROSS

1. French explorer who traveled Mississippi to its mouth
6. Nova Scotia formerly
7. Victim of Pueblo revolt
8. Virginia frontier guardian
10. Primogeniture partner
12. Unorthodox New England colony for short

13. South Carolina's greed for ___ ignited Yamasee War
17. One of King Philip's folks
19. Grande for one
20. A colonial capital
22. Scottish tobacco town
23. Metacom and others

ANSWER KEY

WHO? WHAT? WHERE?
Who Were They?

1. e.   John Eliot, p. 100
2. f.   John Sassamon, p. 101
3. b.   Increase Mather, p. 103
4. k.   William Berkeley, p. 103
5. g.   Lord Shaftesbury, p. 107
6. j.   Sir Robert Walpole, p. 107
7. i.   Sir Edmund Andros, p. 110
8. l.   William of Orange, p. 110
9. c.   Jacob Leisler, p. 111
10. d.   Jacques Marquette, p. 120
11. h.   Robert Carter, p. 121
12. a.   Esther Wheelwright, p. 124

What Was It?

1. e.   enumerated commodities, p. 98
2. i.   Iroquois League, p. 99
3. j.   Mourning War, p. 100
4. k.   praying Indians, p. 100
5. l.   Tories, p. 107
6. f.   Restoration Era, p. 110
7. b.   Board of Trade, p. 114
8. a.   Act of Union, p. 116
9. h.   Iron Act, p. 116
10. c.   brandy, p. 119
11. d.   Choctaws, p. 120

Where Was It?

1. g.   New England, p. 93
2. h.   Sugar Islands, p. 99
3. e.   London, p. 100
4. f.   Natick, p. 102
5. d.   Great Swamp, p. 102
6. i.   Salem Village, p. 113
7. c.   Glasgow, p. 116
8. b.   Deerfield, Massachusetts, p. 123
9. a.   Acadia, p. 124

CHARTS, MAPS, AND ILLUSTRATIONS

1. John White, p. 97
2. Green Spring, p. 105
3. New York, p. 115
4. Fort St. Louis, p. 120
5. St. Augustine, p. 124

MULTIPLE CHOICE

1. b.   (p. 91)
2. c.   (p. 93)
3. a.   (p. 93)
4. d.   (p. 96)
5. c.   (p. 96)
6. a.   (p. 97)
7. c.   (p. 98)
8. b.   (p. 99)
9. c.   (p. 100)
10. d.   (p. 100)
11. c.   (p. 101)
12. a.   (p. 103)
13. d.   (p. 110)
14. a.   (p. 110)
15. a.   (p. 112)

16. a. (p. 113)

17. d. (p. 114)

18. b. (p. 113)

19. b. (p. 117)

20. a. (p. 119)

21. a. (p. 119)

22. c. (p. 120)

23. d. (p. 120)

24. a. (pp. 122–123)

25. c. (p. 123)

3. pp. 116–117

4. pp. 119–120

5. pp. 123–124

Discussion and Analysis

1. pp. 91–93

2. p. 117

What If

1. pp. 94–95

2. pp. 104–106

3. pp. 100–101

ESSAY

Description and Explanation

1. pp. 98–99

2. pp. 99–100

Crossword Puzzle

CHAPTER 4

PROVINCIAL AMERICA AND THE STRUGGLE FOR A CONTINENT

During the eighteenth century, the English colonies developed into distinct regions. The South used extensive slave labor to produce crops to be sold in Europe, thus creating a social structure defined by a rigid social hierarchy. New England, on the other hand, was a land of farmers, fishermen, lumberjacks, shipwrights, and merchants. Few immigrants went to New England in the eighteenth century. In contrast, the middle colonies consisted of an ethnic and religious mix of settlers that began when that area first was settled. Immigration of the Ulster Irish and Germans made the middle colonies even more diverse. The valleys of the Hudson and Delaware Rivers contained the most prosperous family farmers in North America and two large cities by 1760.

These three colonial regions, however, were alike in their interest in replicating British society. In the eighteenth century, printing, the learned professions (such as law and medicine), and the intellectual movement known as the Enlightenment, all made an impact on the British colonies. A powerful religious revival, known as the Great Awakening, also swept over the colonies in the 1730s and 1740s. These forces had an anglicizing effect on the American colonies.

By the 1720s, nearly every colony had an appointed governor, a council, and an assembly elected by the settlers. The assembly was seen as embodying a colony's democratic elements. Over the years, legislatures sat longer and passed more laws, and assemblymen usually took the initiative in drafting major bills. Northern colonies, with their more diverse economic groups and ethnic interests, were more likely to give rise to political factions. Most southern colonies practiced the politics of harmony.

A new era of imperial war began in 1739 and continued, with only a brief interruption, until 1763. The British, French, and Spanish colonies, together with most of the Indians east of the Mississippi, were involved in this period of war. The last of four wars, the French and Indian War, started in the colonies, and from the beginning the Indians were a significant factor in the war. This war was strongly supported by the colonials and, measured by casualties per capita, was the third bloodiest contest Americans ever have fought. By the late 1750s, the British, under William Pitt, had assumed control of the war and were victorious nearly everywhere and conquered extensive territory. The Peace of Paris in 1763 removed France from North America, gave Florida to Britain, and Louisiana to Spain.

LIBERTY, EQUALITY, POWER

The anglicization of the colonies reduced the status of women. The European double standard of sexual behavior for men and women revived in the colonies, and women often had fewer rights of inheritance and property than they had in the previous century. As the population and wealth of each region increased, prestige and power were concentrated in the hands of fewer and fewer families.

This trend set in motion a pattern of dependency of poorer families on fewer wealthy families and, as a result, equality and power for many ordinary families were decreased.

The growth of the learned professions increased the concepts of liberty in America with such ideas as freedom of the press. The flourishing beliefs of the Enlightenment encouraged discussion on abstractions such as liberty and equality. The Great Awakening instilled in congregations the desire to exercise their religious liberty and to establish their own churches. These new churches sometimes allowed more equality and power to ordinary members, thus advancing the idea of the right to liberty in America.

The white English colonists, from both North and South, were convinced that they were free in a way that French and Spanish colonists were not and that Britain was the bastion of liberty. Only when the wars for the empire were unfolding did the colonials insist that liberty itself was at stake in the contest; and they were willing to fight for it.

Some groups had different views from the white colonists. Slaves tended to identify Spain with their liberty. The first free-black community in Florida acted as a beacon for Carolina slaves. During the Stono Uprising in South Carolina, the slaves clearly wanted their liberty. The Indians along the frontier identified France as the protector of their liberty and independence. When France surrendered the frontier to Britain, the Indians were not considered in the final treaty. Many Indians considered Britain an unlikely protector, and they were uniting to protect their freedom and power along the frontier.

OBJECTIVES

After studying this chapter, a student should be able to

1. Describe the effects of anglicization.
2. Compare the life of slaves in the Chesapeake region and the Lower South.
3. Compare the economies of the three colonial regions and their effects on the lifestyles of the region.
4. Trace the origins of professions such as law and medicine in the colonies.
5. Describe the Enlightenment in the colonies.
6. Discuss the Great Awakening and its long-term effects on religion and American life.
7. Analyze the changes in colonial government.
8. Discuss the role of the colonies in the French and Indian War and the effects of the war on the colonies.

CHRONOLOGY

1636   Massachusetts founded Harvard College and, six years later, required every town to have a writing school and larger towns to support a Latin grammar school.

1690	In response to a military emergency, Massachusetts invented fiat money—paper money backed only by a government promise to accept it in payment of taxes.
1693	The first real commitment to education by Chesapeake settlers was the founding of the College of William and Mary and a Latin grammar school in Annapolis about the same time.
1700	Before **1700**, ordinary farmers and small planters often had sat in colonial assemblies. However, after **1700**, those who participated in public life above the local level came increasingly from a higher social status.
1700–1740	A massive influx of slaves over four decades laid the foundation that would form the Old South—a society consisting of wealthy slaveholding planters, a much larger class of small planters, and thousands of slaves. By **1720**, slaves made up 70 percent of South Carolina, 40 percent of Virginia, and almost 30 percent of Maryland.
1704	John Campbell, the city's postmaster, established the *Boston Newsletter.*
1710–1719	Governor Robert Hunter of New York achieved spectacular success by playing off one faction against another in a colony that had been fiercely divided since Leisler's rebellion.
1712	A bloody slave revolt broke out in New York City that killed nine settlers. Afterward, twenty-one slaves were tortured and executed.
1716–1720	To counter French efforts to hold on to the Gulf of Mexico, Spain sent missionaries and soldiers into Texas between 1716 and 1720, establishing a capital at Los Adaes.
1717–1721	The French-owned Company of the Indies shipped seven thousand settlers and two thousand slaves to Louisiana. In less than ten years, half of them had died or fled.
1718	The first Ulsterites from Ireland sailed for New England, expecting to be welcomed by fellow Calvinists. However, they were treated with suspicion and hostility and, after 1718, most Ulster emigrants headed for the Delaware Valley.
1720s	Every colony except Connecticut and Rhode Island had an appointive governor, either royal or proprietary, plus a council and an elective assembly.
1721	Smallpox devastated Boston until Dr. Zabdiel Boylston began inoculating people with the disease on the theory that healthy individuals would survive and develop an immunity to it.
1722	During commencement exercises, the entire Yale College faculty, except for a nineteen-year-old tutor, Jonathan Edwards, stunned observers by announcing their conversion to the Church of England.
	The French founded the city of New Orleans.

1727	Benjamin Franklin and several friends founded the Junto, a debating society that discussed literary and philosophical questions. Later, it evolved into the American Philosophical Society, which still meets near Independence Hall. In **1729**, Franklin took over the *Pennsylvania Gazette* and made it the best-edited newspaper in America.
1729	When the French began to take over the lands of the Natchez Indians, the Natchez killed every French male in the area. In the war that followed, the French and their Choctaw allies destroyed the Natchez as a distinct people, although some refugees found homes among the Chickasaws and the Creeks.
1720–1765	Between these years, especially during the administration of Sir William Gooch (1727–1748), the governor of Virginia and House of Burgesses engaged in only one public quarrel, a remarkable record of political harmony.
1730	Virginia passed an inspection law that guaranteed a high-quality tobacco and raised tobacco prices.
1730s	The Log College at Neshaminy, Pennsylvania, was established by William Tennent, Sr., where he trained evangelical Presbyterian ministers.
1730s–early 1740s	An immense religious revival, known as the Great Awakening, swept across the Protestant world.
1732	A group of trustees obtained a charter for a colony they named Georgia. It reflected a combination of Anglican humanitarianism, Enlightenment beliefs in social improvements, and a military need to protect South Carolina.
1733	Parliament passed a prohibitive tax on all foreign molasses imported to the colonies. The Molasses Act was not strictly enforced and resulted in bribery and smuggling.
1735	John Peter Zenger, editor of a New York newspaper, was acquitted of the crime of "seditious libel," which involved criticizing government officials. This was a major victory for freedom of the press.
1738	The governor of Spanish Florida established a new town, Gracia Real de Santa Teresa de Mose (or Mose for short). Francisco Menéndez, an African, was put in charge, and the town's very existence attracted Carolina slaves, especially those who were Catholic. This was the first community of free blacks in what is now the United States.
1739	The Spanish governor of Florida offered liberty to any slave from the British colonies. This, rumors about Mose, and religious and personal reasons served as contributing factors in touching off the Stono Rebellion in South Carolina, the largest slave revolt in the history of the thirteen colonies.
1739	George Whitefield began a religious speaking tour that included most of the colonies. At times, up to 30,000 people attended his meetings.

1739–1763	A new era of imperial war began and continued with only a brief interruption for over two decades. The British colonies, New Spain, and New France all became involved, and eventually so did all Indians east of the Mississippi River.
1740	Boston had eight printers, New York and Philadelphia each had two. No other community in the colonies had more than one.
	James Oglethorpe, governor of Georgia, invaded Spanish Florida. His invasion was unsuccessful, but he brought back rumors that Spain was sending blacks into the British colonies to start slave revolts.
1740s	Heavy military appropriations sent the value of New England currency to a new low. Observing an opportunity to rid the colonies of paper money, Governor William Shirley and House Speaker Thomas Hutchinson persuaded the legislature to retire all paper money and convert the American economy to silver money. This was an example of anglicization, since Massachusetts repudiated its own form of money in favor of British methods of public finance.
1741	New York City's two thousand slaves were the largest concentration of blacks in British North America outside of Charleston. The New York slave conspiracy trials ended when four whites and eighteen slaves were hanged, thirteen slaves were burned alive, and seventy slaves were banished to the West Indies.
1741–1756	William Shirley, governor of Massachusetts, used judicial and militia appointments and wartime contracts to build a majority in the assembly.
1741–1767	Governor Benning Wentworth of New Hampshire created a powerful political machine that gave something to just about every assemblyman.
1742	Philip V of Spain sent thirty-six ships and two thousand soldiers from Cuba with instructions to devastate Georgia and South Carolina and free the slaves. Governor James Oglethorpe of Georgia and his men ambushed two patrols, and the Spanish morale collapsed.
	In South Carolina, Hugh Bryan, a Savannah River planter, began preaching the evangelical message to his slaves. He announced that slavery was a sin and that God would pour out his wrath on planters unless they rejected it. However, he later renounced his actions and apologized for being "deluded."
1743	James Davenport established the "Shepherd's Tent" in New London in order to train awakened preachers. This outdoor school abandoned the classical curriculum and insisted on a valid conversion experience.
1744	France joined Spain in the war against Britain, and the main struggle shifted northward.
1745	The mighty French fortress, Louisbourg, on Cape Breton Island, fell to the British in **June**.

1747	Virginians organized the Ohio Company of Virginia to settle the area of the Ohio Valley. Their first outpost was to be at the point where the Monongahela and Allegheny Rivers converge to form the Ohio River.
1748	Britain had to return Louisbourg to France in the Treaty of Aix-la-Chapelle, which ended the war in **1748**.
1749	The British government, worried that its hold on Nova Scotia was feeble, recruited 2,500 Protestants from the continent of Europe to settle the colony, accompanied by four regiments of redcoats. In **1749** they founded the town of Halifax.
	Massachusetts retired all paper money and converted to silver, a more orthodox method of public finance.
1750	Germans outnumbered the original English and Welsh settlers of Pennsylvania.
1752	Georgia became a royal colony.
1753	Virginia sent George Washington to the Ohio country to warn Marquis Duquesne to withdraw, and a small Virginia force began building a fort at the fork of the Ohio River. Marquis Duquesne ignored Washington, advanced toward the Ohio, expelled the Virginians, took over the fort, and finished building it.
1754	Virginia sent Washington back to the Ohio, and he ordered an attack that started a world war. He then surrendered to the French at Great Meadows.
	The Albany Congress originally was called to meet with the Iroquois because of fear that they might side with New France. Massachusetts instructed its commissioners to work for a plan of intercolonial union. The congress adopted an amended version of a proposal by Benjamin Franklin for promoting unity among the colonies. Every colony rejected it.
	America's first political cartoon appeared in Benjamin Franklin's *Pennsylvania Gazette*.
1754–1763	Four wars were fought between Britain and France from 1689 to 1763; only the last, which started in the mid-1700s, began in America. That last conflict, popularly known as the French and Indian War, was also the biggest and produced the most sweeping results. Spain's neutrality until 1762 permitted the British to concentrate their resources against New France.
1755	General Edward Braddock landed with regiments of British soldiers in Virginia. He was the commander-in-chief of the British army in North America. He was killed and his army devastated near Fort Duquesne.
	The French built Fort Carillon (the British called it Ticonderoga) at Lake Champlain south of Crown Point.

The modernizing British state with its disciplined professional army came into direct and sustained contact with North America's householder society and its voluntaristic principles.

1756–1763   Britain declared war on France, and the colonial contest merged into a general European struggle that pitted France, Austria, and Russia against Prussia, which was heavily subsidized by Britain. The Seven Years' War created a sharper confrontation between Protestant and Catholic states than Europe had seen in more than a century.

1756–1757   New France under Governor-General Pierre de Rigaud de Vaudreuil kept winning over the British and the provincials. He understood the French need for Indian support. Then Louis-Joseph, marquis de Montcalm, a professional general, was sent to New France to assume command. He tried to turn the conflict into a traditional European struggle.

1757   William Pitt came to power. He sharply reversed the authoritarian emphasis by appealing to the patriotism of the colonials and by opening voluntaristic ways for them to support the war effort.

1758   By this time, the British empire finally had put together a military force capable of overwhelming New France and had learned how to use it. During the last years of the war, the redcoats and provincials began to cooperate, and they became a devastatingly effective force.

The Royal Navy cut Canada off from reinforcements and routine supplies. Britain sent more than thirty regiments to North America.

Spurred on by Quaker intermediaries, the British and colonial governments came to terms with the western Indians, promised not to seize their lands after the war, and arranged an uneasy peace. Few settlers or officials had yet noticed a new trend—few Indians in the northeastern woodlands were willing to attack other Indians.

1759   General James Wolfe ascended the St. Lawrence River with eight thousand redcoats and colonial rangers and laid siege to Quebec, defended by Montcalm with sixteen thousand regulars, Canadian militia, and Indians. In **September**, Wolfe deployed his men on the Plains of Abraham behind Quebec. In the European-style battle, the French were defeated and surrendered Quebec.

1760   After a long winter, the North American war was all but over as armies converged from all sides on Montreal, and Canada finally surrendered.

1762   William Shippen arrived in Philadelphia, where he became the first American to lecture on medicine, publish a treatise on chemistry, and dissect human cadavers.

Spain entered the war in an attempt to prevent a total British victory.

1763   The Peace of Paris ended the war. France surrendered to Britain all of North America east of the Mississippi River, except for New Orleans. In exchange for Havana, Spain ceded Florida to Britain. To compensate its Spanish ally, France gave New Orleans and all of Louisiana west of the Mississippi River to Spain.

GLOSSARY OF IMPORTANT TERMS

bateau   A light, flat-bottomed boat with narrow ends that was used in Canada and the northeastern part of the colonies.

blast   A plant disease that affected wheat and first appeared in New England in the 1660s. There were no known remedies for the disease, and it gradually spread until wheat production in New England nearly ceased.

coverture   A common-law doctrine that prohibited women from making a contract while married. The legal personality of the husband covered the wife, and he made all legally binding decisions.

dower rights   The right of a widow to a portion of her deceased husband's estate (usually one third of the value of the estate). It was passed to their children upon her death.

dowry   The cash or goods a woman received from her father when she married.

enfranchise   To give the right to vote. In colonial America, roughly three fourths of the adult white males could meet all the requirements for voting.

entail   A system of inheritance that prohibited a landowner, or his heir, from dividing up a landed estate.

evangelical   A style of Christian ministry that includes much zeal and enthusiasm. Evangelical ministers tend to emphasize personal conversion and faith rather than religious ritual.

fiat money   Paper money backed only by the promise of the government to accept it in payment of taxes. It originated in Massachusetts after a military emergency in 1690.

gang labor   A system where planters organized their field slaves into gangs, supervised them closely, and kept them working in the fields all day. This type of labor was used on tobacco plantations.

gentleman   A term used to describe a person who performed no manual labor.

Great Awakening   An immense religious revival that swept across the Protestant world.

Gullah   A language spoken by newly imported African slaves. Originally, it was a simple second language for everyone who spoke it, but gradually evolved into another language. Modern black English is derived in part from Gullah and was born in the rice fields and sea islands of South Carolina.

indigo A blue dye obtained from plants that was used by the textile industry. The British government encouraged the commercial production of it in South Carolina.

irregular war A type of war using men who were not part of a permanent or professional regular military force. It also can apply to guerilla-type warfare, usually against the civilian population.

long knives The term Indians used to describe Virginians.

naval stores Items such as pitch, resin, turpentine, and lumber that were used to manufacture ships. Most of them were obtained from pine trees.

new lights A term used to describe prorevival Congregationalists. Old lights were antirevival Congregationalists.

new sides A term used to describe evangelical Presbyterians. Old sides were antirevival Presbyterians.

patriarchal A society dominated by the male or father in a household.

patronage The act of appointing people to government jobs or awarding them government contracts, often based on political favoritism rather than on abilities.

politics of harmony A system of ritualized mutual flattery in which the governor and the colonial assembly worked through persuasion rather than through patronage or bullying.

privateer A privately owned ship that was authorized by a government to attack enemy ships during times of war. The owner of the ship got to claim a portion of whatever was captured. This was a way to damage the ability of the enemy country to engage in shipping without the expense of expanding the navy.

redemptioners This term described servants who were employed in a type of indentured contract that allowed them to find masters after they arrived in the colonies. It was attractive to couples because it allowed them to stay together. Many German settlers were redemptioners.

republics Independent Indian villages that were willing to trade with the British and remained outside the French system of Indian alliances.

revival An emotional religious meeting.

sickle cell A crescent- or sickle-shaped red blood cell sometimes found in African Americans. It helped protect them from malaria but exposed their children to the dangerous condition of sickle cell anemia.

synod The governing body of the Presbyterian church. A meeting or convention of church officials or an assembly of churches.

task system A system of slave labor under which slaves had to complete specific assignments each day. After these assignments were finished, their time was their own. It was used primarily on rice plantations. Slaves often preferred this system over gang labor because it gave them more free time.

Ulster   The northern province of Ireland that provided 70 percent of the Irish immigrants in the colonial period. Nearly all of them were Presbyterians whose forebears had moved to Ireland from Scotland in the previous century. They sometimes are called Scots-Irish today.

WHO? WHAT? WHERE?

WHO WERE THEY?

Complete each statement below (questions 1–16) by writing the letter preceding the appropriate name in the space provided. Use each answer only once.

> a. Benjamin Franklin
> b. Elizabeth Lucas Pinckney
> c. Edward Braddock
> d. George Washington
> e. Hugh Bryan
> f. James Oglethorpe
> g. James Wolfe
> h. John Campbell
> i. John Tillotson
> j. Jonathan Edwards
> k. Pierre de Rigaud de Vaudreuil
> l. William Bradford
> m. William Johnson
> n. William Pitt
> o. William Shippen
> p. William Shirley

_____ 1. Woman planter who pioneered indigo as a cash crop for South Carolina.

_____ 2. Philadelphia's first printer.

_____ 3. City postmaster of Boston who established the *Boston Newsletter* in 1704.

_____ 4. Editor of the *Pennsylvania Gazette*.

_____ 5. Archbishop of Canterbury who preached morality rather than religious dogma. His sermons appeared in more southern libraries than the writings of any other person of the time.

_____ 6. Only member of the Yale faculty who did not defect to the Anglican Church in 1722 and the most profound religious thinker that North America has ever produced.

_____ 7. First American to lecture on medicine, publish on chemistry, and dissect human cadavers.

_____ 8. One of the founding leaders of Georgia.

_____ 9. Savannah River planter who preached the evangelical Christian message to his slaves. He attempted to part the waters of a river and lead the slaves to freedom.

_____ 10. Governor of Massachusetts from 1741 to 1756 who used judicial and military appointments and military contracts to build a majority within the colonial assembly. He later was named second in command of the British army in North America.

_____ 11. Virginian employed by the Ohio Company as a surveyor and militia officer. He discovered a French patrol along the frontier and ordered an attack, which started a world war.

_____ 12. Irish immigrant with great influence among the Mohawk part of the Iroquois League and the first Northern Indian Superintendent.

_____ 13. British professional commander sent to North America who tried to cross the mountains to attack the French fort on the Ohio River.

_____ 14. Canadian who understood New France's need for support from the Indians and under whose leadership tremendous damage was inflicted upon the British colonial frontier during the French and Indian War.

_____ 15. War minister of Britain who reversed the conduct of the war and became the most popular public official of Britain in his century.

_____ 16. British commander who laid siege to Quebec.

WHAT WAS IT?

Complete each statement below (questions 1–17) by writing the letter preceding the appropriate response in the space provided. Use each answer only once.

a. Company of the Indies
b. Dartmouth
c. coverture
d. fiat money
e. French and Indian War
f. Great Awakening
g. Gullah
h. long knives
i. Natchez
j. naval stores
k. Ohio Company of Virginia
l. old lights
m. Philadelphia Synod
n. politics of harmony
o. republics
p. Shepherd's Tent
q. wheat

_____ 1. Common-law doctrine that prohibited women from making a contract while married.

_____ 2. Language spoken by newly imported slaves that gradually evolved in the rice fields of South Carolina.

_____ 3. Items such as pitch, resin, and turpentine used to manufacture ships.

_____ 4. Second cash crop of Virginia.

_____ 5. Paper money backed only by the promise of the government to accept it in payment of taxes.

_____ 6. Immense religious revival that swept across the Protestant world.

_____ 7. Highest governing body of the Presbyterian church in the colonies.

_____ 8. Outdoor school in New London established by James Davenport to train awakened preachers.

_____ 9. Name given to antirevival Congregationalists.

_____ 10. College that would be turning out more graduates than any other by the end of the eighteenth century.

_____ 11. System of ritualized mutual flattery in which the government and colonial assembly worked through persuasion rather than through patronage or bullying.

_____ 12. Group, created by France to protect the Gulf of Mexico, that shipped settlers and slaves to Louisiana.

_____ 13. Independent villages that were willing to trade with the British and remained outside the French-Indian alliance system.

_____ 14. Last of the Mississippian mound-builder societies. It was destroyed by the French and their Choctaw allies.

_____ 15. Term used by some Indians to describe Virginians.

_____ 16. Group organized to settle the Ohio country and establish an outpost where the Monongahela and Allegheny Rivers converge to form the Ohio River.

_____ 17. Third bloodiest contest Americans ever have fought. It was also the only colonial war between Britain and France to start in North America.

WHERE WAS IT?

Complete each statement below (questions 1–14) by writing the letter preceding the appropriate response in the space provided. Use each answer only once.

    a. Albany, New York
    b. Boston, Massachusetts
    c. Charleston, South Carolina
    d. Great Meadows
    e. Louisbourg

f. middle colonies
g. Mose
h. Nantucket, Massachusetts
i. New England
j. Newport, Rhode Island
k. Philadelphia, Pennsylvania
l. Pennsylvania
m. Plains of Abraham
n. Ulster

_____ 1. Only region that had acquired a strong sense of regional identity by the time of the Revolution.

_____ 2. City that imported the greatest number of slaves.

_____ 3. Only colonial seaport deeply involved in slave trading along the African coast.

_____ 4. Second most populous colony by 1770.

_____ 5. Northern province of Ireland that provided 70 percent of the immigrants from that country.

_____ 6. Area known as the "breadbasket."

_____ 7. Largest city in British North America by 1770.

_____ 8. Center of a prosperous whaling industry.

_____ 9. Leading city in the printing industry in colonial America.

_____ 10. First community of free blacks in what is now the United States.

_____ 11. Most formidable fortress in North America. It was located on Cape Breton Island.

_____ 12. Town where a meeting was called by the governor of New York in order to confer with the Iroquois and redress their grievances.

_____ 13. Location where George Washington surrendered his small Virginia force to the French in 1754.

_____ 14. Area behind Quebec where the battle of Quebec began.

CHARTS, MAPS, AND ILLUSTRATIONS

1. The planned eighteenth-century southern city with wide streets and spacious atmosphere was _____.

2. The governor's palace at Williamsburg, Virginia, was built during the period when _____ was governor of the colony.

3. Strings of conch and clam shells along the Atlantic coast were called _____. They served as currency in the _____ trade.

4. The first newspaper cartoon in colonial America appeared in the newspaper edited by
———————————————. The purpose of the cartoon was ———————————————.

5. According to the map on the growth of population (p. 169), Maine was considered a part of the colony of ———————————————.

MULTIPLE CHOICE

Circle the letter that best completes each statement.

1. All of the following examples reflect the changing status of early women, except
   a. Under the common-law doctrine of coverture, women could not make a contract while married, since the legal personality of the husband "covered" the wife.
   b. If the husband died first, his widow was not entitled to any part of the estate, since the estate passed on to the couple's surviving male children.
   c. Seventeenth-century Puritan courts routinely punished men for sexual offenses, such as fornication. However, after about 1700, courts rarely convicted men of a sexual offense, not even for committing serious crimes, such as rape.
   d. In the 1600s, many Chesapeake widows had inherited all of their husbands' property and had administered their own estates. However, these arrangements became rare after 1700.

2. Britain shipped thousands of convicts to North America—mostly to
   a. Maryland and Virginia.
   b. Pennsylvania.
   c. Spanish Florida.
   d. the Carolinas.

3. Slaves preferred the task system over gang labor because
   a. they liked monotonous labor and close supervision.
   b. they did not acquire new skills.
   c. they were kept in the fields all day.
   d. it gave them greater control over their own lives.

4. Many immigrants to the mid-Atlantic colonies often arrived as "redemptioners," a new form of indentured servitude that was attractive because
   a. families could stay together.
   b. it did not allow servants to find and bind themselves to their own masters.
   c. after indentureship expired, they were given forty acres of land and a mule.
   d. it was only for unmarried people and there was no hope of finding a mate.

5. All of the following statements correctly characterize the backcountry settlements of the interior parts of Virginia and the Carolinas, except
   a. Immigrants brought their folkways with them and soon made the backcountry into a region with its own distinctive culture.
   b. The backcountry showed few signs of anglicizing—no newspapers, few clergymen or other professionals, and, in some areas, almost no government.

    c. Most settlers were unable to hunt, farm, or raise cattle, so they turned to fishing.

    d. Settlers were clanish, violent, and drank heavily.

6. New England was a land of all of the following except

    a. fishermen.

    b. lumberjacks.

    c. rice planters.

    d. merchants.

7. In 1721, smallpox devastated Boston until a local doctor began inoculating people with the disease on the theory that healthy people would survive the injection and acquire an immunity. This self-taught doctor was

    a. John Campbell.

    b. William Douglas.

    c. Cotton Mather.

    d. Zabdiel Boylston.

8. All of the following statements correctly describe the Molasses Act of 1733, except

    a. It was passed by the British Parliament.

    b. It generated bribery and smuggling.

    c. It placed prohibitive duty of six pence per gallon on all foreign molasses imported to the colonies.

    d. It was strictly enforced.

9. Seventeenth-century America was almost a society without presses. The first printers were located in

    a. Georgia.

    b. Virginia.

    c. Massachusetts.

    d. Pennslyvania.

10. All of the following statements correctly characterize Benjamin Franklin, except

    a. He helped to found North America's first Masonic lodge in 1730.

    b. He was a Roman Catholic whom Massachusetts prosecuted twice in a vain attempt to silence him.

    c. His greatest fame rested on his electrical experiments during the 1740s and 1750s.

    d. He invented the Franklin stove (a more efficient heating device than the fireplace) and the lightning rod.

11. All of the following statements are true of the English Enlightenment, except

    a. It rejected the idea of a vengeful God.

    b. Its followers liked rigid doctrine, embraced superstition, and were fanatics.

    c. It grew out of the rational and benevolent piety favored by low-church Anglicans in Restoration England.

    d. It exalted man's capacity for knowledge and social improvement.

12. Which of the following men is matched incorrectly with his ideas/occupation?

    a. Sir Isaac Newton—laws of motion

    b. John Locke—astronomer

c. John Tillotson—archbishop of Canterbury
d. John Leveret, Jr.—college president

13. In 1701, in reaction to a trend at Harvard College, the older clergy founded a new college in New Haven, Connecticut. It was named
a. Princeton.
b. William and Mary.
c. Yale.
d. Edinburgh.

14. All of the following statements reflect goals as set up by the sponsors of the colony of Georgia except
a. They hoped to create a society that could make productive use of England's "deserving" poor, as opposed to the lazy criminal poor.
b. They wanted to shield South Carolina's slave society from Spanish Florida by populating Georgia with armed and disciplined freemen.
c. They allowed unregulated slavery and hard liquor.
d. They hoped to strengthen the imperial economy by producing silk and wine, items that no other British colony had yet succeeded in making.

15. Some of the earliest revivals arose in New Jersey in the 1690s among the
a. English.
b. French.
c. Dutch.
d. Spanish.

16. In a 1740 sermon entitled "The Dangers of an Unconverted Ministry," observers were warned against lifeless preachers that would only lead people to hell. A split in the Presbyterian church resulted after this attack by
a. Guiliam Bertholf.
b. Gilbert Tennent.
c. John Wesley.
d. George Whitefield.

17. All of the following are correct about John Wesley except
a. He was one of the founders of the Methodists.
b. He preached extensively in Virginia.
c. He helped establish the Holy Club at Oxford University.
d. He believed that his life's work was to convert sinners.

18. When Charles Chauncy attacked revivals as frauds because of their emotional excesses, a leading Congregational minister replied in "A Treatise Concerning Religious Affections." He was
a. John Trumball.
b. Theodorus Jacobus Frelinghuysen.
c. John Wesley.
d. Jonathan Edwards.

19. In the colonies, approximately three fourths of free adult white males could vote. By contrast, the number of adult males in England who were disfranchised was
    a. one half.
    b. two thirds.
    c. one third.
    d. three fourths.

20. In the southern colonies
    a. the assembly could coerce the governor.
    b. the governor could manipulate the assembly through patronage.
    c. governors learned that they got more done through persuasion than through patronage or bullying.
    d. the assembly tried to create an impasse by avoiding the cultivation of "politics of harmony," a system of ritualized mutual flattery.

21. The governor of New Hampshire created a powerful political machine that gave something to just about every assemblyman between 1741 and 1767. He was
    a. Robert Hunter.
    b. William Gooch.
    c. Benning Wentworth.
    d. Samuel Adams.

22. During the years 1710–1719, New York's governor achieved success by playing off one faction against another in a colony that had been fiercely divided since Leisler's rebellion. He was
    a. Robert Hunter.
    b. Robert Walpole.
    c. Alexander Spotswood.
    d. William Shirley.

23. All of the following were French forts except
    a. Fort Detroit.
    b. Fort St. Frédéric.
    c. Fort Oswego.
    d. Fort Michilimackinac.

24. The city of New Orleans was founded by
    a. France.
    b. Spain.
    c. England.
    d. Russia.

25. In 1738, the governor of Spanish Florida established a new town, partly as a magnet for escaped slaves from Carolina. He put an African in charge who was named
    a. William Gooch.
    b. William Bull.
    c. Francis Drake.
    d. Francisco Menéndez.

26. The Stono Rebellion in South Carolina, the largest slave revolt in the history of the thirteen colonies, was in response to all of the following factors except
    a. treatment of Indians by colonists.
    b. rumors about Mose, a free black community.
    c. the slaves had religious as well as personal reasons for identifying with Spain.
    d. the manifesto in which Spanish Florida offered liberty to slaves in any of the British colonies who could make their way to Florida.

27. In 1741, Fort George burned down in what was probably an accident. But, due to a series of suspicious fires, public anxiety turned into a judicial massacre when Mary Burton swore that John Hughson's tavern was the center of a monstrous popish plot to do all of the following except
    a. murder the city's whites.
    b. free the slaves.
    c. make Hughson king of the Africans.
    d. undermine Spanish control of the area.

28. Britain returned Louisbourg to France and King George's War ended in the 1748 Treaty of
    a. Aix-la-Chapelle.
    b. Ghent.
    c. Hartford.
    d. Paris.

29. Of the four wars fought between Britain and France from 1689 to 1763, which one was the biggest and produced the most sweeping results?
    a. first
    b. second
    c. third
    d. fourth

30. In June 1754, Benjamin Franklin drafted his "Short hints towards a scheme for uniting the Northern Colonies." His plan included all of the following suggestions, except
    a. a "Presidential general."
    b. annexation of Florida.
    c. deputies apportioned according to tax receipts.
    d. the union would have power to raise soldiers, build forts, levy taxes, deal with Indians, and supervise western settlements.

31. Every colony rejected the Albany Plan for all of the following reasons except
    a. The colonies feared the President General might become too powerful.
    b. Despite the French threat, the colonists were not ready to patch up their differences and unite.
    c. The colonies trusted one another.
    d. The colonists did not see themselves as "Americans."

32. After spending miserable years as unwanted Catholic exiles in a Protestant world, some three thousand Acadian refugees finally made it to French Louisiana, where their descendents became known as
    a. Texans.
    b. Amish.
    c. Cajuns.
    d. Hurons.

33. In 1763, the Peace of Paris finally ended the war and resulted in all of the following except
    a. France surrendered to Great Britain several minor West Indian islands and all of North America east of the Mississippi, except the port of New Orleans.
    b. In exchange for Havana, Spain ceded Florida to the British and also paid a large ransom for the return of Manila.
    c. To compensate its French ally, Spain gave all of Louisiana east of the Mississippi and the city of New Orleans to France.
    d. Most of the Spanish and African occupants of Florida withdrew to other parts of the Spanish empire, but nearly all French settlers remained behind in Canada, the Illinois country, and Louisiana.

ESSAY

Description and Explanation (one- to two-paragraph essay)

1. Describe the anglicizing of the role of women and its effects in the eighteenth century.

2. Describe the impact of anglicization on the economic prospects of colonial families.

3. Compare the gang and task systems of slave labor, including the reasons different systems were used and the advantages of each.

4. Describe the purposes for the founding of Georgia and why the colony did not work well at first.

5. Describe the religious views, personal style, and accomplishments of George Whitefield.

6. Describe the changes in the roles of the parts of provincial government, such as the assembly and the governor.

7. Describe French expansion into the Mississippi Valley and the Middle Ground.

8. Describe the activities of New England during King George's War.

9. Describe the importance of the Iroquois along the frontier.

Discussion and Analysis (class discussion or one- to two-paragraph essay)

1. Compare the prosperity of the southern, middle, and New England colonies. How did their different economies affect the lifestyles of the settlers?

2. Discuss the effects of the Enlightenment on the professions in the American colonies.

3. Discuss the long-term consequences of the Great Awakening.

4. Compare professional British soldiers and the provincial militiamen. What caused the problems between them?

5. Discuss Britain's overall planning and operations in the first years of the French and Indian War and compare them with William Pitt's handling of the war. Why was one more successful than the other?

What If (include an explanation of your position)

1. If you were a slave in eighteenth-century colonial America, would you find life better or worse in South Carolina or Virginia?

2. If you were living in colonial America, would you attend one of George Whitefield's revivals?

3. If you were an Indian in the Ohio Valley during the mid-1700s, would you support Britain or France?

Crossword Puzzle: Provincial America and the Struggle for a Continent

ACROSS

1. Site of Crown Point and Ticonderoga
8. Philadelphia company founded by Ben Franklin in 1731
9. Conquerer of Quebec
10. Founder of Mose
12. Musket
14. Man of motion laws
15. Tactic of French and Indians against Braddock
18. Bean initials
19. One of the naval stores
20. Capital region
21. Not sooner
24. Enthusiastic
25. Awakening adjective
26. Scourge of Louisbourg in 1755
28. Compass point
29. Homeland of Scots-Irish

DOWN

1. Former King's College
2. Congress town of 1754
3. Abraham of Quebec
4. Word with time or place
5. Side or Light faction
6. This was the key thing for John Locke
7. Log College evangelist Gilbert
11. His acquittal was victory for freedom of the press
13. Carolina pidgin
16. Indian tribe that was target for merciless British in Nova Scotia
17. Involuntary immigrants
19. Baseball's equivalent to British army
22. Grow weary
23. Sun for one
27. Part of Caesar's inquiry to Brutus

ANSWER KEY

WHO? WHAT? WHERE?

Who Were They?

1. b. Eliza Lucas Pinckney, p. 133
2. l. William Bradford, p. 136
3. g. John Campbell, p. 136
4. a. Benjamin Franklin, p. 138
5. h. John Tillotson, p. 139
6. j. Jonathan Edwards, p. 139
7. o. William Shippen, p. 140
8. f. James Oglethorpe, p. 140
9. e. Hugh Bryan, p. 145
10. p. William Shirley, p. 150
11. d. George Washington, p. 158
12. m. William Johnson, p. 161
13. c. Edward Braddock, p. 161
14. k. Pierre de Rigaud de Vaudreuil, p. 162
15. n. William Pitt, p. 165
16. g. James Wolfe, p. 170

What Was It?

1. c. coverture, p. 129
2. g. Gullah, p. 131
3. h. naval stores, p. 133
4. q. wheat, p. 133
5. d. fiat money, p. 135
6. f. Great Awakening, p. 141
7. m. Philadelphia Synod, p. 143
8. p. Shepherd's Tent, p. 145
9. l. old lights, p. 146
10. b. Dartmouth, p. 148
11. n. politics of harmony, p. 150
12. a. Company of the Indies, p. 151
13. o. republics, p. 152
14. i. Natchez, p. 152
15. j. long knives, p. 158
16. k. Ohio Company of Virginia, p. 158
17. e. French and Indian War, p. 160

Where Was It?

1. i. New England, p. 130
2. c. Charleston, South Carolina, p. 130
3. j. Newport, Rhode Island, p. 131
4. l. Pennsylvania, p. 133
5. n. Ulster, p. 133
6. f. middle colonies, p. 134
7. k. Philadelphia, Pennsylvania, p. 134
8. h. Nantucket, Massachusetts, p. 135
9. b. Boston, Massachusetts, p. 136
10. g. Mose, p. 153
11. e. Louisbourg, p. 157
12. a. Albany, New York, p. 160
13. d. Great Meadows, p. 161
14. m. Plains of Abraham, p. 170

CHARTS, MAPS, AND ILLUSTRATIONS

1. Savannah, p. 141
2. Alexander Spotswood, p. 149

3. Wampum; fur trade, p. 153

4. Benjamin Franklin; a call for a colonial union, p. 160

5. Massachusetts, p. 162

MULTIPLE CHOICE

1. b.   (p. 129)
2. a.   (p. 130)
3. d.   (p. 131)
4. a.   (pp. 133–134)
5. c.   (p. 134)
6. c.   (p. 134)
7. d.   (p. 134)
8. d.   (p. 135)
9. c.   (p. 136)
10. b.   (p. 138)
11. b.   (pp. 138–139)
12. b.   (p. 139)
13. c.   (p. 139)
14. c.   (p. 140)
15. c.   (p. 142)
16. b.   (p. 143)
17. b.   (p. 144)
18. d.   (p. 147)
19. b.   (p. 149)
20. c.   (p. 150)
21. c.   (pp. 150–151)
22. a.   (p. 151)
23. c.   (p. 151)
24. a.   (p. 152)
25. d.   (p. 153)
26. a.   (pp. 153–154)
27. d.   (p. 154)
28. a.   (p. 157)
29. d.   (p. 160)
30. b.   (p. 160)
31. c.   (p. 160)
32. c.   (p. 163)
33. c.   (p. 170)

ESSAY

Description and Explanation

1. pp. 129–130
2. p. 129
3. pp. 131–132
4. p. 140
5. pp. 144–145
6. pp. 149–150
7. pp. 151–153
8. pp. 156–157
9. p. 158

Discussion and Analysis

1. pp. 130–135
2. pp. 138–140
3. pp. 145–147
4. pp. 164–165
5. pp. 163–170

What If

1. p. 131
2. pp. 144–145
3. pp. 161–162

Crossword Puzzle

CHAPTER 5

REFORM, RESISTANCE, REVOLUTION

The world war that ended with the Treaty of Paris left Britain with a tremendous national debt. The British government expected the Americans to pay something for their own future defense, especially along the frontier. As a result, several steps were taken which seriously alienated the colonies.

The British empire in North America was destroyed by three successive crises between 1765 and 1775: the Stamp Act crisis, the Townshend crisis, and the crisis generated by the Tea Act of 1773. The colonies first petitioned for a redress of grievances and, when that failed, turned to more forceful means of resistance until Parliament repealed the tax. In the Townshend crisis, petitioning and overt resistance through the nonimportation movement proceeded simultaneously. The Tea Act escalated to violence without the involvement of a petition. By 1773, the colonists had lost confidence in Parliament. Parliament responded with the Coercive Acts, which were an attempt to punish and control the colonies.

As colonial resistance increased after 1765, the British became convinced, incorrectly, that an organized movement for independence was under way. This erroneous notion led to even more severe British attempts to control the colonies. The colonists denied that they wanted independence, but they feared that the British government was planning to deliberately deprive them of their liberty and rights as Englishmen. Neither the British nor the Americans really understood the distinction between them on such major issues as taxation. The British government experimented with military coercion, and the Americans employed violence as a means of resistance.

As crisis followed crisis, the colonies began to unite against what they perceived to be a common foe. The First Continental Congress was held in Philadelphia in 1774 and began to function as a central government for the colonies. After the violent events of the spring and early summer of 1775, an improvised war was under way in North America. By the time that the Second Continental Congress met in May 1775, a war was clearly under way and Congress organized the forces around Boston into the Continental Army.

By the summer of 1776, there was still some division among various groups and areas about independence, but British policies during these important months continued to alienate the colonists. In July 1776, the Continental Congress passed a resolution favoring independence and adopted the Declaration of Independence. On the same day that the resolution was adopted, the first ships of the largest armada yet sent across the Atlantic began landing British soldiers on Staten Island. The Americans now faced tremendous military challenges.

LIBERTY, EQUALITY, POWER

The idea of liberty was integral to the motivation behind the American Revolution. At first, the colonists denied that they desired independence, but a growing number of men feared that the leaders in the British government were plotting to deprive them of their liberties. British officials were determined to impose control and demonstrate their power over the colonies. To many leaders in London, the collection of taxes and the imposition of control were necessary for the maintenance of the empire. The British tried military coercion as a show of power, but the colonists, especially in Boston, used street violence to resist. Ordinary settlers used violence in the name of liberty in the tenant upheavals in New York and the regulator movements in the Carolinas.

As the issue of equal rights became a topic of concern, a small number of colonists questioned whether equality applied to all—were the slaves to be free as well? Around the middle of the eighteenth century, the inequalities of slavery came under attack for the first time. The Quakers became the first group to prohibit the ownership of slaves. Boston slaves made it clear to General Thomas Gage and to the patriots that they would serve whichever side supported their freedom. For most Americans, however, equality was not the issue. Liberty—meaning freedom from British control—was the paramount concern.

OBJECTIVES

After studying this chapter, a student should be able to

1. Describe Indian and white relations just after the French and Indian War.

2. Discuss the three crises that shattered Britain's Atlantic empire.

3. Describe the distinction between internal and external taxation.

4. Trace the escalating colonial reaction to British taxation from the Sugar Act through the Tea Act.

5. Explore the processes that intensified discontent in the rural areas.

6. Describe the first attacks on slavery.

7. Discuss the purpose and role of the first and second Continental Congresses.

8. Explain who supported or opposed independence and the reasons they did so.

CHRONOLOGY

1750s	In these years, Quakers prohibited any involvement in the slave trade and, in **1774**, would forbid slaveholding altogether.
1760	George II died and was succeeded by his twenty-two-year-old grandson, George III (1760–1820).
	General Amherst cut back sharply on traditional presents to the Indians. This deprived British officials of most of their leverage with western Indians at a serious time.
1761	Pitt was forced to resign from the British government, even though he was the most popular public official of the century.

1763

With a unity never seen before, the Indians struck in the West in a conflict that came to be known as Pontiac's War, after a prominent Ottawa chief. Indian successes so enraged Jeffrey Amherst that he ordered the commander at Fort Pitt to distribute smallpox-infested blankets among the western tribes, touching off a severe epidemic during 1763–1764.

The Paxton Boys murdered a number of Indians along the Pennsylvania frontier. They then planned a march on Philadelphia, but, after meeting with Benjamin Franklin and presenting a list of grievances, they returned home. For the next decade, it was virtually an open season on Indians along the Virginia and Pennsylvania frontiers.

As Parliament adjourned in the spring, John Wilkes, a radical journalist, all but accused the king of lying in an essay that was published in the 45th number of *The North Briton*. The government used a general warrant to arrest Wilkes, who was also a member of Parliament. He was freed when Chief Justice Charles Pratt declared the warrants illegal and freed Wilkes. Wilkes fled to France after Parliament refused to support him.

1764

The British and provincial forces brought Indian resistance to an end and restored peace. In the aftermath, the British government ineptly and reluctantly embraced the role that the French had once played in the Great Lakes region by distributing presents and mediating differences.

The Sugar Act was a major part of George Grenville's war against smuggling. It increased paperwork and encouraged prosecution of violators in vice-admiralty courts, which did not use juries.

The Quartering Act ordered colonial assemblies to provide public housing for the British army.

The Currency Act was a response to the wartime protests of London merchants against Virginia's employment of paper currency, which had been used for the colony's defense. It forbade the colonies to issue any paper money as legal tender.

1765

Parliament approved the Stamp Act. This act required that all contracts, licenses, commissions, and most other legal documents be executed on stamped paper. A stamp duty would have to be paid also on all newspapers and pamphlets, as well as on playing cards and dice.

Colonial resistance to the Stamp Act increasingly alarmed the British that an organized movement for independence was indeed under way, a fear that led to even sterner measures of control.

Patrick Henry, a newcomer to the Virginia House of Burgesses, launched a wave of resistance by introducing five resolutions in **May**.

Nearly all colonial spokesmen concurred that the Stamp Act was an unconstitutional measure and that colonial representation in Parliament was impractical because of distance and expense.

In **August**, Boston awoke to find an effigy of Andrew Oliver, the stamp distributor, hanging on the town's Liberty Tree. Thoroughly intimidated, Oliver resigned from office. In the same month, the elegant mansion of Lt. Governor Thomas Hutchinson was all but demolished by angry colonists.

For political reasons having nothing to do with the colonies, the king dismissed George Grenville and replaced his ministry with a narrow coalition organized primarily by William Augustus, duke of Cumberland, the king's uncle.

By this time, the Indians felt threatened. Though the Proclamation Line of 1763 was still official policy, apparently the British government no longer intended to use force to protect Indian claims to their lands.

In **October**, nine colonies sent delegates to the Stamp Act Congress meeting in New York. It passed a series of resolutions affirming colonial loyalty while condemning the Stamp Act and Sugar Act.

1765–1766   Resistance to the Stamp Act began in the spring and continued for a year until news of the repeal reached the colonies. Everywhere except in Georgia, stamp masters were forced to resign before the act went into effect in **November**.

1765–1767   As violence in South Carolina reached a peak, the more respectable settlers organized themselves as "regulators" (a later generation would call them vigilantes) to impose order in the absence of any organized government. North Carolina regulators, by contrast, attacked corrupt government officials.

1766   The Stamp Act crisis ended with three major pieces of British legislation. The first repealed the Stamp Act because it was detrimental to British commercial interests. The Declaratory Act affirmed that Parliament had the power to make laws and statutes binding on the colonies. The Revenue Act of 1766 amended the Sugar Act by reducing the duty on molasses. A duty was placed on all molasses, British and foreign, imported by the mainland colonies. This act generated more income than all other colonial taxes.

The atmosphere of good will between Britain and the colonies did not last long. The king decided to replace his ministry with William Pitt, earl of Chatham. The colonists admired him more than any other Englishman of his day. They expected sympathy and support from his government.

At that point, several thousand angry farmers, inspired by the Stamp Act riots, took to the fields and roads, threatening to pull down the New York City mansions of absentee landlords. Redcoats were brought in by the landlords to suppress the rioters.

1766–1767   Pitt began to slip into an acute depression that lasted more than two years. He refused to communicate with other ministers or even the king. This left Charles Townshend, known as politically uncompromising, in charge of colonial policy.

1767

Phillis Wheatley, former slave, published her first poem in Boston. In **1772**, a volume of her poetry was printed in London, making her a transatlantic celebrity by age 20.

Britain passed the New York Restraining Act, which forbade the governor from assenting to any legislation until the assembly had complied with the Quartering Act.

Revenue was clearly not the main object of the Townshend Revenue Act. Charles Townshend's real goal was to use the new revenues to pay the salaries of the governors and judges in the colonies, thereby freeing them from dependence on their assemblies.

On **August 31**, the radical *Boston Gazette* proclaimed the death of liberty in America and called for complete nonimportation of all British goods.

After winning approval for his program, Charles Townshend died suddenly in September. The dilemmas created by Townshend were passed on to the new chancellor of the exchequer, Frederick, Lord North.

The Townshend duties became operative in **November** with little opposition, and, beginning in **December**, John Dickinson tried to rouse colonists to action through twelve urgent letters published in *Letters of a Pennsylvania Farmer*. They were reprinted in nearly every newspaper in America.

1768

In **February**, the Massachusetts assembly dispatched a circular letter to the other assemblies, urging colonists to pursue "constitutional measures" of resistance against the Quartering Act, the revenue acts, and the use of the Townshend Act's revenue to pay the salaries of governors and judges. The colonists believed that, at this point, Britain would only respond to organized resistance.

Two dozen Massachusetts towns adopted pacts in which they agreed not to consume British goods. Boston merchants had drafted a nonimportation agreement on **March 1**, conditional on its acceptance by New York and Philadelphia.

John Hancock's ship, *Liberty*, was seized by customs collectors in Boston for smuggling wine on its previous voyage. This seizure produced another disturbance in the city in **June**.

The British fleet entered Boston Harbor in battle array by October 2 and landed about one thousand soldiers. However, the following summer, half the soldiers were withdrawn.

1769

This was the most effective year for the nonimportation agreements. Imports were reduced by one third.

1770

Following the funeral of Christopher Seider, an eleven-year-old boy randomly shot in a crowd by a customs informer, tensions between soldiers and citizens reached a fatal climax known as the Boston Massacre, on **March 5**. The event marked the failure of Britain's first attempt at military coercion.

On the same day as the Boston Massacre, Lord North asked Parliament to repeal the Townshend duties, except the one on tea, which provided nearly three fourths of the revenue under the act. He regarded the duties as an antimercantile restriction on Britain's own exports.

1771

Granville Sharp, an early abolitionist, compelled Chief Justice William Murray, baron Mansfield, to declare slavery incompatible with the "free air" of England. The decision gave ten to fifteen thousand slaves living in England a chance to claim their freedom.

1772

A customs vessel, the *Gaspée*, ran aground near Providence, Rhode Island, while in pursuit of peaceful coastal ships. After dark, men with blackened faces boarded, wounded its commander, and burned the ship. An inquiry into the matter failed because no one would talk.

Twelve colonial assemblies considered the investigation of the *Gaspée* so serious that they created permanent committees of correspondence to keep in touch with one another and to anticipate the next assault on their liberties.

1773

Governor Hutchinson announced that, under the Townshend Act, the judges of the Massachusetts Superior Court henceforth would receive their salaries from the imperial treasury instead of from the General Court. Boston established its own committee of correspondence and urged other towns to do the same. Most of them responded positively.

By this time, several New England newspapers were calling for a political union of the colonies.

Parliament passed the Tea Act to bail out the East India Company, the largest business corporation in Britain. This act repealed the taxes on tea within England, but retained the tax in the colonies. It also gave a monopoly to the company on the shipping and distribution of tea in the colonies. A combination of merchants and artisans rallied against this measure and none of the tea was sold. The most serious problems were in Boston, where radicals disguised themselves as Indians and threw 342 chests of tea into Boston Harbor on the night of **December 16.**

1773–1774

Many of the slaves in Boston began to sense an opportunity for emancipation. On several occasions they petitioned the legislature or the governor for freedom, pointing out that, though they had never forfeited their natural rights, they were being held in bondage.

1774

Convinced that severe punishment was essential to British credibility, Parliament passed four Coercive Acts during the spring of 1774. The Boston Port Act closed the city's port until the tea was paid for. The Quartering Act gave British officers the power to quarter soldiers in the homes of civilians if necessary. The Administration of Justice Act permitted a British soldier or official who was charged with a crime while carrying out his duties to be tried in another colony or in Great Britain. The Massachusetts Government Act made the upper house appointments and sharply restricted the power of town meetings. To enforce the policies, the king made General Thomas Gage, commander-in-chief of the British army in North America, the new governor of Massachusetts.

Passed at the same time, the unrelated Quebec Act established French civil law and the Roman Catholic Church in the province of Quebec. It also reorganized the boundaries of the province to include the area between the Great Lakes and the Ohio River. Many colonists thought that this would be the new model for restructuring the empire. They tended to lump the Quebec Act together with the Coercive Acts and called them the Intolerable Acts.

Gage took over the governorship of Massachusetts in May and closed the port of Boston.

In **September**, the First Continental Congress opened at Philadelphia's Carpenters' Hall. Twelve colonies were represented (Georgia was not present). The members finally agreed to petition the king on their grievances. They did not petition Parliament because the Congress did not recognize it as a legitimate legislature for the colonies. It also created a group they called the Association, citizen committees to enforce trade sanctions against Britain. The creation of the Association was the first step by the Congress in acting as a central government for the colonies.

A Committee of Public Safety began to collect arms and supplies at Concord, Massachusetts.

1775

Lord North ordered Gage to send troops to Concord, destroy the arms stored there, and arrest John Hancock and Samuel Adams. In **April**, Gage made his move. Paul Revere, an energetic Boston silversmith and engraver who had aided in creating the patriot information network, rode through the countryside shouting news—"The redcoats are coming!" His informant was probably the general's American wife. As the British approached Lexington, they found militiamen facing them. The militia began to withdraw when the first shots were fired. The British opened fire and then marched on to Concord. They then were pursued back to Boston, where the British were under siege. As colonists fortified Breed's Hill, they were attacked by the British. When the colonials ran out of ammunition, they withdrew.

In **May**, the Second Continental Congress convened. It voted to form a continental army. On **June 15**, at the urging of John Adams of Massachusetts, George Washington was named commanding general.

Fearing that the British in Canada might recruit a French force to attack New York, Congress authorized an invasion of Canada in **June**. The two forces were led by General Richard Montgomery and Colonel Benedict Arnold.

In **July**, Congress agreed to send an Olive Branch Petition to George III, but he issued a formal proclamation of rebellion.

In **November**, Lord Dunmore, governor of Virginia, offered freedom to any slaves or rebels who joined his forces.

1776   Thomas Paine published his pamphlet *Common Sense*, which sold more than one hundred thousand copies in just a few months. Paine strongly attacked George III and monarchy in general.

In **March**, after Washington fortified the surrounding area, the British pulled out of Boston and sailed for Halifax.

The British government decided to use mercenary soldiers in America. They were from Germany and often were called Hessians because of the German area of their origination.

In **May**, Louis XVI of France authorized covert aid to the Americans.

By the summer, patriot forces had control of all thirteen colonies. The last royal governor to be driven from office was William Franklin of New Jersey. In **June**, Congress appointed a committee of five to prepare a declaration that would justify American independence to the world.

On **July 2**, Congress adopted a resolution drafted by Richard Henry Lee stating "that these United colonies . . . ought to be, Free and Independent." On that same day, the first ships of the largest armada yet sent across the Atlantic began landing British soldiers on Staten Island.

On **July 4**, twelve colonies, with New York abstaining, approved the Declaration of Independence.

GLOSSARY OF IMPORTANT TERMS

artisan
A skilled laborer who works with his or her hands. In early America, artisans often owned their own shops and produced goods either for general sale or for special order.

Association
A group created by the First Continental Congress to enforce its trade sanctions against Britain. The creation of this group was an important sign that Congress was beginning to act as a central government.

benefit of clergy
A medieval practice that exempted the clergy from trial or punishment in civil courts. It was used as a legal technicality in the Boston Massacre trial. The accused asserted that they were "clergy" by proving their ability to read.

committees of correspondence
These committees were formed on both the local and colonial levels, and they played an important role in exchanging ideas and information. They spread primarily anti-British material and were an important step in the first tentative unity of people in different areas.

common-law courts These courts were based on precedents and judicial decisions. They offered due process through such devices as trial by jury, which usually consisted of local men.

external taxes Taxes based on oceanic trade, such as port duties. Some Americans thought of them more as a means of regulating trade than as taxation.

feudal revival The reliance on old feudal charters for all of the profits that could be extracted from them. This took place in several colonies in the mid–eighteenth century and caused serious problems for many of the tenants on the land.

general warrant A warrant that does not specify the person, place, or things to be searched.

Hessians A term used by Americans to describe the seventeen thousand mercenary troops acquired by Britain from the German states, especially Hesse.

internal taxes Taxes that did not deal with overseas trade but were collected for revenue rather than the regulation of trade. Many colonial Americans thought that internal taxes could legally be imposed only by their elected provincial assemblies.

liberty tree A term for the gallows on which enemies of the people deserved to be hanged. The best known was in Boston.

mandamus A legal writ ordering a person, usually a public official, to carry out a specific act. In Massachusetts in 1774, the new royal councillors were appointed by a writ of mandamus.

mercenary A professional soldier hired by a group or a government other than his own.

minutemen A special militia force designed for rapid response to any emergency.

nonimportation agreements Agreements not to import goods from England. They were designed to put pressure on the British economy and force the repeal of unpopular parliamentary acts. They affected only exports from Britain.

poll tax A tax based on people or population rather than property. It was usually a fixed amount per adult.

probable cause Reasonable grounds for an assumption about a crime or suspected criminal.

provincial congress A type of convention elected by the colonists to organize resistance. They tended to be larger than the legal assemblies they displaced, and they played a major role in politicizing the countryside.

specie A term used to describe metal money. In colonial times, it usually meant silver, but it also could be gold coins.

vice-admiralty courts These courts dealt with a restricted royal jurisdiction and dealt with naval and merchant ships and their crews, and cases involving parliamentary regulation of trade. They offered few of the protections normally allowed under the English legal system, such as trial by jury.

virtual representation   The English concept that it was not necessary for everyone to vote. Representation was afforded only to those who could vote. Members of Parliament represented the entire empire, not just a local constituency or a group of voters. According to this theory, settlers had the same representation as British subjects within Great Britain or other portions of the empire.

WHO? WHAT? WHERE?

WHO WERE THEY?

Complete each statement below (questions 1–18) by writing the letter preceding the appropriate name in the space provided. Use each answer only once.

a. Benjamin Franklin
b. Crispus Attucks
c. Ebenezer McIntosh
d. Ebenezer Richardson
e. Frederick Stump
f. Jeffrey Amherst
g. John Adams
h. John Dickinson
i. John Hancock
j. John Mein
k. John Murray, earl of Dunmore
l. Margaret K. Gage
m. Marquess of Rockingham
n. Phillis Wheatley
o. Sarah Osborn
p. William Franklin
q. William Howe
r. William Pitt, earl of Chatham

_____ 1. British commander who ordered the commander of Fort Pitt to distribute smallpox-infested blankets among the Indians. This touched off a severe epidemic.

_____ 2. German settler in backcountry Pennsylvania who murdered ten Indians but was not brought to justice because of the anti-Indian sentiment in the frontier counties.

_____ 3. Poor shoemaker in Boston who organized two riots against the Stamp Act.

_____ 4. British leader who mobilized the major British merchants and manufacturers to petition Parliament for repeal of the Stamp Act.

_____ 5. One of the witnesses who appeared effectively before Parliament to appeal for the repeal of the Stamp Act.

_____ 6. British official whom the colonists admired more than any other Englishman of his day.

_____ 7. Author of twelve letters insisting that all parliamentary taxes for revenue violated the rights of the colonists. These were widely reprinted in colonial newspapers.

_____ 8. Loyalist editor of the *Boston Chronicle*, which caricatured leading patriots.

_____ 9. Customs informer who fired shots from his home into an angry mob and killed an eleven-year-old boy.

_____ 10. Free black sailor who was killed in the Boston Massacre.

_____ 11. English immigrant who opened a school in Newport, Rhode Island, that admitted women and blacks to its classes.

_____ 12. Slave brought to Boston at a very young age who wrote poems rejoicing in the Christianization of Africans while deploring slavery.

_____ 13. Leading ship owner and one of the two men Lord North ordered arrested by General Thomas Gage.

_____ 14. Person who probably informed the Americans about the British raid on Concord.

_____ 15. British officer who launched three bloody frontal attacks on Breed's Hill as a demonstration that mere civilians had no chance against a regular army.

_____ 16. Delegate to the Second Continental Congress from Massachusetts who urged the naming of George Washington as commander-in-chief of the army.

_____ 17. Governor of Virginia who offered some slaves freedom if they would join his forces against the Americans.

_____ 18. Last royal governor to be forced from office.

WHAT WAS IT?

Complete each statement below (questions 1–20) by writing the letter preceding the appropriate response in the space provided. Use each answer only once.

   a. the Association
   b. *Common Sense*
   c. Currency Act of 1764
   d. Declaratory Act
   e. East India Company
   f. feudal revival
   g. Hessians
   h. Intolerable Acts
   i. *Liberty*
   j. liberty tree
   k. Massachusetts Government Act
   l. minutemen
   m. Olive Branch Petition
   n. Paxton Boys
   o. Port Act

p. Proclamation of 1763
q. Quakers
r. Quebec Act
s. regulators
t. tea

_____ 1. Measure that established governments in newly conquered British areas and tried to regulate the pace of western settlement.

_____ 2. Group of Scots-Irish in Pennsylvania who murdered several unarmed Indians. They then marched toward Philadelphia to kill more Indians.

_____ 3. Bill that forbade the colonies to issue any paper money as legal tender.

_____ 4. Symbol for the gallows on which enemies of the people deserved to be hanged.

_____ 5. Parliamentary act that affirmed that Parliament had full power and authority to make laws governing the colonies. Colonists read that act as a face-saving gesture that made repeal of the Stamp Act possible.

_____ 6. Ship belonging to John Hancock that was seized by customs collectors in Boston for taxes on a previous voyage.

_____ 7. Item that provided three fourths of the revenue collected under the Townshend Revenue Act.

_____ 8. Reliance on old feudal charters for all of the profits that could be extracted from them. This practice took place in several colonies in the mid–eighteenth century.

_____ 9. Early form of vigilantes organized in the Carolinas by settlers who wanted to impose order in the absence of any organized government or who resented the corruption of local officials.

_____ 10. Leading antislavery group in the colonies.

_____ 11. Britain's largest business corporation that was in serious financial trouble.

_____ 12. Bill that closed the port of Boston until the tea that was destroyed was paid for.

_____ 13. Most controversial of the Coercive Acts.

_____ 14. Farsighted measure that showed greater toleration for French Catholics than had previously been shown.

_____ 15. Name given to the Coercive and Quebec Acts by the colonists.

_____ 16. Special militia force designed for rapid response to any emergency.

_____ 17. Group created by the First Continental Congress to enforce its trade sanctions against Britain. The creation of this group was a sign that Congress was beginning to act as a government.

_____ 18. Paper sent to King George III by the Continental Congress in 1775 with the hope of ending the bloodshed.

_____ 19. Pamphlet that sold more than one hundred thousand copies within a few months and changed the hearts and minds of many Americans in support of the patriots.

_____ 20. Term used by Americans to describe the seventeen thousand mercenary troops acquired by Britain from the German states.

WHERE WAS IT?

Complete each statement below (questions 1–9) by writing the letter preceding the appropriate response in the space provided. Use each answer only once.

a. Alamance Creek
b. Carpenters' Hall
c. Castle William
d. Georgia
e. Granville district
f. Hudson River Valley
g. Newport, Rhode Island
h. New York
i. South Carolina

_____ 1. Location of the public barracks for British soldiers on an island in Boston Harbor. This location rendered them ineffective.

_____ 2. American colony that donated money to the Bill of Rights Society supporting John Wilkes in his fight for liberty in Britain.

_____ 3. City where the resistance to the Townshend Acts first collapsed.

_____ 4. Area where several thousand angry farmers threatened violence against large estate owners. These farmers had to be suppressed by the British army.

_____ 5. Vast feudal holdings that embraced over one half of the land and two thirds of the population of North Carolina.

_____ 6. Location of the battle between the regulators of North Carolina and Governor William Tryon. This dispute between the regulators and the eastern part of the colony would leave it divided at the beginning of the Revolution.

_____ 7. Only colony that did not send a delegate to the First Continental Congress.

_____ 8. Building in which the First Continental Congress gathered.

_____ 9. Only colony that abstained from voting on the Declaration of Independence.

CHARTS, MAPS, AND ILLUSTRATIONS

1. According to the table dealing with exports from Britain, in which year were exports the highest? _____

Between 1766 and 1770, which section of the colonies received the greatest amount of this trade? _____

In which year did trade decline most? _____

According to the chapter, why was there so much of a decline in that year?

_____

2. The largest proprietary colony indicated on feudal revival was _____.

   The largest estate in Virginia was _____.

3. The title of Phillis Wheatley's work published in 1773 was _____.

MULTIPLE CHOICE

Circle the letter that best completes each statement.

1. Three successive crises destroyed the first British empire between 1765 and 1775. They were the
   a. Tea Act, Quartering Act, and Revenue Act.
   b. Quartering Act, Coercive Acts, and Revenue Act.
   c. Molasses Act, Declaratory Act, and Stamp Act.
   d. Stamp Act, Townshend Acts, and tea crisis.

2. The king honored wartime commitments to the western Indians by issuing the Proclamation of 1763, which did all of the following except
   a. set up governments in Canada, Florida, and other conquered colonies.
   b. try to regulate the pace of western settlement.
   c. establish the Proclamation Line along the Appalachian watershed.
   d. cut back sharply on traditional presents to the Indians.

3. With a unity and determination never seen before, the Indians struck in the spring and summer of 1763 in a conflict that became known as
   a. the French and Indian War.
   b. Pontiac's War.
   c. War of Jenkins' Ear.
   d. the Stono Rebellion.

4. The bill that launched Grenville's war against smuggling was the
   a. Sugar Act of 1764.
   b. Molasses Act of 1733.
   c. Stamp Act of 1765.
   d. Currency Act of 1764.

5. All of the following were objections to the Stamp Act of 1765 except
   a. It violated the principle of no taxation without representation.
   b. Both internal and external taxes violated the British constitution.
   c. Colonists wanted to decide how much to contribute to their own defense.
   d. It was fair for colonists to contribute to their own defense.

6. A wave of resistance to the Stamp Act was launched by a newcomer to the Virginia House of Burgesses. On May 30 and 31, 1765, five resolutions were introduced by
   a. Francis Bernard.
   b. Daniel Dulany.
   c. Patrick Henry.
   d. Amos Doolittle.

7. By 1765, nearly all colonial spokesmen agreed that colonial representation in Parliament was impractical due to
   a. colonial laziness.
   b. distance and expense.
   c. opposing viewpoints.
   d. political alignment.

8. In Boston, angry colonists realized that resolutions and pamphlets alone could not defeat the Stamp Act, so they took to the streets in violent protest. These men were called
   a. Sons of Liberty.
   b. Redcoats.
   c. Hurons.
   d. Deputies.

9. All of the following statements correctly depict Lt. Governor Thomas Hutchinson except
   a. Most Bostonians believed that he had defended and even helped to draft the Stamp Act in letters to British friends.
   b. He had quietly opposed the Stamp Act.
   c. He was widely liked and supported since leading the fight to replace paper money with silver in 1749.
   d. On August 26 he became the target of an angry crowd that all but demolished his mansion.

10. The real goal of the Townshend Revenue Act was to
    a. repeal duties in colonial ports on certain imports that the colonies could legally get only from Britain.
    b. place more duties on tea within Britain.
    c. prohibit the colonies from importing tea, paper, glass, red and white lead, and painter's colors.
    d. use the new revenues to pay the salaries of governors and judges in the colonies, thereby freeing them from dependence on their assemblies.

11. John Dickinson's *Letters of a Pennsylvania Farmer* did all of the following except
    a. They denied the distinction between internal and external taxes.
    b. They insisted that all parliamentary taxes for revenue violated the rights of colonists.
    c. They explicitly attacked King George III.
    d. They questioned what Townshend's real motives must have been.

12. To warn the public against the dangers of a standing army in times of peace, the patriots compiled a "Journal of the Times" that described ways in which British soldiers were undermining public order in Boston. All of the following examples were included except
    a. The soldiers helped with the town watch.
    b. The soldiers endangered the virtue of young women.
    c. The soldiers disturbed church services.
    d. The soldiers started fights.

13. Which of the following people was an outlaw since 1765, returned from France, ran for Parliament, won a seat for the county of Middlesex, submitted to the law, received a one-year sentence in King's Bench Prison, was expelled from the House of Commons, and was admired in South Carolina as the leading patriot of England?
    a. John Mein
    b. James Bowdoin
    c. John Wilkes
    d. Richard Dana

14. Following the funeral of the 11-year-old boy, tensions between soldiers and citizens reached a fatal climax known as the
    a. Revolution.
    b. Boston Massacre.
    c. Boston Tea Party.
    d. French and Indian War.

15. The Boston Massacre trials and the *Gaspée* affair convinced London that it was pointless to
    a. involve colonists in British government.
    b. send British troops to the colonies.
    c. impose British law on colonists.
    d. prosecute individual patriots for breaking the law.

16. For elite families in the colonies, any direct challenge to British authority carried high risks. They depended on the Crown for all of the following except for their
    a. public offices.
    b. official honors.
    c. staple goods.
    d. government contracts.

17. The discipline imposed by vigilante groups in South Carolina, typically whippings and forced labor, outraged its victims, who organized as
    a. deputies.
    b. regulators.
    c. moderators.
    d. loyalists.

18. All of the following men attacked slavery as a sin except
    a. John Wesley.
    b. Jonathan Edwards.

   c. Adam Smith.

   d. Hugh Bryan.

19. In England, an early abolitionist brought a case to court in 1771 and compelled a reluctant Chief Justice William Murray, baron Mansfield, to declare that slavery was incompatible with the "free air" of England. That decision gave ten thousand to fifteen thousand slaves living in England a chance to claim their freedom. The abolitionist was

   a. John Woolman.

   b. Benjamin Lay.

   c. Granville Sharp.

   d. Anthony Benezet.

20. Convinced that there was no way to block a ship from landing, Boston radicals disguised themselves as Indians and threw 342 chests of tea into Boston Harbor on the night of December 16. The incident became known as the

   a. Revolution.

   b. Boston Massacre.

   c. Boston Tea Party.

   d. French and Indian War.

21. After colonists dumped tea into Boston Harbor, British officials were convinced that severe punishment was essential to maintain their own credibility. North's government passed the following four Coercive Acts:

   a. Quartering Act, Administration of Justice Act, Massachusetts Government Act, and Port Act.

   b. Stamp Act, Massachusetts Government Act, Administration of Justice Act, and Townshend Revenue Act.

   c. Tea Act, Townshend Revenue Act, Quartering Act, and Quebec Act.

   d. Declaratory Act, Stamp Act, Tea Act, and Administration of Justice Act.

22. Following the example of Massachusetts in 1768, individual colonies began to elect conventions in 1774, usually called

   a. boards of directors.

   b. continental congresses.

   c. provincial congresses.

   d. state conventions.

23. All of the following statements correctly describe the demands of the Suffolk County Convention, except that they called for

   a. the emancipation of slaves in the North American colonies.

   b. a purge of unreliable military officers.

   c. the creation of a special force of minutemen capable of rapid response to any emergency.

   d. the payment of all provincial taxes to the congress in Concord, not to Governor Gage in Boston.

24. In May 1775, the Second Continental Congress voted to turn the undisciplined men besieging Boston into a
    a. religious sect.
    b. state militia.
    c. Continental Army.
    d. missionary force.

25. In late June 1775, Congress, fearing that the British in Canada might recruit a French force to attack New York, authorized an invasion of Canada. The two American forces were led by
    a. Richard Montgomery and Benedict Arnold.
    b. Paul Revere and Joseph Galloway.
    c. John Murray and Thomas Paine.
    d. James Wilson and Thomas Jefferson.

26. *Common Sense* was written by
    a. Thomas Paine.
    b. William Franklin.
    c. John Murray.
    d. George Washington.

27. The longest section of the Declaration of Independence
    a. was a detailed discussion of the rights of man.
    b. indicted George III as a tyrant.
    c. established a new government for the colonies.
    d. was a guarantee of American independence.

ESSAY

Description and Explanation (one- to two-paragraph essay)

1. Describe relations between Indians and whites after the French and Indian War.

2. Describe the effectiveness or lack of effectiveness of nonimportation as a means of repealing unpopular British acts.

3. Describe the misunderstandings between the British government and the Americans over the repeal of the Stamp Act.

4. Describe Boston's role in resistance to the Stamp Act and the Townshend duties.

5. Describe the events leading up to the Boston Massacre and the significance of the event.

6. Describe General Thomas Gage's role in the events around Boston in 1774 and 1775.

Discussion and Analysis (class discussion or one- to two-paragraph essay)

1. Discuss George Grenville's and Britain's effort to centralize control over the North American colonies.

2. Discuss the three interrelated processes that magnified social tensions in rural areas.

3. Discuss the provisions and significance of the four Coercive Acts and the colonial reaction to them.

4. Discuss the events from the end of 1775 through the summer of 1776 that led to an increased support for independence.

What If (include an explanation of your position)

1. If you were living in Massachusetts in the 1760s, what would be your reaction to the Stamp Act? Would it be different if you were living in North Carolina?

2. If you were a British soldier stationed in Boston, would you find the conditions there tense or pleasant?

3. If you were a member of the Second Continental Congress, would you vote for independence?

Crossword Puzzle: Reform, Resistance, Revolution

[crossword grid]

ACROSS

1. Paine no-brainer (2 words)
6. Boston Massacre victim
7. Statesman formerly known as William Pitt
8. Short for John Dickinson's state
9. He was the information highway in April 1775
11. Part of peace petition from Second Continental Congress
12. Prime minister when American Revolution began (2 words)
18. Mr. Van Winkle
20. Color for Gage and Howe
21. Tea Party etc. to British
22. Governor who offered freedom to Virginia slaves
25. Clairvoyance
26. Minuteman's equipment
27. Famous first name at Continental Congress
29. Loyalists were defeated at ___ Creek Bridge in North Carolina

DOWN

1. Fight over troubled waters in April 1775 was here (2 words)
2. Canadian conquest for Montgomery
3. Grenville gummy of 1765 tax
4. Hancock was one
5. Torched tax ship of 1772
10. Be wrong
13. Part of Pontiac's domain
14. British crapped out when they tried to tax these
15. Andrew of effigy fame in Boston
16. Liberty symbol of Boston
17. Homeland of German mercenaries
19. Revenue Act of 1766 put this tax on gallon of molasses
23. W
24. Neolin's taboo
27. Ms. Peep
28. Compass point

ANSWER KEY

WHO? WHAT? WHERE?

Who Were They?

1. f. Jeffrey Amherst, p. 176
2. e. Frederick Stump, p. 178
3. c. Ebenezer McIntosh, p. 181
4. m. Marquess of Rockingham, p. 182
5. a. Benjamin Franklin, p. 183
6. r. William Pitt, earl of Chatham, p. 184
7. h. John Dickinson, p. 186
8. j. John Mein, p. 187
9. d. Ebenezer Richardson, p. 189
10. b. Crispus Attucks, p. 190
11. o. Sarah Osborn, p. 197
12. n. Phillis Wheatley, p. 197
13. i. John Hancock, p. 204
14. l. Margaret K. Gage, p. 205
15. q. William Howe, p. 206
16. g. John Adams, p. 207
17. k. John Murray, earl of Dunmore, p. 208
18. p. William Franklin, p. 209

What Was It?

1. p. Proclamation of 1763, p. 176
2. n. Paxton Boys, p. 177
3. c. Currency Act, p. 179
4. j. liberty tree, p. 181
5. d. Declaratory Act, p. 182
6. i. *Liberty*, p. 186
7. t. tea, p. 187
8. f. feudal revival, p. 195
9. s. regulators, p. 195
10. q. Quakers, p. 196
11. e. East India Company, p. 198
12. o. Port Act, p. 199
13. k. Massachusetts Government Act, p. 199
14. r. Quebec Act, p. 199
15. h. Intolerable Acts, p. 201
16. l. minutemen, p. 203
17. a. the Association, p. 204
18. m. Olive Branch Petition, pp. 207–208
19. b. *Common Sense*, p. 209
20. g. Hessians, p. 209

Where Was It?

1. c. Castle William, p. 190
2. i. South Carolina, p. 189
3. g. Newport, Rhode Island, p. 191
4. f. Hudson River Valley, p. 193
5. e. Granville District, p. 193
6. a. Alamance Creek, p. 196
7. d. Georgia, p. 203
8. b. Carpenters' Hall, p. 203
9. h. New York, p. 209

CHARTS, MAPS, AND ILLUSTRATIONS

1. 1771; Chesapeake; 1775; the Revolutionary War began, p. 191
2. Pennsylvania, Fairfax, p. 194
3. *Poems on Various Subjects*, p. 198

MULTIPLE CHOICE

1. d.   (p. 173)
2. d.   (p. 176)
3. b.   (p. 176)
4. a.   (p. 178)
5. d.   (p. 179)
6. c.   (p. 180)
7. b.   (p. 180)
8. a.   (p. 181)
9. c.   (p. 181)
10. d.   (p. 185)
11. c.   (p. 186)
12. a.   (p. 187)
13. c.   (p. 188)
14. b.   (p. 189)
15. d.   (p. 192)
16. c.   (p. 192)
17. c.   (p. 195)
18. c.   (p. 196)
19. c.   (p. 196)
20. c.   (p. 197)
21. a.   (p. 199)
22. c.   (p. 202)
23. a.   (p. 203)
24. c.   (p. 207)
25. a.   (p. 207)
26. a.   (p. 209)
27. b.   (p. 209)

ESSAY

Description and Explanation

1. pp. 176–178
2. pp. 182–183, 186–187, 191
3. pp. 180–181, 184
4. pp. 181, 186–187
5. pp. 189–190
6. pp. 202–205

Discussion and Analysis

1. pp. 175–756, 178–180
2. pp. 193–196
3. pp. 199–203
4. pp. 208–209

What If

1. p. 181
2. Chapter 5 *passim*
3. pp. 208–209

Crossword Puzzle

CHAPTER 6

THE REVOLUTIONARY REPUBLIC

The Revolutionary War was one of the bloodiest conflicts in American history. Once independence became the goal, the price of resistance escalated. British leaders believed that the loss of the colonies would be a fatal blow to British power, and they raised more soldiers and larger fleets than ever before. After the excitement of the first years and the French alliance, the war turned into a struggle of attrition and survival. The British loyalists became an increasing source of manpower as resistance shifted to the southern regions. The Revolution became a partisan, or civil, war in which neighbors were far more likely to shoot at neighbors than during even the Civil War in the nineteenth century, when the geographical line separating the two sides was much clearer.

In the early days of the Revolution, colonists were actively drafting state constitutions and bills of rights. They knew that they were attempting something new, daring, and experimental; they embraced republicanism with enthusiasm. With virtually no dissent, Americans decided that every state would need a written constitution that would limit the powers of government. They also moved toward ever-expanding expressions of popular sovereignty, the theory that all power must be derived from the people themselves. This process sparked lively debates and ignited a learning process of immense importance.

The long war badly damaged the American economy and trade, and the years just after the war were difficult times. Debtors and creditors quarrelled fiercely. Social tensions racked some states, which were buried under their own war debts and divisions among their leaders. Demands quickly aroused the need to do something about the new country and its government.

These needs led to the summoning of the Constitutional Convention in Philadelphia in 1787. After much study and debate, compromises were developed that formed a new national or federal government. The delegates at the convention knew that they were proposing change in the existing legal order. Nothing that resembled American federalism ever had been tried before. Sovereignty would be removed from the government and bestowed on the people, who then would empower different levels of government through separate constitutions. After it had been ratified by the required number of states, the new Constitution went into effect in April 1789. The American federal system was the most lasting contribution of the Revolutionary generation. It was a new order for the ages.

LIBERTY, EQUALITY, POWER

Independence transformed whole areas of American life. Issues such as liberty, equality, and rights were seriously and openly debated. This debate affected American views of slavery, women, and religious freedom. Many slaves won their freedom, but, in the North, freedom brought no equality and little power. Some southern slave owners questioned the institution of slavery and emancipated some slaves; but, in parts of the South, slavery continued to expand. Religious liberty became something to admire, and most states disestablished the Church of England. Women struggled to win greater dignity with some success, especially in the increase in literacy among northern women. But there was little interest or support for true equality of the sexes.

The big losers in the Revolutionary War were the loyalists who lost their property, and many were forced out of the United States. Most Indians had supported the British during the war but were abandoned by the British when the war was over. They shared little of the liberty, equality, or power won by white male householders in the Revolution.

OBJECTIVES

After studying this chapter, a student should be able to

1. Describe the early campaigns of the Revolution, including the effects on Britain and France.

2. Examine the constitutions produced by the states and the experimental nature of them.

3. Describe the campaigns in the South and the end of the war.

4. Discuss the role of the loyalists, slaves, and Indians who sided with the British.

5. Examine the effects of the Revolution on women, slavery, and religion.

6. Describe the problems with the West and purposes of the Northwest Ordinances.

7. Trace the processes that led to the new Constitution and the compromises of the Convention.

8. Discuss the drive to ratify the Constitution, including which groups of people and what regions supported it or opposed it.

CHRONOLOGY

1769	Spain founded a base in San Diego but sent few soldiers. Instead, for the last time in the history of North America, missionaries would set the tone for a whole province—California. During the next few years, Spain explored the Pacific coastline as far north as southern Alaska.
1775	Westward expansion continued during the Revolutionary War. Daniel Boone, a North Carolina hunter, along with thirty axmen, hacked out the Wilderness Road from Cumberland Gap to the Kentucky bluegrass country.
1775–1776	Early successes kept morale high in the American army and helped sustain the *rage militaire* (enthusiasm for the cause) that prompted thousands to volunteer for service, including about four thousand veterans who reenlisted in 1776.
1776	The approach of independence touched off an intense American debate on constitutionalism. Settlers knew that they would have to reconstitute their

governments along more popular lines now that the British Crown no longer provided the basis for legitimacy.

The first setback for Americans in the Revolutionary War came in Canada. Americans besieging Quebec were forced to retreat when British reinforcements sailed up the St. Lawrence in **May**.

In **June**, Virginia became the first state to adopt a permanent constitution, one that envisioned a republican future. Other states adopted variations of this model.

Congress began serious debates on an American union in the summer, but then took nearly a year and a half to draft a final text of what became the "Articles of Confederation and perpetual Union."

In **September**, there were 27,000 Americans fit for duty in the northern theater, but by December only 6,000 remained. Most of them intended to go home when their enlistments expired on **December 31**.

In **November**, at a cost of 460 casualties, the British compelled three thousand men to surrender at Fort Washington. In **December**, as British forces swept across New Jersey, they captured Charles Lee, next in command after Washington, and Richard Stockton, a signer of the Declaration of Independence. Washington knew he had to do something dramatic to restore morale and encourage some of his men to reenlist. On the night of **December 25**, he crossed the ice-choked Delaware River and marched south, surprising the Trenton garrison at dawn.

Also in **December**, Benjamin Franklin arrived in France as an agent of the American Congress and took French society by storm.

The New Jersey constitution allowed women to vote if they headed a household and paid taxes. This privilege was revoked in 1807.

1777

Washington's victories at Trenton and Princeton in **January** helped him recruit what was virtually a new army. With stricter discipline and longer terms of service, military training was now a real possibility.

In northern New York, little went right for the British after Ticonderoga fell to Burgoyne on **June 2**. Seven hundred Hessians were detached to forage in the Green Mountains, but they ran into 2,600 militia fighters raised by John Stark of New Hampshire. At Bennington, Vermont, Stark killed or captured nearly all of the Hessians in **August**. Burgoyne retreated to Saratoga, where he surrendered the entire army on **October 17**. The American victory at Saratoga helped bring France into the war.

Indians began entering the war on the side of Britain, including such groups as the Mohawks of the Iroquois, the Shawnee, and other nations.

The growth of racism along the frontier increased the bitterness and the number of atrocities. In some areas, the frontier was ravaged by one side or the other.

In the **fall**, Washington and his army headed to Valley Forge, where they endured a miserable winter. While there, Baron von Steuben devised a drill manual, which he modified for Americans, thus improving the quality of the American army.

In **November**, Congress asked the states to ratify the Articles by **March 10, 1778**, but only Virginia met the deadline. Most states tried to attach conditions, which Congress rejected.

1778

Burgoyne's disaster convinced Louis XVI (1774–1793) that the Americans could win and that intervention was a good risk. Franklin and French foreign minister, the comte de Vergennes, signed two treaties in **February**.

News of the Franco-American treaties stunned London, and William Pitt, earl of Chatham, warned that American independence would be a disaster for Britain. After finishing his speech, he collapsed on the floor of the House of Lords and died a month later.

Lord North assembled a plan of conciliation that conceded virtually everything to the Americans but independence. In **June**, Congress rejected the proposals.

In **December**, a small British amphibious force took Savannah, Georgia, and held it through **1779** against an American and French counterthrust. The British government even managed to restore royal government in Georgia between **1780** and **1782**.

1779

King Charles III of Spain, who understood that it was dangerous for one imperial power to urge the subjects of another to revolt, never made a direct alliance with the Americans during the war. However, he did join with France in its war against Britain.

With the economy deteriorating in what seemed to be an endless war, the value of Continental money fell to less than a penny on the dollar.

Nearly all Indians, from the Creeks on the Gulf coast to the nations of the Great Lakes, exchanged emissaries and planned an all-out war against frontier settlers, but George Rogers Clark of Virginia thwarted their offensive by cutting off their supplies.

Benedict Arnold, who thought that Congress never really appreciated his heroism, began trading intelligence to the British for cash.

1779–1780

This winter was the most severe of the century and marked a low point in morale, especially among the main force of Continentals snowed in with Washington at Morristown, New Jersey. Many deserted.

1780   The Massachusetts Constitution became the first in the world to be drafted by a special convention and ratified by the people.

Congress agreed to stop the printing presses from making paper money and to rely instead on requisitions from the states and on foreign and domestic loans.

The number of loyalists under arms probably exceeded the number of Continentals by two to one.

General Clinton, who had been in charge of the British war effort since **1778**, moved to Georgia to concentrate on the southern theater of the war. On **May 12**, Charleston, South Carolina, surrendered to the British, giving them the largest number of prisoners Britain had captured in one battle in the entire war. Clinton turned loose his loyalists under Banastre Tarleton and Patrick Ferguson, and Tarleton caught 350 Continentals near the North Carolina border on **May 29**. In what became known as "Tarleton's quarter," he killed them. On **August 16**, the British routed about 3,000 Continentals and militia at Camden, South Carolina.

General Nathanael Greene was sent to the Carolinas with a small Continental force. At King's Mountain on **October 7**, an army of frontiersmen and militia fought a British group, mainly composed of loyalists. This was the first British setback in the Deep South and it halted the British drive into North Carolina.

Pennsylvania adopted the modern world's first gradual emancipation statute. Instead of freeing current slaves, it declared further that all children born to Pennsylvania slaves would become free at age 28.

Esther de Berdt Reed organized the Philadelphia Ladies Association to relieve the sufferings of Continental soldiers. It was the first women's society to take a public role in American history.

1780s   Tragically, the few Indian nations that had supported the colonists suffered the most. In the 1780s, after Joseph Brant led most of the Iroquois north to Canada, New York confiscated most of the land of the friendly Iroquois who had stayed.

The American Revolution created thirty refugees for every one thousand people. About 35,000 found their way to Nova Scotia, the western half of which became the province of New Brunswick in the 1780s. Another 6,000 to 10,000 fled to Quebec, settled upriver from the older French population and, in **1791**, became the new province of Upper Canada (later Ontario).

This decade was a difficult time for the American people. The economy did not rebound, debtors and creditors quarrelled fiercely, and state politics displayed persistent cleavages. Out of this turmoil arose the demand to amend or even to replace the Articles of Confederation.

1781

In **January**, Clinton sent Benedict Arnold with 1,600 men, mostly loyalists, up the James River. They took the new capital of Richmond, almost without resistance, and destroyed the city. When Jefferson called out the militia, few responded.

On **January 17**, at a place known as Cowpens, the Americans clearly outfought the British army without an advantage of numbers or terrain. This was the first time this had happened in the war.

In **March**, the Confederation finally went into effect as the last state ratified it.

By **July**, after Greene outmaneuvered Cornwallis, the British held only Savannah and Charleston in the Deep South.

In **September**, Washington cut off all retreat routes with the help of the French navy and a combined French and American army, and besieged Lord Cornwallis and his men at Yorktown, Virginia. On **October 19**, Cornwallis surrendered his entire army of 8,000 men.

1782

News of British failure in North America brought down the British government in **March**. Lord North resigned and George III even drafted an abdication message, though he never delivered it.

Against the advice of Benjamin Franklin, John Jay and John Adams opened secret peace negotiations with the British. The treaty they signed established the boundaries of the United States and officially ended the war in **February 1783**, although the treaty was not ratified until months later.

1785

Washington invited delegates from Virginia and Maryland to a conference at Mount Vernon to discuss navigation rights on the Potomac. James Madison then persuaded the Virginia legislature to call a convention of all states at Annapolis, Maryland, to discuss ways to improve trade.

In the Land Ordinance of 1785, Congress authorized the survey of the Northwest Territory and its division into townships. It also established a method for selling the land.

1786

Virginia passed Thomas Jefferson's Statute for Religious Freedom. In Virginia, church attendance and the support of ministers became purely voluntary activities.

In **September**, the delegates who had attended the Annapolis conference adopted a report drafted by Alexander Hamilton of New York. It urged all states to send delegates to a general convention in Philadelphia.

During the **winter**, protestors loosely organized under a Continental Army veteran, Captain Daniel Shays, and tried to storm the federal arsenal at Springfield. In early **1787**, this attempt failed due to the efforts of volunteers under Benjamin Lincoln.

1787	Congress passed the Northwest Ordinance of 1787 to provide government for the region. Colonialism clearly was rejected for frontier settlers, though not for the Indians.
	In **May**, delegates of twelve states began work on a new form of government. After four months of secret sessions, they were able to complete a new constitution.
	In **September**, the Constitution was submitted to the states for ratification. In **December**, Delaware became the first state to ratify it.
1788	Additional states ratified the new Constitution, with hotly contested struggles in some of the stronger states. When eleven states adopted it, the government was put into effect in **April 1789**.
1790	John Carroll of Maryland became the first Roman Catholic bishop in the United States and, as part of the new atmosphere of tolerance, hardly anyone protested.
	Rhode Island became the thirteenth state to ratify the Constitution.
	Georgia and South Carolina reopened the Atlantic slave trade to make up for the loss of slaves during the war and to meet the demand for cotton after 1790.

GLOSSARY OF IMPORTANT TERMS

abolition	A term used to describe the end of slavery.
attrition	A type of warfare where an effort is made to exhaust the manpower, supplies, and morale of the other side.
blockhouse	A small wooden fort with an overhanging second floor. The white settlers of Kentucky used blockhouses in wars with the Indians.
convention	A type of legislature in England and colonial America that met only to handle an emergency and then was replaced by a legitimate legislature.
coup d'état	The sudden overthrow of the government.
electoral college	The group that elected the president. Each state received as many electors as it had congressmen and senators combined and could decide how to choose its electors. Every elector voted for two candidates, one of whom had to be from another state.
emancipation	Refers to release from slavery or bondage. **Gradual emancipation** was introduced in Pennsylvania and provided for the protection of property rights and the eventual freeing of slaves, born after a certain date, when they reached age 28.

Federalists	Supporters of the Constitution during the ratification process. Antifederalists were opponents of constitutional ratification.
free householders	A term used to describe small-property owners.
loyalist	People in the thirteen colonies who remained loyal to Britain during the Revolution.
manumission of slaves	The act of freeing a slave, done at the will of the owner.
popular sovereignty	The theory that all power must be derived from the people themselves.
public virtue	To the Revolutionary generation, this meant patriotism and the willingness of a free and independent people to subordinate their interests to the common good and even to die for their country.
rage militaire	A French term used to describe enthusiasm for the cause that encouraged thousands to volunteer for military service in 1775 and 1776.
river gods	A group of wealthy intermarried families in the Connecticut River Valley towns, most of whom subsequently became loyalists.
Shaysites	Farmers in western Massachusetts who took up arms in 1786–1787 to resist taxes and creditors.
sovereign power	A term used to describe supreme or final power.
stay law	A law that delays or postpones something. During the 1780s many states passed stay laws to delay the due date on debts because of the serious economic problems of the times.
unicameral legislature	A legislature with one chamber or house.

WHO? WHAT? WHERE?

WHO WERE THEY?

Complete each statement below (questions 1–17) by writing the letter preceding the appropriate name in the space provided. Use each answer only once.

> a. Alexander Hamilton
> b. Baron von Steuben
> c. Benedict Arnold
> d. Benjamin Franklin
> e. François, compte de Grasse
> f. Elizabeth Freeman
> g. George Washington

  h. James Madison
  i. John Adams
  j. John Burgoyne
  k. John Carroll
  l. Joseph Brant
  m. Lord Cornwallis
  n. Nathanael Greene
  o. Richard Stockton
  p. Robert Morris
  q. Thomas Jefferson

_____ 1. Rhode Island Quaker who gave up pacifism to become a general in the Continental army. He later successfully commanded Americans in the lower South.

_____ 2. Signer of the Declaration of Independence who was captured in New Jersey by British forces.

_____ 3. Prussian officer who volunteered to serve with the Continental army and devised a drill manual modified for American conditions.

_____ 4. Poet and playwright who was ordered to move his army from Canada to New York, but surrendered his entire army at the battle of Saratoga.

_____ 5. Agent of the American Congress in France who signed a military alliance with that government.

_____ 6. Author of a tract entitled *Thoughts on Government* that strongly influenced the drafting of the Virginia constitution.

_____ 7. Literate, educated Indian leader who led the Mohawks in support of Britain.

_____ 8. American general who attempted to negotiate the surrender of West Point to the British. He later served as a general in the British army and destroyed much of Richmond, Virginia.

_____ 9. Wealthy Philadelphia merchant who became the first secretary of finance and helped keep the army fed and clothed.

_____ 10. Commander of the French fleet in the Chesapeake area who helped defeat the British at Yorktown.

_____ 11. British commander who surrendered his army at Yorktown to the victorious George Washington.

_____ 12. Author of the Virginia Statute for Religious Freedom.

_____ 13. First Roman Catholic bishop in the United States.

_____ 14. African-American woman who sued her master for her freedom, based on the Massachusetts Bill of Rights, and won her liberty.

_____ 15. Author of a resolution adopted at the Annapolis meeting asking all the states to send delegates to a general convention at Philadelphia to revise the government.

_____ 16. Presiding officer at the Constitutional Convention at Philadelphia.

_____ 17. Virginian who spent the months before the Philadelphia Convention studying government and planning a stronger American union.

WHAT WAS IT?

Complete each statement below (questions 1–10) by writing the letter preceding the appropriate response in the space provided. Use each answer only once.

    a. *The Federalist*
    b. Massachusetts Bill of Rights
    c. Philadelphia Ladies Association
    d. popular sovereignty
    e. Protestant Episcopal Church
    f. public virtue
    g. *rage militaire*
    h. Roderique Hortalez et Compagnie
    i. Spanish dollar
    j. three fifths

_____ 1. Enthusiasm for the cause that encouraged thousands to volunteer for service in 1775 and 1776.

_____ 2. Firm established as a front to smuggle supplies past the British blockade of the American coastline.

_____ 3. Theory that all power must be derived from the people themselves.

_____ 4. Patriotism and willingness of free and independent people to die for their country or to subordinate their interests to the common good.

_____ 5. Basic monetary unit in the first days of the Revolution.

_____ 6. Name under which the Church of England reorganized itself in the United States in the 1780s.

_____ 7. Document that included the statement that all people are "born free and equal."

_____ 8. Group organized in 1780 by Esther de Berdt Reed to relieve the suffering of Continental soldiers. It was the first women's society in American history to take a public role.

_____ 9. Number of slaves counted in apportioning representation and direct taxes.

_____ 10. Most comprehensive body of political thought produced by the Revolutionary generation.

WHERE WAS IT?

Complete each statement below (questions 1–12) by writing the letter preceding the appropriate response in the space provided. Use each answer only once.

a. Cowpens, South Carolina
b. Delaware
c. Gnadenhutten
d. Kentucky
e. Maryland
f. Massachusetts
g. Newburgh, New York
h. New Jersey
i. Pennsylvania
j. Rhode Island
k. Trenton, New Jersey
l. Virginia

_____ 1. Location of a battle on the day after Christmas 1776, when Washington and his men attacked a garrison housing many Hessians suffering from holiday hangovers.

_____ 2. First state to adopt a permanent state constitution.

_____ 3. State that adopted the first written state constitution to be drafted and ratified by the people. It is today the oldest constitution in the world.

_____ 4. State that refused to ratify the Articles of Confederation for more than three years because of concern about the large western land grants of states such as Virginia.

_____ 5. Location of a Moravian Indian mission where a frontier group massacred unarmed Indians. This event led some Indians to resume the custom of ritual torture of prisoners for punishment.

_____ 6. Battle where, for the first time in the Revolutionary War, an American force clearly outfought the British army without an advantage of numbers or terrain.

_____ 7. Encampment where General Washington made the emotional appeal, "I have grown old in the service of my country, and now find that I am growing blind."

_____ 8. State that enacted the modern world's first gradual emancipation statute.

_____ 9. State whose constitution allowed women to vote if they headed a household and paid taxes.

_____ 10. Area referred to as "the best poor-man's country" and also as the "dark and bloody ground."

_____ 11. Only state that refused to participate in the Philadelphia Convention.

_____ 12. First state to ratify the Constitution.

CHARTS, MAPS, AND ILLUSTRATIONS

1. The Spanish mission founded at Carmel, California, was

_____ .

2. The best surviving example of Jewish artistic taste in the eighteenth century is _____ .

3. One state that claimed the present-day area of Vermont at the end of the Revolution was _____ .

4. The state with the largest western land claims was _____ .

MULTIPLE CHOICE

Circle the letter that best completes each statement.

1. Washington's victories at Trenton and Princeton helped him recruit what was virtually a new army in 1777. After this
   a. he demanded less discipline.
   b. the men were required to serve for a single campaign.
   c. the men were promised a cash bonus to anyone enlisting for three years and a land bounty to anyone serving for the duration.
   d. Congress reduced the number of lashes a soldier could receive from thirty to ten.

2. Men who volunteered for longer terms usually
   a. were poor.
   b. held a secure place in their local communities.
   c. were more religious.
   d. were rich.

3. Washington received help from other European volunteers except
   a. marquis de LaFayette of France.
   b. John Burgoyne and Richard, viscount Howe, of Britain.
   c. Thaddeus Kosciuszko and Casimir, count Pulaski, of Poland.
   d. Johann, baron de Kalb, of France.

4. By the time Burgoyne's surviving soldiers in Bennington, Vermont, reached the Hudson River and advanced toward Albany, they were outnumbered three to one by the Americans under
   a. George Mason.
   b. Horotio Gates.
   c. Thomas Paine.
   d. John Stark.

5. Benjamin Franklin, serving as an agent of the American Congress, signed two treaties in February 1778 with the French foreign minister,
   a. Johann, baron de Kalb.
   b. Charles Gravier, comte de Vergennes.
   c. Pierre Augustin Caron de Beaumarchais.
   d. Roderique Hortalez et Compagnie.

6. In February 1778, France and the American colonies signed two treaties. One, a commercial agreement, granted Americans generous trading terms with France. In the other agreement, all of the following items were agreed to, except that France
   a. established a perpetual alliance with the United States.
   b. recognized American independence.
   c. agreed to receive some territorial concessions on the North American continent.
   d. agreed to fight until Britain conceded independence.

7. Once formally allied with France, Americans expected a quick victory. During this time, the British reevaluated their military strategy. North's government did all of the following except
   a. declare war on France.
   b. sign an alliance with Spain.
   c. recall the Howe brothers.
   d. order General Clinton to abandon Philadelphia.

8. Charles III of Spain, who understood that it was dangerous for one imperial power to urge the subjects of another to revolt, never made a direct alliance with the Americans during the war. However, he did join with France in its war against
   a. Russia.
   b. Sweden.
   c. Italy.
   d. Britain.

9. According to John Adams, government should be divided into all of the following branches except
   a. an executive armed with veto power.
   b. a hereditary monarchy with limited power.
   c. a bicameral legislature.
   d. an independent judiciary.

10. The first state to adopt a permanent constitution that envisioned a republican future was
    a. Virginia.
    b. Delaware.
    c. New Jersey.
    d. Rhode Island.

11. Who was the highly respected planter who drafted a declaration of rights affirming the right to life, liberty, and the pursuit of happiness, while condemning all forms of hereditary privilege?
    a. Joseph Brant
    b. Samuel Kirkland
    c. Thomas Burke
    d. George Mason

12. Most loyalists
    a. strongly rejected American ideas of liberty.
    b. supported the Stamp Act and other British measures and felt that the British government was preparing a general assault on representative government in the colonies.
    c. thought that an untried American union was a far riskier venture than remaining part of the British empire.
    d. decided which side to shoot at or flee from long before the fighting reached their neighborhood.

13. When given the choice, most slaves south of New England sided with the
    a. British.
    b. Americans.
    c. French Canadians.
    d. Spanish.

14. The struggle for loyalties created an enormous stream of refugees, black and white, chiefly at the end of the war. For every one thousand people, the American Revolution created
    a. one refugee.
    b. ten refugees.
    c. thirty refugees.
    d. ninety refugees.

15. Most Indians saw that an American victory threatened their survival as a people on their ancestral lands. Nearly all of them sided with Britain
    a. out of loyalty.
    b. out of affection.
    c. because they considered themselves British subjects.
    d. because they hoped a British victory would stem the flood of western settlement.

16. In the Deep South, the only Indians willing to fight on the American side were the
    a. Huron.
    b. Pawnee.
    c. Blackfoot.
    d. Catawbas.

17. After 1778, as the struggle became a global war of attrition, much of the British public began to suspect that the war could not be won for all of the following reasons except
    a. Trade had expanded.
    b. Taxes and national debt had soared.
    c. A cross-Channel invasion became a serious threat.
    d. Political dissent rose sharply.

18. In 1779, with the economy deteriorating in what seemed to be an endless war, the value of Continental money fell to less than
    a. a penny on the dollar.
    b. a nickel on the dollar.

c. ten cents on the dollar.

d. twenty-five cents on the dollar.

19. Continental soldiers grew discontented and mutinous for all of the following reasons except
    a. They were unpaid.
    b. They were ill-clothed.
    c. They were poorly fed.
    d. They were overworked.

20. Contrary to the French Treaty of 1778 and against Franklin's advice, secret peace negotiations with the British were opened by
    a. John Jay and John Adams.
    b. Jean Baptists Donatier and Hiram Saunders.
    c. Daniel Morgan and Patrick Ferguson.
    d. Francis Marion and John André.

21. The Treaty of Paris ended the Revolution in February 1783 and included all of the following terms except
    a. The British must recognize the Mississippi, without New Orleans, as the western boundary of the United States.
    b. New Englanders retained the right to fish off Newfoundland.
    c. British merchants received recognition of the validity of prewar debts owed them.
    d. Congress refused to urge the states to restore confiscated loyalist property.

22. All of the following occurred in the decade after 1776 except
    a. Religious dissenters supported and reestablished the Church of England in every southern state.
    b. Religious liberty and the pluralism it created became not just tolerated but also admired.
    c. Many slaves won their freedom.
    d. Women struggled to win greater dignity.

23. To make up for their loss of slaves during the war and to meet the demand for cotton after 1790, which two states reopened the Atlantic slave trade?
    a. New York and Connecticut
    b. Maryland and South Carolina
    c. Georgia and South Carolina
    d. Virginia and Georgia

24. Westward expansion continued during the Revolutionary War. Who was the North Carolina hunter who, along with thirty axmen, hacked out the Wilderness Road from Cumberland Gap to the Kentucky bluegrass country in early 1775?
    a. William Clark
    b. Meriwether Lewis
    c. Daniel Boone
    d. David Crockett

25. In the Land Ordinance of 1785, Congress authorized all of the following except
    a. the survey of the Northwest Territory.
    b. the division of the Northwest Territory into townships six miles square, each composed of 36 sections of 640 acres.
    c. all land to be sold at auction beginning at twenty dollars an acre.
    d. alternate townships to be sold in sections or as a whole, to satisfy settlers and speculators, respectively.

26. Congress passed the Northwest Ordinance of 1787 to provide government for the region, which included all of the following provisions except the
    a. creation of from three to five states.
    b. government by an appointive governor and council until the population reached five thousand.
    c. adoption of a constitution once the population reached sixty thousand.
    d. protection of civil liberties, setting aside four sections of each township for education, and allowing slavery forever within the region.

27. In the winter of 1787, who was the Continental Army veteran who led protestors in an attempt to storm the federal arsenal at Springfield?
    a. Daniel Shays
    b. James Bowdoin
    c. James Wilson
    d. Daniel Morgan

28. Which of the following statement completions is not true? Governor Edmund Randolph's Virginia Plan presented at the Constitutional Convention
    a. was drafted largely by James Madison.
    b. proposed a bicameral legislature with representation apportioned according to population.
    c. included explicit provisions to tax and regulate trade.
    d. allowed the legislature to choose the national executive officer.

29. The Connecticut Compromise
    a. settled the state's boundary with New York.
    b. ceded Connecticut's western lands to Congress.
    c. apportioned representation according to population in the lower house but affirmed state equality in the upper house.
    d. established the electoral college.

30. The Constitution was to go into effect when it was
    a. ratified by special conventions in nine states.
    b. debated extensively throughout the country.
    c. published in all of the newspapers in the country.
    d. accepted by ten state legislatures.

31. Which of the following men did not collaborate on a series of eighty-five essays known as *The Federalist Papers*, which were meant to rally support for ratification of the Constitution?
    a. Alexander Hamilton
    b. James Madison
    c. William Duer
    d. John Jay

ESSAY

Description and Explanation (one- to two-paragraph essay)

1. Describe the views of John Adams on government and public virtue. Did they change over the course of the Revolution?

2. Describe the differences among the newly established state governments. What were the main issues and problems with which the founders of these state governments dealt?

3. Describe the effects of the Revolution on women and on gender relations.

4. Describe the effects of the Revolution on organized religion.

5. Compare the cosmopolitan and localist coalitions, and describe the type of people who were members of the two groups.

6. Compare the large and small state plans at the Philadelphia Convention and compare them with the Connecticut Compromise. Was it a real compromise?

Discussion and Analysis (class discussion or one- to two-paragraph essay)

1. Discuss the dispersal of loyalists, slaves, and Indians as a result of the American Revolution.

2. Discuss the Revolution as a partisan or civil war among Americans.

3. Discuss slavery and the American Revolution, including the effects of war on slaves, British use and treatment of slaves, the new state governments, and nationality through the Northwest Ordinance and the federal Constitution.

What If (include an explanation of your position)

1. If you were an official with the French government, would you agree to help the Americans after the battle of Saratoga?

2. If you were a slave living in America during the Revolution and had to decide between supporting the British or the patriots, which side would you select? Would it make a difference if you were living in Connecticut or Virginia?

3. If you were a delegate to the Philadelphia Convention of 1787, would you vote for the Constitution? Which part would you support strongly? Is there any part you would oppose?

Crossword Puzzle: The Revolutionary Republic

ACROSS

1. Ohio company town
6. Spain's Pacific rival
8. Part of a new order for the ages
9. Cap material for Franklin
10. Battle of the ___ kept Cornwallis from leaving Yorktown by sea
11. Carolina partisan leader
13. Trying to turn West Point over to the British was Benedict Arnold's dramatic way of ___
14. Delaware hazard of December 1776
15. Consequences for a Continental
16. Von Steuben's nationality
18. Compass point
20. Abbreviation for "that is"
21. Short for Guilford Courthouse state
23. Leaves army as many at Morristown did, 1779–1780
24. *Thoughts on Government* author

DOWN

1. Gardoqui Treaty proposed closing ___ to Americans for 25 years
2. Washington's Yorktown ally
3. What Indians resumed after Gnadenhutten
4. What the Continental Line was
5. Boone's road to Kentucky
7. Clinton's Conquest of December 1778
9. Tory commander and kin killed at King's Mountain
12. Robert Morris was Secretary of ___ during the Revolution
15. Postwar veterans' bounty
17. Leader of Philadelphia Ladies Association
19. One of the Floridas
22. Number in which Publius argued the virtues of a large republic

ANSWER KEY

WHO? WHAT? WHERE?
Who Were They?

1. n. Nathanael Greene, p. 215
2. o. Richard Stockton, p. 215
3. b. Baron von Steuben, p. 218
4. j. John Burgoyne, p. 218
5. d. Benjamin Franklin, p. 219
6. i. John Adams, p. 221
7. l. Joseph Brant, p. 228
8. c. Benedict Arnold, p. 232
9. p. Robert Morris, p. 237
10. e. François, compte de Grasse, p. 238
11. m. Lord Cornwallis, p. 238
12. q. Thomas Jefferson, p. 240
13. k. John Carroll, p. 241
14. f. Elizabeth Freeman, p. 242
15. a. Alexander Hamilton, p. 249
16. g. George Washington, p. 250
17. h. James Madison, p. 249

What Was It?

1. g. *rage militaire*, p. 215
2. h. Roderique Hortalez et Compagnie, p. 219
3. d. popular sovereignty, p. 221
4. f. public virtue, p. 221
5. i. Spanish dollar, p. 230
6. e. Protestant Episcopal Church, p. 241
7. b. Massachusetts Bill of Rights, p. 241
8. c. Philadelphia Ladies Association, p. 242
9. j. three fifths, p. 250
10. a. *The Federalist*, p. 249

Where Was It?

1. k. Trenton, New Jersey, p. 217
2. l. Virginia, p. 222
3. f. Massachusetts, p. 224
4. e. Maryland, p. 225
5. c. Gnadenhutten, p. 228
6. a. Cowpens, South Carolina, p. 235
7. g. Newburgh, New York, pp. 239–240
8. i. Pennsylvania, p. 241
9. h. New Jersey, p. 242
10. d. Kentucky, p. 243
11. j. Rhode Island, p. 249
12. b. Delaware, p. 251

CHARTS, MAPS, AND ILLUSTRATIONS

1. San Carlos Borromeo, p. 220
2. Touro Synagogue, p. 240
3. New York, Massachusetts, or New Hampshire, p. 246
4. Virginia, p. 246

MULTIPLE CHOICE

1. c. (p. 217)
2. a. (p. 217)
3. b. (p. 218)
4. b. (pp. 218–219)
5. b. (p. 219)
6. c. (p. 219)
7. b. (p. 220)

8. d. (p. 221)

9. b. (p. 221)

10. a. (p. 222)

11. d. (p. 222)

12. c. (p. 226)

13. a. (p. 226)

14. c. (p. 227)

15. d. (p. 227)

16. d. (p. 228)

17. a. (p. 230)

18. a. (p. 230)

19. d. (p. 230)

20. a. (p. 238)

21. d. (p. 239)

22. a. (pp. 240–242)

23. c. (p. 242)

24. c. (p. 243)

25. c. (p. 245)

26. d. (pp. 245–246)

27. a. (p. 248)

28. c. (p. 250)

29. c. (p. 250)

30. a. (p. 251)

31. c. (p. 252)

ESSAY

Description and Explanation

1. pp. 221–222

2. pp. 222–224

3. p. 242

4. p. 240–241

5. pp. 248–249

6. p. 250

Discussion and Analysis

1. pp. 226–228

2. p. 233

3. pp. 241, 244–246

What If

1. pp. 219–220

2. pp. 226–227

3. p. 250

Crossword Puzzle

CHAPTER 7

THE DEMOCRATIC REPUBLIC, 1790–1820

In the democratic republic of the post-Revolutionary period, farming was still the basis of the American economy. American farmers were increasingly engaged in the market economy, particularly during the tremendous expansion of the overseas markets from the wars in Europe.

New equipment was developing that changed the role of women on farms and rejuvenated the use of slavery. In some areas, rural overcrowding forced the price of land upward, pushing many young people into new western areas or into cities. A more individualistic, democratic, and insecure order was taking its place.

Americans freed from the constraints of patriarchal authority often seized the opportunity to think and act for themselves. This trend increased as literacy among Americans increased and a print culture emerged that could cater to popular taste. There was also a redefinition of republican citizenship and a new insistence on equal rights for all white men. New laws dissolved the old connection between political rights and property. This happened at a time when the changing economy was producing growing numbers of landless tenants and wage earners.

The collapse of established churches, social dislocations of the period, and increasingly anti-authoritarian, democratic sensibilities of ordinary Americans provided fertile fields for the growth of new democratic religious sects. The variety of choices increased dramatically, but the fastest-growing churches had a democratic theme. Religion was now a matter of the heart, not the head. Most of the newer churches, such as the Methodist Church, granted responsibility to the individual believer. The religious revival of the late eighteenth and early nineteenth centuries also appealed to many African Americans, who increasingly considered themselves Christians.

LIBERTY, EQUALITY, POWER

The post-Revolutionary republic bestowed freedom and equality on most white men, but powerlessness and dependence on nearly everyone else. By 1820, the agrarian republic, with its promise of widespread land ownership and well-ordered paternal authority, was in deep peril. Most Americans witnessed the initial stirring of changes as a withering of paternal authority in their own households. For some slaves and many women, this was a welcome event. For others, it was a disaster of unmeasured proportions.

There was a noticeable advance in equal rights for all white men, but no other race benefited in this way. Many laws that expanded voting rights for white men specifically excluded or restricted votes for blacks, signifying a lack of liberty, equality, or power for nonwhites. While there was a blurring of the emerging distinctions of social class, the boundaries set by sex and race were hardened. Many of the rising church groups emphasized liberty and equality, but they gradually excluded many groups, such as African Americans. Most of these churches reached their own acceptance of slavery. Slaves from the 1790s onward whispered of natural rights and imagined themselves as part of the democratic republic. This was not yet to be. With or without property, liberty, and equality, power in the democratic republic was for white males only.

OBJECTIVES

After studying this chapter, a student should be able to

1. Examine the changes in agriculture and their effects on rural life.

2. Describe the decline of woodlands Indians.

3. Describe life in backcountry.

4. Explain the rise of cotton as a commercial crop and its role in the revival of slavery.

5. Compare slavery in the Chesapeake area with that of the lower South.

6. Trace the growth of the seaport cities and the changes in the status of workers.

7. Explain changes in patriarchal authority and parental power.

8. Analyze the changes in religion, especially the growth of the new democratic religious sects.

CHRONOLOGY

1780	A conference of Methodist preachers ordered circuit riders to free their slaves and advised all Methodists to do the same. Four years later, Methodists declared that they would excommunicate members who failed to free their slaves within two years.
1782	The free black population of Virginia stood at two thousand in 1782, when the state passed a law permitting manumission. The number of free blacks rose to 12,766 in 1790; to 20,124 in 1800; and 30,570 in 1810. In all, the proportion of Virginia blacks who were free increased from 4 percent in 1790 to 7 percent in 1810.
1783	Baptists and Methodists were by far the most successful at preaching. In 1783, there were only 50 Methodist churches in the United States; by 1820 there were 2,700.
1783–1793	Alexander McGillivray tried to unite the Creek Indians under a national council that could override local chiefs. McGillivray's premature death in 1793 prevented the realization of his vision.
1788–1808	Approximately 250,000 slaves were brought directly from Africa to the United States—nearly all of them to Charleston and Savannah. That figure equaled the number of Africans who had been brought to North America during the whole colonial period.
1790	No paper money had been issued by the states or the federal government, and the widespread use of Spanish, English, and French coins testified to the shortage of specie.

When the first federal census takers made their rounds in 1790, they found that 94 percent of the population was living on farms and in rural villages. The remaining 6 percent lived in twenty-four towns with a population of 2,500 or more, the census definition of urban. Most Americans still were living in a thin line of settlements along the Atlantic coast and along the navigable rivers that emptied into the Atlantic. Only ten thousand settlers lived west of the Appalachians, about one American in forty.

Though many woodland tribes still were intact and living on ancestral lands, their future was threatened. The once-powerful Cherokees had been punished severely for fighting on the British side during the Revolution; by 1790, they ceded three fourths of their territory to the Americans. Many Iroquois fled to Canada or were restricted to reservations in New York and Pennsylvania.

Artisans constituted about half of the male work force of the seaport cities, and their respectability and usefulness, together with the role they had played in the Revolution, earned them an honorable status.

Approximately 85 percent of adult men in New England and 60 percent of those in Pennsylvania and the Chesapeake area could read and write.

Only Vermont granted the right to vote to all free men.

Ninety newspapers were being published in the United States. By 1830, there were 370. This expansion in printed matter sped up the democratizing process.

1790s

The movement of slaves out of the Chesapeake was immense. During this period, one in twelve Virginia and Maryland slaves was taken south and west. The figure rose to one in ten between 1800 and 1810, and one in five between 1810 and 1820. In 1790, planters in Virginia and Maryland owned 56 percent of all American slaves; by 1860, they owned only 15 percent.

Improved winter feeding of cattle and better techniques for making and storing butter and cheese kept dairy products on the tables of the more prosperous farm families throughout the year.

1793–1815

With the outbreak of war between Britain and France in 1793, the overseas demand for American foodstuffs and shipping services to carry products from the Caribbean islands to Europe further strengthened American seaport cities. The economic boom created unprecedented poverty as well as wealth on a scale never seen before. Epidemics in the seaports became more frequent and increasingly deadly. Usually, a disease entered through the port and spread rapidly through the slums.

1793

Eli Whitney invented a cotton gin that combed seeds from fibers with metal pins fitted into rollers. This hand-driven innovation made it possible for a person to clean fifty pounds of short-staple cotton a day.

1794	General Anthony Wayne, commander of the third army sent against the northwestern Indians, defeated them at Fallen Timbers, near present-day Toledo. The next year, the Treaty of Greenville forced the cession of two thirds of what is now Ohio and southeastern Indiana. The British decided to abandon the forts they still occupied in the Northwest.
	African American preachers Richard Allen and Absolom Jones rebelled against the segregated seating at a Methodist church in Philadelphia. They founded separate black congregations.
1800	Plantation agriculture was rejuvenated with the development of the cotton gin. Cotton production grew to 73,000 bales in 1800. By 1820, cotton accounted for more than half the value of all agricultural exports.
	There were 903 post offices in the United States—a considerable increase from 1790, when there were only 75.
	A slave blacksmith in Richmond named Gabriel led a well-planned conspiracy to overthrow the Virginia slave regime. He hoped to make a republican revolution, not a slave revolt. He and many of his followers were hunted down, and twenty-seven were hanged.
1800–1810	For the first time in American history, the growth of urban population exceeded the growth of rural population.
1801	The first full-blown religious camp meeting took place at Cane Ridge, Kentucky. Estimates of the crowd at the outdoor event ranged from ten thousand to twenty thousand people.
1803	By this time, four frontier states had entered the union: Vermont (1791), Kentucky (1792), Tennessee (1796), and Ohio (1803).
1808	A group of young Cherokees, angered by the willingness of the old chiefs to be bribed and flattered into selling land, and by the departure of tribal members to remote locations in the Appalachians or to government lands in Arkansas, staged a revolt. By 1810, the Cherokee had transformed themselves from a defeated and divided tribe into a nation within a nation.
1811	William Henry Harrison of Indiana Territory led an army to Prophetstown and defeated Tenskwatawa at the battle of Tippecanoe.
1812	Louisiana entered the union.
1815	It was evident that wartime commerce had transformed the seaports and institutions of American business. New York City became the nation's largest urban center. The maritime economy, construction work, shipbuilding, the clothing trades, and other specialized crafts were undergoing change. Most young craftsmen could no longer hope to own their own shops, since artisans were being replaced by cheaper labor.
1816–1821	Six states entered the union: Indiana (1816), Mississippi (1817), Illinois (1818), Alabama (1819), Maine (1820), and Missouri (1821).

1820	Few southern evangelists were speaking out against slavery. Those who held antislavery views were concentrated in the upcountry, where few whites owned slaves. Most blacks outside the Deep South considered themselves Christians. There were approximately 700 independent black churches in the United States. Thirty years earlier, there had been none. The creation of an independent Christian tradition among the majority of African Americans who remained plantation slaves took place only after 1830.
1830	Per capita consumption of distilled spirits was over five gallons per year, the highest it has ever been, and three times what is in the United States today.
1840	Only Rhode Island retained property qualifications for voting. Fully 93 percent of northern blacks lived in states that banned or severely restricted their right to vote.

GLOSSARY OF IMPORTANT TERMS

backcountry	A term used in the early days of the republic to refer to the wilderness and the supposed misfits who lived in the western settlements.
changing system	This system was used primarily in the South and West where there was little cash money available. Farmers basically remembered what they owed one another and created an elaborate system of neighborhood debts.
camp meeting	An outdoor religious meeting often lasting days and conducted enthusiastically.
circuit-riding preachers	Methodist ministers who traveled from church to church, usually in rural areas. Where there were no formal church buildings, services were held in other buildings or outdoors.
competence	Defined in the early republic as the ability to live up to neighborhood economic standards while protecting the long-term independence of the household.
cotton	A semitropical plant that produced white, fluffy fibers that could be made into textiles. Two main types were grown in the United States. **Long-staple cotton** produced high-quality fiber and had a smooth seed that was easy to remove. However, it required a longer growing season and a higher moisture level. It was produced along the southeast coast of the United States and on the Sea Islands off Georgia and South Carolina. **Short-staple cotton** was hardier and could be produced throughout a large part of the Deep South. The main problem with it was the sticky, dark seed had to be removed by hand. It took one day for a person to clean a pound of short-staple cotton.
crisis conversion	Understood in evangelical churches as a personal transformation that resulted from directly experiencing the Holy Spirit.

deism The belief that God created the universe but did not intervene in its affairs.

frontier The term used by 1820 to replace "backcountry." The frontier was considered an area that was on the advancing edge of American civilization.

girdled trees Trees that had a line cut around them so sap would not rise in the spring. They then would die and fall down by themselves. Since they did not leaf out, it was possible to plant a crop among the dying trees.

grog shops Places that sold alcoholic beverages, generally cheap rum diluted with water.

household industry City merchants would provide rural workers with raw materials and would pay them for finished goods, such as shoes, furniture, cloth, and brooms. Usually work was done in the home by women and children, and the money earned would be given to the male head of the household.

itinerant preachers Ministers who traveled from place to place.

journeyman A wage-earning craftsman.

private fields Farms of up to five acres on which slaves were allowed to produce items for sale in a nearby market. It was permitted because slaves on the task system worked hard, required minimal supervision, and made money for their owners. The system was used most commonly in South Carolina and Georgia.

restorationism The belief that all theological and institutional changes since the end of biblical times were man-made mistakes and that religious organizations must restore themselves to the purity and simplicity of the apostolic church. This creed rejected learning and tradition and raised to priesthood all believers.

tenancy Farmers working land they did not own.

WHO? WHAT? WHERE?

WHO WERE THEY?

Complete each statement below (questions 1–13) by writing the letter preceding the appropriate name in the space provided. Use each answer only once.

a. Alexander McGillivray
b. Anthony Wayne
c. Cherokee
d. Davy Crockett
e. Eli Whitney
f. Francis Asbury
g. Gabriel
h. Hector St. John de Crevecoeur

    i. James McGready
    j. Mike Fink
    k. Tecumseh
    l. Tenskwatawa
    m. William Henry Harrison

_____ 1. French soldier who settled in rural New York and described an idealistic view of American farmers.

_____ 2. American commander who defeated the northwestern Indians in 1794 at Fallen Timbers.

_____ 3. Mixed-blood Creek who tried to unite Indians under a national council and formed an alliance with Spain.

_____ 4. Native American group that transformed itself from a defeated and divided tribe into a nation within a nation.

_____ 5. Shawnee prophet who encouraged his followers to return to their traditional lifestyles.

_____ 6. Shawnee leader who took control of the Indian movement in the Northwest and who received supplies and encouragement from the British in Canada.

_____ 7. American commander who led an army against Prophetstown and defeated Tenskwatawa at the battle of Tippecanoe.

_____ 8. Tennessee hero whose legendary status included tales about wrestling bears and making recipes for Indian stew.

_____ 9. Pennsylvania boatman who brawled and drank his way along the rivers of the interior.

_____ 10. Connecticut Yankee who went south to work as a tutor and produced a model of the cotton gin with only a few days' work.

_____ 11. Head or bishop of the Methodist Church during its fastest-growing years.

_____ 12. Minister in rural North Carolina who openly condemned local plantation owners.

_____ 13. Slave blacksmith in Richmond who dreamed of a truly democratic republic for Virginia. He organized a well-planned conspiracy to overthrow the state's slave-owning regime.

WHAT WAS IT?

Complete each statement below (questions 1–11) by writing the letter preceding the appropriate response in the space provided. Use each answer only once.

    a. Baptists
    b. camp meeting
    c. cotton
    d. cotton gin
    e. circuit-riding preachers
    f. deism
    g. household industry
    h. personal letters

  i. *The Power of Sympathy*
  j. private fields
  k. whiskey

_____ 1. City merchants would provide rural workers, usually women and children, with raw materials and then return to pick up the finished product.

_____ 2. Crop most responsible for the resurgence of slavery.

_____ 3. Machine that combed seeds from fiber with metal pins fitted into a roller.

_____ 4. Slave farmers of up to five acres who were allowed to produce items for sale in a nearby market.

_____ 5. National drink of Americans in the early nineteenth century.

_____ 6. Most intimate expression of increased literacy.

_____ 7. First best-selling novel in the United States.

_____ 8. Belief that God created the universe but did not intervene in its affairs.

_____ 9. Rapidly growing religious group that based much of its appeal on localism and congregational democracy.

_____ 10. Ministers who traveled from church to church, generally in rural areas.

_____ 11. Outdoor religious meeting.

WHERE WAS IT?

Complete each statement below (questions 1–9) by writing the letter preceding the appropriate response in the space provided. Use each answer only once.

  a. Cane Ridge, Kentucky
  b. Delaware
  c. Greenville
  d. New York City, New York
  e. North Carolina
  f. Philadelphia, Pennsylvania
  g. Rhode Island
  h. Saint Domingue
  i. Vermont

_____ 1. Site where a treaty was signed by the Indians of the Northwest ceding two thirds of present-day Ohio and part of Indiana to the Americans.

_____ 2. State where over nine tenths of the slaves had been freed by the 1860s.

_____ 3. Largest American city in 1790.

_____ 4. Largest American city in 1815.

_____ 5. Only state that granted the vote to all free men in 1790.

_____ 6. Only state that retained a property requirement for voting by 1840.

_____ 7. Southern state that gave the vote to "all men" who met the qualifications, including the tiny group of propertied African Americans. Later, this was changed.

_____ 8. Location of the first big camp meeting in 1801.

_____ 9. French island where a half million slaves fought for freedom.

CHARTS, MAPS, AND ILLUSTRATIONS

1. The Cherokee who developed the eighty-six-symbol alphabet that became the first Native American written language was _____.

2. In the maps on the distribution of the slave population (p. 269), the areas that had the highest concentration of slaves in 1790 were _____.

   In what directions had the concentration of slave population moved by 1820?

   _____

3. The farm product that used a complex system of irrigation, perhaps developed in Africa, was _____.

4. The large building in New York City that housed the Stock Exchange and insurance offices was _____.

5. The area where the concentration of Methodists was strongest in 1775 was

   _____

   Was this group still strong in the same area in 1850? _____

6. The founder of the Bethel AME Church in Philadelphia was _____.

MULTIPLE CHOICE

Circle the letter that best completes each statement.

1. It was women's labor and ingenuity on farms that helped create a more varied and nutritious rural diet. All of the following statements correctly characterize the rural diet by the 1790s except
   a. Improved winter feeding for cattle and better techniques for making and storing butter and cheese kept dairy products on the tables of the more prosperous farm families throughout the year.
   b. Women discontinued using bread and salted meats as staples.
   c. Chickens became more common.
   d. Women on farms began to fence and manure their kitchen gardens, planting them with potatoes, turnips, cabbages, squashes, beans, and other vegetables that could be stored in the root cellars that were becoming standard features of farm houses.

2. Most industrial outwork was taken on by
   a. relatively poor families.
   b. middle- to upper-class families.
   c. wealthy families.
   d. slave families.

3. In the South and West, farmers arranged debts through a "changing system" in which they
   a. exchanged money.
   b. signed a written agreement.
   c. simply remembered what they owed.
   d. used notarized contracts specifying services rendered.

4. Outside New England, farm tenancy was
   a. nonexistent.
   b. stagnant.
   c. on the increase.
   d. quickly decreasing.

5. Relegated to smaller territory, but still dependent on the European fur trade, the natives of the Northwest and Southwest fell into competition with settlers and other Indians for the diminishing supply of
   a. women.
   b. game.
   c. lumber.
   d. water.

6. To easterners, backcountry whites who replaced Indians were no different from the defeated aborigines in all of the following ways except
   a. To clear the land, backcountry farmers simply girdled trees, left them to die and fall down by themselves, and plowed the land by navigating between stumps.
   b. The fields were always worked by men.
   c. They depended on game for food and animal skins for trade.
   d. They often spent long periods away on hunting trips, leaving women to do the work.

7. Cotton requires all of the following conditions except
   a. a hot, humid climate.
   b. a long growing season.
   c. intensive labor.
   d. large quantities of land because it cannot be grown on a small scale.

8. The principal crop of coastal South Carolina and Georgia during the eighteenth century was
   a. cotton.
   b. rice.
   c. peanuts.
   d. wheat.

9. On the rice and cotton plantations of lowland South Carolina and Georgia, what percentage of the population was made up of slaves?
   a. 20
   b. 30
   c. 50
   d. 80

10. Due to the environment in South Carolina and Georgia, which included deadly summer diseases, white owners and overseers often stayed out of the fields by implementing the "task system." The task system was characterized by all of the following except
    a. Each morning, owners and overseers assigned specific tasks to a slave; when the tasks were complete, the rest of the day belonged to the slave.
    b. It encouraged slaves not to work and to relax, unsupervised, in the fields.
    c. Often, slaves would work together until all their tasks were completed, and stronger young slaves sometimes would help older and weaker slaves.
    d. Slaves won the right to cultivate land as "private fields" of up to five acres, on which they grew produce and raised livestock for market.

11. As a testimonial to the key of international commerce in the economy of early America, in 1790 all five cities with a population of over ten thousand were located on the
    a. Gulf of Mexico.
    b. Great Lakes.
    c. Atlantic coast.
    d. Pacific coast.

12. With the growth of the maritime economy, the nature of construction work, shipbuilding, the clothing trades, and other specialized crafts were undergoing change. Artisans were being replaced by
    a. cheaper labor.
    b. highly skilled workers.
    c. older craftsmen.
    d. higher-paid workers.

13. As wage earners, few men could support their families unless the wife and children earned money to increase the family income. Working-class women participated in all of the following except
    a. taking in boarders and doing laundry.
    b. working as domestic servants.
    c. peddling fruit, candy, vegetables, cakes, or hot corn.
    d. sending their children out to scavenge in the businesses.

14. The growing thirst of Americans was not driven by neighborliness and social drinking, but by a desire to get drunk. Most Americans drank regularly, though there were wide variations. Which of the following generalizations is incorrect?
    a. Men drank far more than women.
    b. The emerging middle class drank more than the poor and the rich.
    c. City dwellers drank more than farmers.
    d. Westerners drank more than easterners, and southerners drank more than northerners.

15. The most widely distributed publications were
    a. magazines.
    b. books.
    c. newspapers.
    d. sheet music.

16. After the collapse of established churches, there was an increase in the variety of choices on the American religious landscape. Within the turmoil of emerging churches was a roughly uniform democratic style shared by the fast-growing sects, which included all of the following attributes except
    a. They renounced the need for an educated, formally authorized clergy.
    b. They emphasized that crisis conversion was a necessary credential for preachers.
    c. New preachers substituted emotionalism and storytelling for ritual theological lectures.
    d. New churches regarded the Bible as one of many sources of religious knowledge.

17. The belief that all theological and institutional changes since the end of biblical times were man-made mistakes, and that religious organizations must restore themselves to the purity and simplicity of the church of the Apostles is known as
    a. transcendentalism.
    b. restorationism.
    c. Catholicism.
    d. Marxism.

18. Blacks were drawn to revival religion for many of the same reasons as whites. Which of the following statements incorrectly explains this phenomenon?
    a. They found the formal lectures of evangelical preachers more attractive than the informal storytelling of the old Anglican missionaries.
    b. Revivalists welcomed slaves and free blacks to their meeting and sometimes recruited them as preachers.
    c. Evangelical, emotional preaching and the revivalists' emphasis on singing and other forms of audience participation were much more attractive than the cold preaching of Anglicans.
    d. Slaves respected Methodist missionaries who entered their own cabins and talked with them on their own terms.

ESSAY

Description and Explanation (one- to two-paragraph essay)

1. Compare gender role differences between the North and the South and between rural and urban areas.

2. Describe how the decline of parental power affected courtship and marriage.

3. Describe the redefinition of republican citizenship.

4. Describe the decline of established churches in the North and South.

5. Describe the democratic sects, their views on slavery, and the compromises involved in justifying slavery rather than seeing it as a sin.

6. Describe the appeal of Christianity to African Americans and how they turned it into a religion of their own.

Discussion and Analysis (class discussion or one- to two-paragraph essay)

1. Discuss the changes in agriculture in the early republic and how this affected gender roles and the position of the head of the family.

2. Discuss the growing disparity between rich and poor in the seaport cities and explain the reasons for it.

3. Discuss the rise of the democratic sects and the groups involved. Analyze their appeal to ordinary Americans.

What If (include an explanation of your position)

1. If you were of the Chesapeake planters of Virginia active in the Revolution, what would be your view of slavery? Would it change with the invention of the cotton gin?

2. If you were an African American in the nineteenth century, would you adopt evangelical religion?

Crossword Puzzle: The Democratic Republic, 1790–1820

ACROSS

1. Francis Asbury, principal founder of American ___
5. Carolina crop
7. Wayne's treaty with Indians
8. Obligation or tax
9. Elder's title
10. Message if Morse had been at Mims
11. New York City by 1810
13. New state in 1816
14. Jefferson's view of God's relation to the universe
15. Industry spurred by wartime commerce of early 1800s
17. Jefferson called artisans "___ of the cities"
18. Anthony Wayne country
19. Cubed cotton
20. Crevecoeur's spokesman

DOWN

1. Chief Alexander of the Creeks
2. What southern evangelicalism rejected (2 words)
3. Old for several, modern with sky
4. Preserves meat by pickling
5. Traditionalist Creek follower of Tecumseh (2 words)
6. Full name of Whitney machine (2 words)
9. Long staple locale (2 words)
12. Indians' horizontal hideout near Toledo
16. White instrument rejected by Tenskwatawa
18. Boat accessory

ANSWER KEY

WHO? WHAT? WHERE?

Who Were They?

1. h. Hector St. John de Crevecoeur, p. 256
2. b. Anthony Wayne, p. 262
3. a. Alexander McGillivray, p. 264
4. c. Cherokee, p. 264
5. l. Tenskwatawa, pp. 264–265
6. k. Tecumseh, p. 265
7. m. William Henry Harrison, p. 265
8. d. Davy Crockett, p. 266
9. j. Mike Fink, p. 266
10. e. Eli Whitney, p. 268
11. f. Francis Asbury, p. 280
12. i. James McGready, p. 283
13. g. Gabriel, p. 286

What Was It?

1. g. household industry, p. 258
2. c. cotton, pp. 268–269
3. d. cotton gin, p. 268
4. j. private fields, p. 272
5. k. whiskey, p. 276
6. h. personal letters, p. 277
7. i. *The Power of Sympathy*, p. 277
8. f. deism, p. 279
9. a. Baptists, p. 279
10. e. circuit-riding preachers, p. 281
11. b. camp meeting, p. 283

Where Was It?

1. c. Greenville, p. 262
2. b. Delaware, p. 268
3. f. Philadelphia, Pennsylvania, p. 272
4. d. New York City, New York, p. 272
5. i. Vermont, p. 278
6. g. Rhode Island, p. 278
7. e. North Carolina, p. 278
8. a. Cane Ridge, Kentucky, p. 283
9. h. Saint Domingue, p. 286

CHARTS, MAPS, AND ILLUSTRATIONS

1. Sequoya, p. 264
2. Chesapeake Bay or Virginia and Maryland; South and West, p. 269
3. rice, p. 271
4. Tontine Coffee House, p. 273
5. Maryland and Virginia; yes, p. 280
6. Richard Allen, p. 285

MULTIPLE CHOICE

1. b. (p. 257)
2. a. (p. 258)
3. c. (p. 260)
4. c. (p. 260)
5. b. (p.264)
6. b. (pp. 265–266)
7. d. (p. 269)
8. b. (p. 270)
9. d. (p. 271)

10. b. (pp. 271–272)

11. c. (p. 272)

12. a. (p. 274)

13. d. (p. 275)

14. b. (p. 276)

15. c. (p. 277)

16. d. (p. 279)

17. b. (p. 280)

18. a. (p. 285)

ESSAY

Description and Explanation

1. pp. 257–258

2. p. 275

3. pp. 277–278

4. p. 279

5. p. 283

6. pp. 284–286

Discussion and Analysis

1. pp. 256–258

2. pp. 272–274

3. pp. 279–283

What If

1. pp. 267–269

2. pp. 284–286

Crossword Puzzle

CHAPTER 8

COMPLETING THE REVOLUTION, 1789–1815

When George Washington took office as the first president under the Constitution, in April 1789, he and his closest advisers arrived in New York determined to make a national government strong enough to command respect abroad, to counter democratic excesses, and to impose order at home. For the most part, they succeeded. This group, which became known as the Federalists, thought that a strong executive and centralization of power were necessary to the survival of the republic. Generally, they were successful in building the national government they wanted, but in the process they aroused a determined opposition—the Democratic Republicans. These self-styled men, led by Thomas Jefferson, were firmly tied to the revolutionary idea of limited government and an agrarian republic.

The fight between Federalists and Democratic Republicans echoed the revolutionary contest between liberty and power; it intensified when a world war began in Europe. Governmental affairs were conducted at this time against an ominous backdrop of international intrigue and war. This increased the fervor of American politics to the point that the republic almost failed to protect liberty and freedom. National politics were all but consumed with the struggle over international republicanism. By intervening in the internal affairs and maritime rights of the United States, Britain and France made American isolationism virtually impossible.

Through all of this, political parties developed and conducted elections, the national debt was managed, the country greatly increased its geographic territory, and the United States survived possible military disasters in the War of 1812. When the war in Europe ended in 1815, Americans could survey the kind of society and government that their Revolution had made.

LIBERTY, EQUALITY, POWER

In the process of completing the Revolution and forming a permanent national government, issues of liberty, equality, and power remained important. Very quickly, two different views of what these issues meant evolved. Federalists foresaw a stable, orderly, commercial society; Jeffersonians fought for an agrarian society.

Both groups believed that an important contest for power and liberty was taking place in the new federal government. Federalists wanted to expand the power of the national government. Jeffersonian Democratic Republicans wanted to limit power as a way to preserve liberty.

OBJECTIVES

After studying this chapter, a student should be able to

1. Analyze the issues involved in the establishment of the new government, especially the role of Hamilton and his financial proposals.

2. Describe foreign affairs in the early republic under Washington and Adams.

3. Discuss the impact of the frontier on foreign affairs from Washington's administration to the end of the War of 1812.

4. Explore the Alien and Sedition Acts and the Republican reaction in the Virginia and Kentucky Resolutions.

5. Analyze the elections of 1796 and 1800.

6. Describe the Jeffersonian Republican conflicts with the federal courts.

7. Discuss the problem with France and Britain involving shipping and overseas trade.

8. Describe the War of 1812 along the Canadian border.

CHRONOLOGY

1789

George Washington moved from Mount Vernon to the temporary capital of New York City on **April 23**, and was inaugurated seven days later. Every branch of the United States government was staffed by supporters of the Constitution.

The Judiciary Act established a Supreme Court with six members, along with thirteen district courts and three circuit courts of appeal. The act made it possible for certain cases to be appealed from state courts to federal circuit courts, which would be presided over by traveling Supreme Court justices.

Congress passed the ten amendments to the Constitution, which were ratified by the states. They became known as the Bill of Rights.

Congress asked the secretary of the treasury, Alexander Hamilton, to report on the public credit.

1790

Hamilton responded to congressional inquiries concerning the public debt in the Report on Public Credit. He proposed that Congress assume state debts and combine them with the federal government's foreign and domestic debts, thus creating a national debt.

1791

Enacted in **April**, the national bank and the federal excise measures completed Hamilton's organization of government finances.

1792

Thomas Jefferson joined the opposition, insisting that Hamilton's schemes would dismantle the Revolution. Within only three years, the consensus of 1789 had deteriorated into an angry argument over what sort of government would finally result from the American Revolution.

French revolutionaries rejected monarchy and proclaimed the French Republic.

1793

In **January**, French revolutionaries beheaded King Louis XVI. Eleven days later, the French, already at war with Austria and Prussia, declared war on Britain.

As Britain and France went to war, President Washington declared American neutrality, thus negating the obligations made in the 1778 treaties with France.

In **April**, the French sent Citizen Edmond Genêt as minister to the United States. Genêt's mission came to an abrupt end by summer, when the Girondists fell from power. Learning that he would be guillotined if he returned to France, he accepted the hospitality of Americans, married a daughter of George Clinton, and lived out the rest of his life in America.

1793–1815

Throughout the war years, both Great Britain and France, by intervening freely in the internal affairs of the United States, made American isolationism impossible.

1794

In the Northwest, Washington sent General Anthony Wayne against the northwestern Indian tribes, culminating in a decisive victory at Fallen Timbers.

In **September**, Washington ordered federalized militiamen from eastern Pennsylvania, Maryland, Virginia, and New Jersey to crush the Whiskey Rebellion.

1795

Jay's Treaty was ratified by the Senate by a bare two-thirds majority. The treaty granted British trade a most-favored-nation basis in exchange for the agreement of the British to abandon their northwestern forts. It was during the fight over this treaty that dissension within the government was first aired in public.

1796

In **March**, Washington released the details of a treaty Thomas Pinckney had negotiated with Spain. In the treaty, Spain recognized American neutrality and set the border between the United States and Spanish Florida on American terms. Most importantly, the treaty put an end to Spanish claims to territory in the Southwest and gave Americans the unrestricted right to navigate the Mississippi River and to transship produce at the Spanish port of New Orleans.

George Washington refused to run for reelection—thus setting a two-term limit that was observed by every president until Franklin Roosevelt.

John Adams narrowly won the presidential election, and Thomas Jefferson was relegated to the vice presidency. Adams took office with justifiable mistrust of many members of his own party and with the head of the opposition party as his second in command.

1797   France expelled the American minister and refused to carry on relations with the United States until it addressed French grievances. The XYZ Affair was the first foreign crisis during the administration of President Adams. French agents demanded a bribe, loan, and apology in return for the American delegation to be officially received in Paris.

1798   President Adams asked Congress to prepare for war, and the French responded by seizing more American ships. Thus began, in **April 1798**, an undeclared war between France and the United States in the Caribbean.

            Without consulting President Adams, the Federalist-dominated Congress passed the Alien and Sedition Acts.

            Thomas Jefferson and James Madison constructed the Kentucky and Virginia Resolutions to denounce the Alien and Sedition Acts as unconstitutional.

1800   Democratic Republican candidates Jefferson and Aaron Burr won the election, but each received 73 electoral votes. The election then went to the House of Representatives, which was controlled by the Federalists. After 35 hotly contested votes, Jefferson was elected.

1801   Jefferson took the presidential oath of office from Chief Justice John Marshall in **March**.

            The Judiciary Act, which was passed just before Jefferson's inauguration, assured long-term Federalist domination of the federal courts.

            A half million Americans lived west of the Appalachian Mountains.

            Spain controlled New Orleans and, under Pinckney's Treaty, allowed Americans to transship produce from the interior. The year before, however, Spain had secretly ceded New Orleans and the Louisiana Territory to France.

1802   Jeffersonians hit on a simple solution to the Judiciary Act of 1801. Congress repealed the Judiciary Act and thus did away with the "midnight judges."

1803   In the *Marbury* v. *Madison* decision, the Supreme Court ruled on the constitutionality of a federal law for the first time and laid the basis for the practice of judicial review.

            The United States purchased the Louisiana Territory from France for $15 million.

            A few weeks after closing the deal for Louisiana, Napoleon Bonaparte declared war on Great Britain.

1803–1807   Americans resumed their role as neutral carriers and suppliers of food. For a time, Americans made huge profits as U.S. exports (mostly foodstuffs and plantation staples) rose from $66.5 million to $102.2 million.

1803–1812	Over the course of nine years, an estimated 6,000 American citizens were impressed into the Royal Navy.
1804	Prior to the ratification of the Twelfth Amendment in 1804, the presidential candidate with the majority of electoral votes became president, and the second-place candidate became vice president. After this, electors voted separately for president and vice president.
	Thomas Jefferson easily defeated Federalist candidate Charles Pinckney in the presidential election.
1805	In the Essex Decision, the British decreed that the Royal Navy could seize American ships engaged in reexport trade with France.
1805–1807	Beginning in **1805** and ending with the Milan Decree in **December 1807**, the barrage of European decrees and counterdecrees meant that virtually all American commerce with Europe had been outlawed by one or the other of the warring powers.
1806	In the **spring**, Congress, angered by British seizures of American ships, passed the Non-Importation Act, forbidding the importation of British goods that could be bought elsewhere or that could be manufactured in the United States.
1807	In **June**, the American naval frigate *Chesapeake* was fired upon and boarded by the British. The incident resulted in three Americans dead and eighteen wounded. It set off huge anti-British demonstrations in seaport towns and angry cries for war throughout the country.
	Jefferson asked Congress to suspend all U.S. trade with foreign countries and thus keep American ships out of harm's way. However, the Embargo Act, passed in **December**, devastated American commerce.
1808	In the elections of 1808, Republican James Madison, Jefferson's old ally and chosen successor, won the presidency, but the Federalists made significant gains in Congress and on the state levels.
1809	Congress passed the Non-Intercourse Act, which retained the ban on trade with Britain and France but reopened trade with other nations. It also gave President Madison the power to reopen trade with either Britain or France once it had agreed to respect American rights. Neither complied, and the Non-Intercourse Act proved nearly as ineffective as the embargo.
1811–1812	In the winter and spring of 1811–1812, the War Hawks led Congress into a declaration of war. In **November**, they voted for military preparation for war with Great Britain. In **April**, they enacted a ninety-day embargo, not to coerce the British, but to get American ships safely into port before the war.

1812	On **June 1**, Madison sent a war message to Congress. This was to be the first war declared under the Constitution, and the president stayed out of congressional territory by refusing to ask explicitly for a declaration of war. Instead, he presented a list of British crimes that could not be interpreted in any other way.
	Congress declared war on **June 18**. The vote was far from unanimous. The United States opened its offensive against Canada with disastrous results.
1812–1815	Throughout the War of 1812, citizen soldiers proved that Jefferson's confidence in the militia could not be extended to the invasion of other countries.
1813	A wiser U.S. Army returned to Canada, where it raided and burned the Canadian capital at York (Toronto) in **April** and then fought inconclusively through the summer.
	In **September**, Commodore Oliver Hazard Perry cornered the British fleet at Put-in-Bay and destroyed it. Control of Lake Erie enabled the United States to cut off supplies to the British in the Northwest and to continue into Canada.
1813–1814	With the battle of Thames in **1813** and Horseshoe Bend in **1814**, the military power of the Native American peoples east of the Mississippi River was broken.
1814	The British defeated Napoleon in **April**, thus ending the larger war of which the War of 1812 was a part, and the British decided to concentrate their resources on the American war. During the summer, they marched on Washington, D.C., and burned a public building. This was considered a moment of great embarrassment.
	In **August**, the British and Americans opened peace talks in the Belgian city of Ghent and, on Christmas Eve, the war ended with the Treaty of Ghent. The treaty simply put an end to the war.
1815	Andrew Jackson and the Americans overwhelmingly defeated the British at New Orleans. This made Jackson a national hero.

GLOSSARY OF IMPORTANT TERMS

abrogating a treaty	The process of abolishing a treaty so that it is no longer in effect.
alien	A person from another country who is living in the United States. Aliens are not citizens.
Bill of Rights	The first ten amendments to the Constitution. These contain the basic protection of the rights of individuals from abuses by the federal government.

circuit court	A court that meets at different places within a district.
Directory	The five-member revolutionary committee of France that replaced the beheaded king, Louis XVI.
embargo	A government order prohibiting the movement of merchant ships or goods in or out of its ports.
excise tax	An internal tax on goods or services.
Girondists	The revolutionary group in France that declared war on monarchies.
High Federalists	A term used to describe Alexander Hamilton and some of his less-moderate supporters. They wanted the naval war with France to continue and also wanted to severely limit the rights of an opposition party.
impeachment	The act of charging a public official with misconduct in office.
impressment	The removing of sailors from American ships by British naval officers. It was the most significant problem between Britain and the United States, leading to the War of 1812.
judicial review	The Supreme Court's power or practice to rule on the constitutionality of congressional acts.
lame-duck administration	The period between when a candidate or party loses an election and when the successor takes office. John Adams had the first lame-duck administration after he lost the election of 1800 to Jefferson.
midnight judges	Federal judicial officials appointed to office in the closing period of a presidential administration. The Republicans accused Adams of staying awake until midnight in order to sign the commissions for Federalist officeholders.
naturalization	The process by which people born in a foreign country are granted full citizenship with all of its rights.
strict constructionist	A person who believes that the federal government had no powers beyond those specified in the Constitution. This view was first expressed by Thomas Jefferson in the debates over the Bank of the United States.
tariff	A tax on imports. Under the federal Constitution, exports cannot be taxed.
Twelfth Amendment	This amendment requires electors to vote on separate ballots for president and vice president. This was added to the Constitution as a result of the election of 1800.
War Hawks	Members of the Twelfth Congress who promoted the war with Britain. They were usually young, nationalist, and from southern and western areas.
yeoman	A farmer who works his own farm. Jefferson considered them to be the most important group in the democratic republic.

WHO? WHAT? WHERE?

WHO WERE THEY?

Complete each statement below (questions 1–17) by writing the letter preceding the appropriate name in the space provided. Use each answer only once.

    a. Aaron Burr
    b. Alexander Hamilton
    c. Charles C. Pinckney
    d. Edmond Genêt
    e. Francis Scott Key
    f. George Washington
    g. Henry Knox
    h. James Madison
    i. John Adams
    j. John Jay
    k. John Neville
    l. John Randolph
    m. Matthew Lyon
    n. Oliver Hazard Perry
    o. Richard M. Johnson
    p. Thomas Pinckney
    q. William Marbury

_____ 1. First vice president of the United States.

_____ 2. Virginia representative who was the leader of the First Congress and proposed the first amendments to the Constitution.

_____ 3. Old comrade of President Washington from the Revolution who was appointed the first secretary of war.

_____ 4. Most single-minded nationalist in the new government and the leading cabinet member in directing the making of national government.

_____ 5. French diplomat sent to the United States to enlist American aid with or without the support of the Washington administration. He married into a prominent New York family and became a gentleman farmer.

_____ 6. One of the most hated of the federal excise collectors. His house was attacked, looted, and burned by militiamen from the Pittsburgh area.

_____ 7. Chief justice of the Supreme Court who was sent to Britain by President Washington to negotiate a treaty.

_____ 8. American who negotiated a treaty with Spain that gave westerners the right to use the Mississippi River for shipments and awarded the disputed territory to the United States.

_____ 9. American leader who warned against entangling alliances and thought that the United States should stay free to operate on its own in international waters.

_____ 10. Republican congressman from Vermont convicted under the Sedition Act of criticizing President Adams.

_____ 11. Political leader who played skillfully on the interests and resentments of craftsmen and merchants of New York City who worked outside the British trade.

_____ 12. Virginia Republican congressman who was most involved in the attack on the federal court system. At times, he took over the prosecution.

_____ 13. One of the justices of the peace whose office was eliminated by Jefferson. He sued Secretary of State James Madison for the nondelivery of his commission.

_____ 14. Federalist candidate for president in 1804 and 1808.

_____ 15. Naval officer who destroyed the British fleet on Lake Erie at Put-in-Bay, thus cutting the British supply line in the Northwest.

_____ 16. War Hawk congressman acting as commander of the Kentucky militia who was given credit for killing Tecumseh at the battle of the Thames.

_____ 17. Author of the poem "The Star-Spangled Banner," written about the battle around Fort McHenry at Baltimore.

WHAT WAS IT?

Complete each statement below (questions 1–14) by writing the letter preceding the appropriate response in the space provided. Use each answer only once.

a. First Amendment
b. High Federalists
c. impressment
d. Jay's Treaty
e. judicial review
f. midnight judges
g. peaceful coercion
h. red sticks
i. Sedition Act
j. strict constructionist
k. tariff
l. Twelfth Amendment
m. War Hawks
n. whiskey rebels

_____ 1. Chief source of income of the federal government when it first was established.

_____ 2. Person who believed that the federal government had no powers beyond those specified in the Constitution.

_____ 3. Group along the frontier who refused to pay the excise tax and launched a direct challenge to federal authority.

_____ 4. It was during the fight over this that dissension within the new federal government first was aired in public.

_____ 5. Congressional act that set jail terms and fines for persons convicted of advocating disobedience to the federal law or who wrote, printed, or spoke "false, scandalous, and malicious statements against the government of the United States."

_____ 6. Basic principle the Republicans thought the Alien and Sedition Acts violated.

_____ 7. Term used to describe Hamilton and some of his more extreme followers during the Adams administration.

_____ 8. This required electors to vote separately for president and vice president. It was ratified to prevent a repetition of the disputed election of 1800.

_____ 9. New judicial officials appointed by President Adams just before he left office. They were all members of the Federalist Party.

_____ 10. Supreme Court's power or practice to rule on the constitutionality of congressional acts.

_____ 11. What Jefferson hoped to use to keep the United States out of a war with Britain and to ensure respect of American neutral rights.

_____ 12. Removing of sailors from American ships by British naval officers. It was the most important problem between Britain and the United States and led to the War of 1812.

_____ 13. Group of young congressmen who were primarily Republicans from the South and West, strong nationalists, and more than willing to declare war on Britain.

_____ 14. Creeks who joined Tecumseh's Confederacy and fought on the side of Britain on the southern frontier.

WHERE WAS IT?

Complete each statement below (questions 1–10) by writing the letter preceding the appropriate response in the space provided. Use each answer only once.

  a. Canada
  b. Caribbean
  c. Detroit
  d. Ghent
  e. Hartford, Connecticut
  f. New England
  g. New Orleans
  h. New York City
  i. South Carolina
  j. western Pennsylvania

_____ 1. Temporary first capital of the new federal government.

_____ 2. Only southern state that had not paid off most of its Revolutionary War debts by 1790.

_____ 3. Area where the whiskey rebels where most active.

_____ 4. Area where most of the naval war with France was fought.

_____ 5. According to Jefferson, the "one single spot, the possessor of which is our natural and habitual enemy."

_____ 6. Attacking this area seemed the easiest and most logical place in which to damage the British. If it could be captured, it could be held hostage, forcing Britain to back down on the issues.

_____ 7. Fort surrendered by General William Hull during the War of 1812. He surrendered to a small force, and this surrender left British forces in control of much of the Northwest.

_____ 8. Area most opposed to the War of 1812. It was not included in the British blockade of the coastline for the first part of the war.

_____ 9. Location where a group of moderate Federalists met to try to protect the position of New England.

_____ 10. City where peace negotiations that ended the War of 1812 were held.

CHARTS, MAPS, AND ILLUSTRATIONS

1. The location of the first presidential inauguration was _____.

   The oath of office was administered by _____.

2. In the map on securing the West (p. 298), two of the forts on American territory controlled by Britain were _____ and _____.

3. The distant relative of Thomas Jefferson who used the Supreme Court as a conservative centralizing force was _____.

4. The battle of Tippecanoe was in the present state of _____.

   Horseshoe Bend was in _____ territory.

5. One of the greatest military embarrassments ever suffered by the United States was _____.

MULTIPLE CHOICE

Circle the letter that best completes each statement.

1. Which of the following amendments guaranteed the freedom of speech, press, and religion against federal interference?
   a. First
   b. Second
   c. Seventh
   d. Ninth

2. Which of the following amendments stated that powers not assigned to the national government by the Constitution remained with the states and the citizenry?

a. Third
b. Fourth
c. Eighth
d. Tenth

3. The Judiciary Act of 1789
   a. prohibited Supreme Court justices from presiding over federal circuit courts.
   b. established a Supreme Court, district courts, and circuit courts of appeal.
   c. made it impossible for cases to be appealed from state courts to the federal level.
   d. weakened national authority.

4. Alexander Hamilton asked Congress to charter a Bank of the United States for all of the following purposes except to
   a. store government funds.
   b. print and back the national currency.
   c. regulate other banks.
   d. prevent the sale of government securities and stock in banks.

5. In exchange for accepting Hamilton's proposals on the debt, Madison and members of the congressional opposition won his promise to locate the permanent capital of the United States at a site on the
   a. Ohio River.
   b. Hudson River.
   c. Potomac River.
   d. Mississippi River.

6. Jefferson and his associates viewed the war between Britain and France in all of the following ways except
   a. They applauded the French for carrying on the republican revolution Americans had begun in 1776.
   b. They had no affection for the "monarchical" politics of the Federalists or for America's continued dependence on British trade.
   c. The faction led by Jefferson and Madison wanted to abandon the English mercantile system and trade freely with all nations.
   d. They agreed that the United States should enter the war.

7. George Washington refused to run for reelection in 1796, thus setting an unofficial term limit that was observed by every president until Franklin Roosevelt. What was the length of the unofficial term limit?
   a. one term
   b. two terms
   c. three terms
   d. four terms

8. Before leaving office, Washington accomplished all of the following except
   a. He presided over the creation of a national government.
   b. He lost control over the western settlements to British, Spanish, and Indian military threats.

c. He secured free use of the Mississippi River for western produce.

d. He made it evident that the U.S. government could and would control its most distant regions.

9. France expelled the American minister and refused to carry on relations with the United States until it addressed French grievances. President Adams decided to send a mission to France, made up of all of the following statesmen except
   a. John Beckley.
   b. Charles Cotesworth Pinckney.
   c. John Marshall.
   d. Elbridge Gerry.

10. The U.S. delegation to Paris became embroiled in the
    a. Zimmerman telegram.
    b. XYZ Affair.
    c. Watergate scandal.
    d. temperance movement.

11. The troubles with France precipitated a crisis at home that many Federalists wanted to use to destroy their political opponents. Without consulting President Adams, the Federalists-dominated Congress passed all of the following measures except
    a. set jail terms and fines for persons who advocated disobedience to federal law.
    b. a federal property tax.
    c. a decreased naturalization period for immigrants.
    d. empowered the president to detain enemy aliens during wartime and to deport those he considered dangerous to the United States.

12. Thomas Jefferson and his Democratic Republicans approached the election of 1800 better organized and more determined than they had been four years earlier. Moreover, all of the following events in the months preceding the election worked in their favor except
    a. The Alien and Sedition Acts, the direct tax of 1798, and the Federalist military build-up were always popular and widely supported.
    b. Prosecutions under the Sedition Act revealed its partisan origins.
    c. The army suppressed a minor tax rebellion led by Jacob Fries in Pennsylvania.
    d. The Federalists showed no sign of repealing the tax or abandoning the Alien and Sedition Acts and the new military, even when peace seemed certain.

13. The Constitution created the Supreme Court but left the creation of lesser federal courts to
    a. the Supreme Court chief justice.
    b. Congress.
    c. the president.
    d. the vice president.

14. Coupled with President Adams's appointment of the Federalist John Marshall as chief justice, the Judiciary Act of 1801 resulted in all of the following except
    a. It assured long-term Republican domination of the federal courts.

b. It reduced the number of associate justices of the Supreme Court from six to five when the next vacancy occurred, thus reducing Jefferson's chances of appointing a new member to the Court.

c. It took Supreme Court justices off the circuit and created a new system of circuit courts.

d. It allowed Adams to appoint sixteen new judges, along with a full array of marshals, federal attorneys, clerks, and justices of the peace, who were all Federalists.

15. Congress continued on its impeachment quest by going after Supreme Court Justice Samuel Chase. However, this time the quest was plagued by all of the following problems except

a. Chase's "crimes" were not alcoholism or insanity but mere partisanship.

b. Chase was unpleasant, overbearing, and an unashamedly partisan member of the Supreme Court; but these were not constitutional grounds for impeachment.

c. Chase hated the Jeffersonians and had prosecuted sedition cases with real enthusiasm, but within the law.

d. Chase was a much less prominent figure than Pickering.

16. In 1803, the United States purchased the Louisiana Territory from

a. France.
b. Spain.
c. Mexico.
d. England.

17. Napoleon Bonaparte sold the Louisiana Territory only after a slave revolt ended his plans for Saint Dominique, which is the present-day country of

a. Jamaica.
b. Haiti.
c. Hawaii.
d. Cuba.

18. The Louisiana Territory sold for

a. $5 million.
b. $8 million.
c. $15 million.
d. $22 million.

19. In 1805, the British minister dusted off what was known as the Rule of 1756, which stated that a European country could not use a neutral merchant marine to conduct its wartime trade with its colonies unless that trade was legal during peace. This was known as the

a. Non-Importation Act.
b. Milan Decree.
c. Berlin Decree
d. Essex Decision.

20. In 1806, Congress, angered by British seizures of American ships, passed a Non-Intercourse Act

a. outlawing all trade with the British Isles.

b. demanding that neutral ships trading with Europe stop first for inspection and licensing in a British port.

c. stating that any vessel that obeyed the British decrees or allowed itself to be searched by the Royal Navy was subject to seizure by France.

d. forbidding the importation of British goods that could be bought elsewhere or could be manufactured in the United States.

21. In June 1807, the British fired upon and boarded an American naval frigate. Three Americans were killed and eighteen were wounded; the incident set off anti-British demonstrations and cries for war. What was the name of the American naval frigate?

a. *Chesapeake*

b. *Alabama*

c. *Leopard*

d. *Clermont*

22. Jefferson wanted to avoid war because it

a. inevitably brought low taxes.

b. created a deflated military and civil service.

c. carried the danger of defeat and thus the possible failure of America's republican experiment.

d. decreased government debt.

23. The Embargo Act of 1807 resulted in all of the following except

a. It boosted American commerce in all sections of the country, especially in the Northeast.

b. It dropped exports by $86 million in one year.

c. Unemployed sailors, dockworkers, and other maritime workers and their families sunk to new levels of economic despair.

d. It rotted the oceangoing merchant fleet at anchor.

24. On June 1, Madison sent a war message to Congress. He presented a list of British crimes that included all of the following except

a. the enforcement of the Orders of Council, even within the territorial waters of the United States.

b. the impressment of American seamen.

c. the use of spies and provocateurs within the United States.

d. the influence over the French in the Southeast Territory.

25. The Treaty of Ghent, signed on Christmas Eve 1814, provided for all of the following except

a. an end to a war that neither the British nor Americans desired.

b. for the border between Canada and the United States to remain where it had been in 1812.

c. British maritime violations were not mentioned.

d. Indians south of the Canadian-American border were left to the mercy of the British.

ESSAY

Description and Explanation (one- to two-paragraph essay)

1. Explain why the dispute over executive titles was important for the new national government.

2. Describe the parts of the Bill of Rights.

3. Describe the differences in the manner in which the two different political groups viewed the Constitution as expressed during the debates over the Bank of the United States.

4. Describe the differences between the Federalists and Jeffersonians over the war in Europe and the role of the United States.

5. Describe the political maneuvering involved in the election of 1796.

6. Describe the role of foreign affairs in the administration of John Adams, concentrating on the problems with France.

7. Describe the social changes and differences in general tone in Jefferson's administration and what they reflected.

8. Describe what peaceful coercion was and explain why it did not work.

9. Describe New England's role in the War of 1812.

Discussion and Analysis (class discussion or one- to two-paragraph essay)

1. Discuss the issues involved in the public debts, Hamilton's purposes in handling them the way he did, the provisions of the Report on Public Credit, and the main reasons opposition developed. Is there any value in permanent national debt in the 1990s?

2. Discuss the Alien and Sedition Acts, including their provisions and purposes, and the Republican response to them.

3. Discuss the Republican conflict with the federal courts. Why were they so opposed to them and what did they do about it?

What If (include an explanation of your position)

1. If you were in Congress in 1790 and had to choose between Thomas Jefferson and Alexander Hamilton, which one would you support?

2. If you were Jefferson after the election of 1800, how would you regard Aaron Burr?

Crossword Puzzle: Completing the Revolution, 1789–1815

DOWN

1. Waters of Jefferson's "one single spot"
2. Hamilton was the most single-minded ___ of the new government
3. Christmas Eve peace
4. Popular pictures of Hamilton
5. Payment of this debt was windfall to speculators
6. 1805 decision that resurrected Rule of 1756
9. Pawn in Hamilton's 1796 intrigue
11. Tecumseh's Waterloo
14. Rebels of Santo Domingo
16. Redcoats' revenge in Washington
18. Occupies a chair
20. Napoleon's salt-free domain

ACROSS

1. Adams's appointee (2 words)
7. Jefferson was strong in these states
8. 1814 threat of some Federalists
10. Taxable item in first Congress
11. Jay or Pinckney document
12. ___ bomber
13. British actions at McHenry, New Orleans
15. Short for Whiskey Rebellion state
17. First Amendment freedom
19. Ninth word for key
21. Form of "to be"
22. Results like those of the election of 1800
23. He triumphed at Trafalgar
24. Courageous Federalist of 1800

ANSWER KEY

WHO? WHAT? WHERE?

Who Were They?

1. i.   John Adams, p. 290
2. h.   James Madison, p. 291
3. g.   Henry Knox, p. 292
4. b.   Alexander Hamilton, p. 292
5. d.   Edmond Genêt, p. 297
6. k.   John Neville, p. 297
7. j.   John Jay, p. 299
8. p.   Thomas Pinckney, p. 299
9. f.   George Washington, p. 299
10. m. Matthew Lyon, p. 302
11. a. Aaron Burr, p. 303
12. l. John Randolph, p. 308
13. q. William Marbury, p. 308
14. c. Charles C. Pinckney, p. 309
15. n. Oliver Hazard Perry, p. 316
16. o. Richard M. Johnson, p. 317
17. e. Francis Scott Key, p. 318

What Was It?

1. k.   tariff, p. 296
2. j.   strict constructionist, p. 295
3. n.   whiskey rebels, p. 297
4. d.   Jay's Treaty, p. 299
5. i.   Sedition Act, p. 302
6. a.   First Amendment, p. 302
7. b.   High Federalists, p. 302
8. l.   Twelfth Amendment, p. 304
9. f.   midnight judges, p. 307
10. e. judicial review, p. 308
11. g. peaceful coercion, p. 312
12. c. impressment, p. 312
13. m. War Hawks, p. 314
14. h. red sticks, p. 316

Where Was It?

1. h.   New York City, New York, p. 290
2. i.   South Carolina, p. 292
3. j.   western Pennsylvania, p. 297
4. b.   Caribbean, p. 301
5. g.   New Orleans, p. 309
6. a.   Canada, p. 315
7. c.   Detroit, p. 315
8. f.   New England, p. 319
9. e.   Hartford, p. 319
10. d. Ghent, p. 319

CHARTS, MAPS, AND ILLUSTRATIONS

1. Dutchman's Point, Pointe au Fer, Oswegatchie, Oswego, Niagara, Detroit, or Michillimackinac, p. 298
2. John Marshall, p. 308
3. Indiana, Mississippi, p. 317
4. The burning of the Capitol, p. 318

MULTIPLE CHOICE

1. a.   (p. 291)
2. d.   (p. 291)
3. b.   (p. 292)
4. d.   (p. 293)
5. c.   (p. 294)
6. d.   (p. 297)

7. b. (p. 299)

8. b. (p. 299)

9. a. (p. 301)

10. b. (p. 301)

11. c. (p. 301)

12. a. (p. 303)

13. b. (p. 306)

14. a. (p. 307)

15. d. (p. 307)

16. a. (p. 309)

17. b. (p. 309)

18. c. (p. 310)

19. d. (p. 311)

20. d. (p. 311)

21. a. (p. 312)

22. c. (p. 312)

23. a. (p. 312)

24. d (p. 314)

25. d (p. 319)

ESSAY

Description and Explanation

1. p. 290

2. pp. 291–292

3. pp. 293–294

4. pp. 295–297

5. p. 300

6. pp. 300–301

7. pp. 304–305

8. p. 312

9. p. 319

Discussion and Analysis

1. pp. 292–293

2. p. 302

3. pp. 306–307

What If

1. pp. 291–295

2. pp. 303–304

Crossword Puzzle

CHAPTER 9

THE MARKET REVOLUTION, 1815–1860

In 1815, the United States was a predominantly rural nation stretching from the old settlements on the Atlantic coast to the trans-Appalachian frontier. Transportation facilities ranged from primitive to nonexistent. After 1815, however, dramatic improvements—better roads, steamboats, canals, and railroads—tied communities together and penetrated previously isolated neighborhoods. It was these improvements that made the transition to a market-oriented, capitalist society physically possible. Overall, the cost of moving goods over long distances dropped 95 percent between 1815 and 1860.

Of equal importance were the decisions made by thousands of farmers, planters, craftsmen, and merchants that pulled farmers and workshops out of old household and neighborhood relationships and into production for distant markets. By the 1830s and 1840s, the northern United States was experiencing a full-blown market revolution. New cities and towns provided financing, retailing, and manufacturing, while increasingly profitable commercial farms traded food for what was available in the urban areas. The great engine of economic growth in the North and the West was not the old colonial relationship with Europe, but a self-sustaining internal market.

The cotton belt of the South expanded dramatically as a result of international trade and textile production in Europe and the United States. Over the years, the South produced three fourths of the world's supply of cotton. The cotton plantations were among the most intensively commercialized farms in the world. At the same time, most southern households remained marginal to the market economy. The result was not simply an unequal distribution of wealth in the South, but the creation of a dual economy. The South's commitment to cotton and slavery deepened its dependence on the world's financial and industrial centers and left it increasingly isolated by the economic developments in the other areas.

The market revolution produced commercial agriculture, a specialized labor force, technological innovation, and flourishing commercial cities in the North. In the South, it produced more slavery.

LIBERTY, EQUALITY, POWER

In the new economy, there was little interest in creating a classless society. The very rich, the middle class, and the impoverished lived together in communities that recognized the reality of social class. There was little or no emphasis on social equality at that time. For commercial farmers, economic prosperity brought equality and the liberty of a secure social status. With the transportation revolution, the Northeast and the Northwest were integrated into a unified national market economy. This integration influenced the way each section viewed the other and the power structure between them.

While the Jeffersonian society denigrated wage labor, it was a way to gain independence for the young women who worked in the early textile mills. These jobs gave them more liberty and control of their lives. The position of women in general was changing as their role in the new market economy developed.

The slaveholder's republic persisted in the southern states, which reinforced the dominance of white men who owned the land and the slaves. There was a growing concentration of wealth and power in fewer hands—producing economic inequality.

OBJECTIVES

After studying this chapter, a student should be able to

1. Describe the American system.

2. Analyze the work of John Marshall and the Supreme Court.

3. Describe the new types of transportation and the results of their development.

4. Explore changes in the role of women in an agricultural society and differences in "female work."

5. Compare the lifestyles of yeoman farmers in the North and South, including the use of new techniques and new equipment.

6. Describe the origins of the early textile mills and their work force.

7. Evaluate how the market revolution affected different regions of the country, rural and urban.

CHRONOLOGY

1790	Working from memory, Samuel Slater reproduced the first Arkwright spinning mill in America at Pawtucket, Rhode Island.
1801–1835	John Marshall presided over the Supreme Court.
1805	In *Palmer* v. *Mulligan*, the New York Supreme Court asserted that the right to develop property for business purposes was inherent in the ownership of property, no matter the consequences to neighboring landowners. By the 1830s, northern courts routinely granted property owners such rights, even when their exercise inflicted damage on neighbors.
1807	Robert Fulton launched the *Clermont* on an upriver trip from New York City to Albany, thus proving steamboat navigation was possible.
1812–1815	U.S. involvement in the War of 1812 demonstrated that the United States was unable to coordinate a fiscal and military effort. It also convinced many Republicans that reliance on foreign trade rendered the United States dependent on Europe.

1813	After touring English factory districts and making secret drawings, Francis Cabot Lowell returned to the United States and joined with wealthy friends to build the first mill at Waltham, Massachusetts.
1813–1815	State banks increased in number from 88 to 208 over two years.
1815	Congress resumed construction on the National Road that linked the Potomac River with the Ohio River at Wheeling, Virginia. It first was authorized in 1802 and reached the Ohio River in 1818.
1816	Congress chartered a second Bank of the United States that was headquartered in Philadelphia.
	Congress drew up the first overtly protective tariff in U.S. history. Shepherded through the House by Henry Clay and his fellow nationalist John Calhoun, the Tariff of 1816 raised tariffs an average of 25 percent, extending protection to the nation's infant industries.
	In *Dartmouth College* v. *Woodward*, John Marshall ruled that the corporate charter of Dartmouth College could not be altered by a state legislature, thus upholding the sanctity of the contract.
	John Marshall's most explicit blow against Jeffersonian strict constructionism came in *McCulloch* v. *Maryland*. Marshall stated that the Constitution granted the federal government "implied powers" that included chartering a national bank.
1816–1860	The transportation revolution dramatically cut costs and time to move goods. For example, turnpikes cut the cost of wagon transport in half between 1816 and 1860, from 30 cents per ton-mile to 15 cents. Freight rates on the Ohio-Mississippi system had been 1.3 cents per ton-mile for downriver travel and 5.8 cents for upriver travel; steamboats dramatically cut both costs to more than a third of a cent. Between the end of the War of 1812 and 1860, the cost of moving goods over long distances dropped by 95 percent.
1817	Governor DeWitt Clinton talked the New York legislature into building a canal linking the Hudson River and Lake Erie. After six years, the Erie Canal was completed at a cost of $7.5 million. This feat opened a continuous water route between the Northwest and New York City.
1820s	The manufacture of shoes and textiles began to be concentrated in factories. For the outworkers who remained, the dependence on merchants who provided them with imported raw materials increased.
	By the late 1820s, Samuel Slater and most other mill owners were eliminating outworkers and were buying power looms, thus transforming villages into disciplined, self-contained factory towns.

1820s–1830s	The commercial classes transformed the look and feel of American cities, as retailing and manufacturing became separate activities, and clerks now worked in quiet offices on downtown business streets.
1820s–1870s	In the years following 1820, American cities grew faster than ever before or since. The fastest growth was in new cities that served commercial agriculture and in factory towns.
1824	In *Gibbons* v. *Ogden*, the Marshall Court broke a state-granted steamship monopoly in New York, since the monopoly interfered with federal jurisdiction over interstate commerce.
1820s–1840	Approximately three thousand miles of railroads were built during this time, thus helping the market positions of some cities, but still not constituting a national or even a regional rail network.
pre-1830	Before 1830, most toll roads were built and owned by corporations chartered by state governments, with the governments providing $5 million of the $30 million that it cost to build the roads.
1830	Around 1830, a stream of northeastern migrants entered the Northwest. They filled the new lands of Wisconsin and Michigan and the northern counties of the older northwestern states.
1830s	New England courts routinely were granting owners of industrial mill sites unrestricted water rights, even when the exercise of those rights inflicted damage on their neighbors.
	Although outwork still helped poor families maintain their independence, control of their labor had passed to merchants and other agents of the regional economy.
1831	Cyrus McCormick tested the first model of his mechanical reaper in Virginia in 1831. By the 1850s, his Chicago factory was turning out twenty thousand reapers each year.
1835	Canals and roads from New York, Philadelphia, and Baltimore became the favored passageways for commodities entering the West. By 1855, 55 percent of the West's imported sugar, salt, and coffee entered the region via the Great Lakes, Pennsylvania, or Wheeling routes. Within the next two decades, the rate grew to 71 percent.
1830s–1840s	By this time, the market revolution had transformed the rural landscape of the Northeast as forests were reduced, streams and rivers were dammed, and wildlife disappeared.
1840	When construction began in 1819 on the Erie Canal, there were fewer than 100 miles of canal in the United States. By 1840, there were 3,300 miles, nearly all of them in the Northeast and Northwest.

Travel time between the big northeastern cities had been reduced from one fourth to one eleventh of what it had been in 1790, with people, goods, and information traveling at an average of fifteen miles an hour.

The Northwest exported 27 percent of its agricultural produce, in contrast with 12 percent twenty years earlier.

After the War of 1812, the cotton belt of the South expanded dramatically from 178,000 bales of ginned cotton in 1810 to 1,350,000 bales in 1840.

1840s   A national railway system was initiated by the five thousand miles of track laid in the 1840s.

The women of Lowell were among the leaders of a labor movement in the region.

pre-1843   Before 1843, over one third of the $137 million spent on roads was put up by the states.

1840s–1850s   The new transportation networks turned the increasingly industrial Northeast, Middle Atlantic region, and commercial farms of the Old Northwest into a unified market society.

1859   Seventy-nine percent of American cotton was produced in the states of Alabama, Mississippi, Louisiana, and Georgia.

1860   America's budding railway system had developed into a rail network of thirty thousand miles.

Few farmers in the North and West lived more than twenty road miles from railroads, canals, and rivers that could deliver their produce to regional, national, and international markets.

In **1815**, American exports stood at $52.6 million and imports at $113 million. A market revolution spurred on by improved transportation rapidly increased exports sixfold to $333.6 million and tripled imports to $353.6 million in 1860.

The Northwest became intensively commercialized and was tied by canals and railways to eastern markets. It was exporting 70 percent of its wheat, and, in this year alone, it produced 46 percent of the nation's wheat crop.

The twelve wealthiest counties in the United States were in the South—illustrating the opportunities for profit from plantation agriculture.

By **1860**, 26 percent of southern white households owned at least one slave—a full 10 percent decrease in thirty years.

Forty percent of the northern work force and 84 percent of the southern work force were employed in agriculture by 1860. The passage of sixty years saw a dramatic change for the North, which had recorded 70 percent employed in agriculture in 1800. However, the southern work force had increased by only 2 percent from 1800.

Twenty-five thousand women worked in manufacturing jobs in New York City, fully two thirds in the clothing trades. This was about one fourth of the work force of the city.

The geographic center of the population was near Chillicothe, Ohio.

GLOSSARY OF IMPORTANT TERMS

American System The program headed by Henry Clay to foster national economic growth and interdependence among the geographical sections. It included a protective tariff, national bank, and internal improvements.

aqueduct A bridgelike device designed to carry water. Along the Erie Canal, stone aqueducts crossed eighteen rivers.

Boston Brahmins A group of wealthy Boston merchant families who were urbane, elite, and socially responsible. They prospered in the new market economy in banking, insurance, and urban real estate.

economy of scale This term can be applied to both industry and agriculture. As farms or industries became larger, the costs of operation did not always rise in direct relation to the increase in production. Therefore, the larger farms were often more profitable and had more capital for future expansion. This economic advantage led to a greater concentration of wealth in a few hands and was especially noticeable in the cotton-producing South, where planters with more land and many slaves prospered.

internal improvements A nineteenth-century term for transportation facilities such as roads, canals, and railroads.

neo-Federalist A nationalist Republican who favored many Federalist economic programs, such as a protective tariff and a national bank.

protective tariff A tariff that increases the price of imported goods that compete with American products and thus protects American manufacturers from foreign competition.

sweated Describes a type of worker, mostly women, who worked in their homes producing items for subcontractors. They worked mainly in the clothing industry and were paid by the piece or item, rather than by the hour.

toll roads Roads for which travelers were charged a fee for each use. Most of the first toll roads were in the Northeast and were built by private corporations with some state support.

ton-mile The cost of moving one ton a distance of one mile. This is a basic form of measuring the cost of transportation.

WHO? WHAT? WHERE?

WHO WERE THEY?

Complete each statement below (questions 1–7) by writing the letter preceding the appropriate name in the space provided. Use each answer only once.

  a. DeWitt Clinton
  b. Francis Cabot Lowell
  c. Henry Clay
  d. James H. Hammond
  e. John Chapman
  f. Robert Fulton
  g. Samuel Slater

_____ 1. Leading spokesman of the neo-Federalists in Congress.

_____ 2. Person who launched the first steamboat upriver from New York City to Albany.

_____ 3. New York governor who persuaded the legislature to build a canal that would link the Hudson River and Lake Erie.

_____ 4. Eccentric Yankee who was called "Johnny Appleseed" because he planted apple trees in southern Ohio and Indiana.

_____ 5. English immigrant who built the first cotton spinning mill in America in 1790.

_____ 6. Wealthy Bostonian who toured English factories, secretly made drawings, and returned to Massachusetts to build a major textile business.

_____ 7. Slaveholding senator from South Carolina who coined the phrase "Cotton is King."

WHAT WAS IT?

Complete each statement below (questions 1–13) by writing the letter preceding the appropriate response in the space provided. Use each answer only once.

  a. American System
  b. Boston Brahmins
  c. cattle and pigs
  d. *Dartmouth College* v. *Woodward*
  e. *DeBow's Review*
  f. fences
  g. household broom
  h. *McCulloch* v. *Maryland*
  i. National Road
  j. needlework
  k. razorbacks
  l. Rhode Island system
  m. steamboat

_____ 1. Program that fostered national economic growth and interdependence among regions.

_____ 2. Highway crossing the Appalachian Mountains that linked the Chesapeake area with the Ohio River.

_____ 3. Supreme Court case in which corporate charters were granted the legal status of contracts.

_____ 4. Case in which Chief Justice John Marshall ruled that the Bank of the United States was constitutional and that "the power to tax" is the "power to destroy."

_____ 5. Largest part of the eastbound traffic on the National Road.

_____ 6. First form of transportation to transform the interior from an isolated frontier into a busy commercial region.

_____ 7. Type of southern hog that survived by roaming through the woods.

_____ 8. One of the first mass-produced commodities in the United States.

_____ 9. System whereby mill owners built whole villages surrounded by company-owned farm land. The mill workers were usually children.

_____ 10. Elite group of very wealthy families who made fortunes as seaport merchants and prospered in the new economy.

_____ 11. First sweated trade in America.

_____ 12. Farm items that demonstrated the differences in the attitudes and practices of northern and southern farmers more distinctively than any other.

_____ 13. Leading business journal in the South.

WHERE WAS IT?

Complete each statement below (questions 1–10) by writing the letter preceding the appropriate response in the space provided. Use each answer only once.

a. Adams County, Mississippi
b. Buffalo, New York
c. Chillicothe, Ohio
d. New York City
e. Northwest
f. Ohio
g. Pawtucket, Rhode Island
h. Pearl Street
i. Waltham, Massachusetts
j. Wheeling, Virginia

_____ 1. Point at which the National Road reached the Ohio River.

_____ 2. City where the Erie Canal met Lake Erie.

_____ 3. State that built the most ambitious system of canals in the Northwest.

_____ 4. Location of the first spinning mill in America in 1790.

_____ 5. Geographic center of population in 1860.

_____ 6. One of the world's great wheat-producing regions, exporting 70 percent of its wheat in 1860.

_____ 7. Location of the first factory built by the Boston Manufacturing Company. It was heavily capitalized and as fully mechanized as possible.

_____ 8. Area in New York City that contained the greatest concentration of wholesale firms.

_____ 9. Center of the national market in ready-made clothes.

_____ 10. Richest county in the United States in 1860.

CHARTS, MAPS, AND ILLUSTRATIONS

1. According to the map on rivers, roads, and canals (p. 330), the state in the Ohio Valley with the greatest number of canals was _____.

   The only state on the Gulf coast with a canal was _____.

2. Among the most admired engineering feats of the 1820s and 1830s were the _____.

3. The state where Cyrus McCormick tested his mechanical reaper was _____.

4. Examine the soap advertisement from the 1850s (p. 340). Are there any ways that it is similar to advertisements of today? _____

5. In the maps on cotton production (p. 348), which state was the leading producer in 1801? _____

   Which was the leader in 1859? _____

6. The technological improvement that helped in the packing of cotton for shipment was _____.

MULTIPLE CHOICE

Circle the letter that best completes each statement.

1. In 1816, Congress chartered the second Bank of the United States. Which of the following statements incorrectly describes the bank?
   a. It was headquartered in Philadelphia and was empowered to establish branches wherever it saw fit.
   b. The government agreed to deposit its funds in the bank.

c. The government agreed to accept the bank's notes as payment for government land, taxes, and other transactions.

d. Stock in the bank was sold only to private investors, not to the government.

2. The Tariff of 1816, the first avowedly protective tariff in U.S. history, extended protection to the nation's infant industries and raised tariffs an average of
   a. 5 percent.
   b. 14 percent.
   c. 25 percent.
   d. 75 percent.

3. The most spectacular of the canal systems was New York's
   a. Huron Canal.
   b. Erie Canal.
   c. Michigan Canal.
   d. Superior Canal.

4. Which of the following statements incorrectly characterizes John Marshall, who presided over the Supreme Court from 1801 to 1835?
   a. He saw the Court as a conservative hedge against the excess of democratically elected legislatures.
   b. Many of his early decisions protected the independence of the courts and their right to review legislation.
   c. From 1816 onward, his decisions encouraged agriculture and strenghtened the states at the expense of national government.
   d. Many of his most important decisions protected the sanctity of contracts and corporate charters against state legislatures.

5. In 1824, the Marshall Court broke a state-granted steamship monopoly in New York, since the monopoly interfered with federal jurisdiction over interstate commerce. The case was
   a. *Cherokee Nation* v. *Georgia*.
   b. *Dred Scott* v. *Sanford*.
   c. *Gibbons* v. *Ogden*.
   d. *Worcester* v. *Georgia*.

6. In 1805, the New York Supreme Court asserted that the right to develop property for business purposes was inherent in the ownership of property. The case was
   a. *Brown* v. *Board of Education*.
   b. *Marbury* v. *Madison*.
   c. *Palmer* v. *Mulligan*.
   d. *Dred Scott* v. *Sanford*.

7. Which of the following statements does not characterize the Erie Canal?
   a. It was designed by European-educated engineers.
   b. It was built by gangs of Irish immigrants, local farm boys, and convict laborers.
   c. It stretched 364 miles from Albany to Buffalo.
   d. It required a complex system of eighty-three locks, and it passed over eighteen rivers on stone aqueducts.

8. Which railroad paralleled the Erie Canal and rendered it obsolete?
   a. Baltimore and Ohio
   b. New York Central
   c. Illinois Central
   d. Pennsylvania

9. By 1852, the Erie Railroad and its connectors could make the Cincinnati to New York City run—though at a higher cost than via water routes—in
   a. 6 to 8 days.
   b. 12 to 14 days.
   c. 21 to 23 days.
   d. 40 to 42 days.

10. An early nineteenth-century New England farm geared toward family subsistence required all of the following except
    a. forty acres of cultivated land.
    b. twelve acres of pasture and meadow.
    c. an acre of land for a house, outbuildings, and a vegetable garden.
    d. a thirty-acre wood lot to make fires for cooking and heating.

11. In the Northwest until about 1830, most settlers were
    a. yeomen from Kentucky and Tennessee.
    b. former slaves from South Carolina.
    c. Irish immigrants.
    d. resettled Indians.

12. Around 1830, a stream of northeastern migrants entered the Northwest. They filled the lands of Wisconsin and Michigan and the northern counties of the older northwestern states. Most of these migrants were from
    a. Canada.
    b. the upland South.
    c. Georgia.
    d. New England and western New York.

13. The northeastern migrants to the Northwest did all of the following except
    a. They duplicated the intensive, market-oriented farming they had known at home.
    b. They penned their cattle and hogs to fatten them, thus increasing their value.
    c. They planted their land with grain.
    d. They concentrated primarily on outwork and subsistence farming.

14. The new settlers of the Northwest were notably receptive to all of the following improvements in farming techniques except
    a. the traditional shovel plow that dug shallow furrows and skipped over roots.
    b. the grain cradle used in harvesting.
    c. the McCormick reaper used in harvesting.
    d. the treadmill threshers and hand-cranked fanning mills to clean the grain.

15. As the market revolution transformed eighteenth-century households into nineteenth-century homes, all of the following changes were evident except
    a. Americans began to increase the size of their families because, as they converted to newer farming techniques or switched to livestock, more children were needed.
    b. A new emphasis was placed on personal hygiene.
    c. They began to plant shade trees, keep their yards free of trash, paint their houses, arrange woodpiles in neat stacks, and plant shrubs to hide their privies from view.
    d. Oil lamps began to replace homemade candles.

16. In New England, mill owners built villages surrounded by company-owned farm land that they rented to the husbands and fathers of their mill workers. Which of the following statements incorrectly characterizes this environment?
    a. The workplace was closely supervised.
    b. Drinking and other troublesome practices were forbidden in the villages.
    c. Fathers and sons either worked on rented farms or as laborers at mills.
    d. Income from the outwork of women and children provided 90 percent of family income.

17. The mills built by the Boston Manufacturing Company differed from the early Rhode Island mills in all of the following ways except
    a. They used only young male orphans from large cities.
    b. They were heavily capitalized.
    c. They were as fully mechanized as possible.
    d. They turned raw cotton into finished cloth with little need for skilled workers.

18. All of the following statements correctly characterize the Lowell girls except
    a. They were young, single women who never drank.
    b. They seldom stayed out late.
    c. They attended church faithfully.
    d. They were illiterate and uneducated.

19. The commitment to cotton and slavery
    a. made the South independent of the world's financial and industrial centers.
    b. permanently stablized the economy of the South.
    c. isolated the South politically.
    d. isolated the southern states from economic recessions and depressions.

ESSAY

Description and Explanation (one- to two-paragraph essay)

1. Describe state support of internal improvements.

2. Describe the effects of the building of the Erie Canal.

3. Compare agriculture in New England before and after the market revolution.

4. Compare the origin and agricultural practices of settlers in the northern and southern parts of the Ohio Valley.

5. Compare the labor system used by Samuel Slater and the Boston Associates.

6. Explain how the exploitation of slave labor after 1820 became more systematic and more humane.

7. Describe why the South built fewer internal improvements.

Discussion and Analysis (class discussion or one- to two-paragraph essay)

1. Discuss John Marshall and the sanctity and protection of contracts and charters from the states. Explain how this helped encourage business over the years.

2. Discuss the building of transportation facilities and how this helped the development of the national market. Which new form of transportation affected the United States the most at the time it was built? Would it be different from section to section and decade to decade?

3. Describe how the market revolution transformed eighteenth-century households into nineteenth-century homes and how it changed the expectations of the role of women and housework.

What If (include an explanation of your position)

1. If you were John Marshall, how would you react to the changes of the Jacksonian era and its growing emphasis on democracy?

2. If you were traveling in the United States before the Civil War, which form of transportation would you like to use?

3. If you were a woman living in the Northeast, how would you regard the changes brought to the role of women by the market revolution? Include both rural areas and small towns.

Crossword Puzzle: The Market Revolution, 1815–1860

DOWN

1. Ordinal for Bank of the U.S.
2. Industrial ___ helped start textiles in U.S.
3. Western terminus of Erie Canal
4. Nineteenth-century mall
5. Challenge
6. By 1830, most of New England was no longer ___
7. Word with American or Rhode Island
11. Money savers for freight haulers
14. Product of cotton press
17. Mill town known for its women workers
18. Land shark
19. Wizard's world
20. Ohio tributary
21. Rodent
23. Palm-leaf products
25. Tariff

ACROSS

1. *Clermont* for one
6. 15 MPH in 1840
8. Investment for Boston Associates
9. Canal state
10. Rarity for black belt slaves
12. *Et ___ , Brute?*
13. Dartmouth's attorney
15. Word with last or least
16. Twin Cities abbreviation
18. Mike Fink at work on his keelboat
20. What Samuel Slater did with designs for spinning machinery
22. Tail motion
24. ___revolution affected the North and South differently
25. Road to Natchez
26. Class that was proud to work with "heads not hands"
27. If states could tax the Bank of the U.S., it couldn't ___

ANSWER KEY

WHO? WHAT? WHERE?

Who Were They?

1. c. Henry Clay, p. 324
2. f. Robert Fulton, p. 328
3. a. DeWitt Clinton, p. 329
4. e. John Chapman, p. 339
5. g. Samuel Slater, pp. 341–342
6. b. Francis Cabot Lowell, p. 342
7. d. James H. Hammond, p. 352

What Was It?

1. a. American System, p. 324
2. d. *Dartmouth College* v. *Woodward*, p. 326
3. h. *McCulloch* v. *Maryland*, p. 326
4. i. National Road, p. 328
5. c. cattle and pigs, p. 328
6. m. steamboat, p. 328
7. k. razorbacks, p. 337
8. g. household broom, p. 340
9. l. Rhode Island system, p. 342
10. b. Boston Brahmins, p. 344
11. j. needlework, p. 346
12. f. fences, p. 350
13. e. *DeBow's Review*, p. 351

Where Was It?

1. j. Wheeling, Virginia, p. 328
2. b. Buffalo, New York, p. 329
3. f. Ohio, p. 329
4. g. Pawtucket, Rhode Island, p. 342
5. c. Chillicothe, Ohio, p. 337
6. e. Northwest, p. 338
7. i. Waltham, Massachusetts, p. 342
8. h. Pearl Street, p. 344
9. d. New York City, p. 345
10. a. Adams County, Mississippi, p. 350

CHARTS, MAPS, AND ILLUSTRATIONS

1. Ohio, Alabama, p. 330
2. locks on the Erie Canal at Lockport, p. 322
3. Virginia, p. 338
4. yes, p. 340
5. South Carolina, Mississippi, p. 348
6. cotton press, p. 351

MULTIPLE CHOICE

1. d. (p. 324)
2. c. (p. 325)
3. b. (p. 329)
4. c. (p. 326)
5. c. (p. 326)
6. c. (p. 327)
7. a. (p. 329)
8. b. (p. 331)
9. a. (p. 331)
10. a. (p. 333)
11. a. (p. 337)
12. d. (p. 338)
13. d. (p. 338)
14. a. (pp. 338–339)
15. a. (p. 339)
16. d. (p. 342)

17. a. (p. 342)

18. d. (pp. 342–343)

19. c. (p. 352)

ESSAY

Description and Explanation

1. p. 329

2. pp. 329–330

3. pp. 333–337

4. pp. 337–339

5. pp. 342–343

6. pp. 347–349

7. p. 351

Discussion and Analysis

1. pp. 326–327

2. pp. 329–333

3. pp. 339–340

What If

1. pp. 326–327

2. pp. 327–330

3. pp. 339–340, 342–343

Crossword Puzzle

CHAPTER 10

TOWARD AN AMERICAN CULTURE

Americans after 1815 experienced wave after wave of social change that broke many old patterns. In the process, they reinvented family life. They created distinctively American forms of popular literature and art and found new ways of having fun. They flocked to evangelical revivals in which they remade American religious life. The emerging American culture was more or less uniformly republican, capitalist, and Protestant.

Across the nation, however, Americans formed subcultures as diverse as their origins, based on region, class, and race. From the 1830s on, the urban middle class of the Northeast, successful northwestern farmers, and rural southerners thought differently about parenthood, the proper way to raise a family, and the efficient way to conduct domestic life. Northeastern businessmen, slave-holders, slaves, factory hands, rich and poor farmers, and middle-class women all heard the same Bible stories and learned different lessons from them.

The new northern middle class nourished a cosmopolitan culture and domestic sentimentalism that changed the roles of fathers, mothers, and children in the family. It increasingly emphasized a reformist view of life that often was at odds with the varied groups that made up the plain folk of the North. These ordinary people were culturally conservative patriarchal families that rejected sentimentalism and reformist religion. They saw much of the popular culture as a melodramatic contest between good and evil.

The white antebellum southerner remained localistic and culturally conservative. Routines of family life and the possibility of economic prosperity for most whites remained rooted in inherited land and in help that was obtained from family members. Southerners tended to distrust outsiders and to isolate themselves within their rural neighborhoods. The South became a conservative minority within a democratic and capitalistic nation.

In the law, the census, and the minds of planters, slaves were members of a plantation household over which the owner exercised absolute authority. Wise slaveholders learned that allowing slaves some measure of privilege and autonomy encouraged discipline and obedience among the slaves far more than terror and torture did. These privileges allowed some slaves to improve the quality of their lives within slavery.

LIBERTY, EQUALITY, POWER

Middle-class evangelicals claimed that neither the social order, nor the troubles of the world, nor the spiritual state of individuals was divinely ordained. People could make themselves and their world better by choosing right over wrong, considered a form of personal liberty. It also elevated the role of women by placing increasing emphasis on domestic life—separate from economic activities.

"Plain-folk" religions were locally organized and emphasized democracy or liberty. They were culturally conservative and rejected the middle-class view that women were the continuation of the power of the father over the family.

Both the middle class and the plain folk, though, still viewed their world through the lens of religion. They applied the theories of democracy to the spiritual world and saw a fight to the finish between the forces of good and evil as necessary and unavoidable.

The code of honor in the South forged some equality and respect among white men, but it created rigid distinctions between men and women and between whites and blacks. Southern life was not about liberty, freedom, individual fulfillment, or social process; it was about honoring the obligations to which one was born. A father must govern and protect; a mother must assist the father in raising the family; and the women, children, and slaves must carry out the duties of their stations in life. The agrarian republic had become a noisy, somewhat violent, divided democracy that applied the principles of liberty to only some.

OBJECTIVES

After studying this chapter, a student should be able to

1. Compare the role of religion and its ideas in the life of the northern middle class and among the common people.

2. Discuss the development of American literature and fine arts.

3. Describe the rise of popular culture, especially in the cities and towns.

4. Describe the development of the popular print.

5. Explain the relationship between southern Christianity and southern conservatism.

6. Trace the development of the slave family and culture.

7. Contrast the North and South in religious ideas, popular culture, literature, and general social environment.

CHRONOLOGY

1790s   Sunday schools first appeared with the purpose of teaching working-class children to read and write by inducing them to copy long passages from the Bible.

1815   Americans experienced wave after wave of social change. Territorial expansion, market revolution, and the spread of plantation slavery uprooted Americans and broke old social patterns.

After 1815, improvements in transportation and communication, along with the rapid growth of cities, created a much broader American theater audience.

1817   The first theater riot occurred when an English actor refused a New York audience's demand that he stop what he was doing and sing "Black-Eyed Susan."

1820s	By this time, southern evangelicalism had long since abandoned its hostility toward slavery, and slaveholders commonly attended camp meetings and revivals.
1822	Denmark Vesey, a free black from Charleston and a leading member of an independent African Methodist congregation, attempted to lead a slave insurrection. It failed when news of the uprising was leaked by the slaves.
1825	Completion of the Erie Canal ended the isolation of Niagara Falls and brought tourists to the area. It became the most venerated spot in the United States.
post-1825	In acting out the imperatives of the new evangelicalism, entrepreneurial families of the East and Northwest created an American middle-class culture after 1825. That culture was based, paradoxically, on an intensely private and emotionally loaded family life coupled with an aggressively reformist stance toward the world at large.
1827	In a vision, the angel Moroni appeared to Joseph Smith and led him to golden plates that translated into The Book of Mormon. Joseph Smith used his model of brotherly cooperation and patriarchal authority to found the Church of Jesus Christ of Latter-Day Saints several years later.
1830	By this time, the South was an increasingly conservative minority within a democratic and capitalistic nation. The northern middle class espoused a link between material and moral progress, identifying both with individual autonomy and universal rights. Radical northerners agitated for the abolition of slavery.
	Charles Grandison Finney began a six-month revival of preaching and praying at Rochester, New York. He preached what became the ongoing principle of northern middle-class evangelicalism.
	After 1830, most southern states outlawed black preachers, but the laws could not be enforced.
1830s	New England was the first center of factory production, and southern New England farms were thoroughly commercialized by the 1830s.
	In Utica, New York, women who began having children averaged only 3.6 births each; those who entered their child-bearing years only ten years earlier had an average of 5.1. Housewives also began to plan their pregnancies, commonly at five-year intervals, which meant that they could give each child close attention.
	After the revivals of the 1820s and 1830s, the emphasis of Sunday schools shifted from promoting the memorization of extraordinary amounts of Bible verses to preparing children's souls for conversion. Middle-class children now were included in the schools, corporal punishment was forbidden, and Sunday-school teachers tried to develop the moral sensibilities of their charges.

From this time on, northern middle-class evangelists held out their religious and domestic values as a national culture for the United States. But even in their own regions, they were surrounded and outnumbered by Americans who rejected their cultural leadership.

Throughout the 1830s, William Miller publicized his predictions that the world would end by **March 23, 1844**, and, as that date approached, his followers gathered to read the Bible, pray, and attend meetings.

By this time, separate theaters and types of performances were established for the rich and poor in a failed attempt to limit violence and theater riots.

1830s–1850s   Improvements in printing and paper making enabled entrepreneurs to sell daily newspapers for a penny. Cheap "story papers" became available in the 1830s, "yellow-backed" fiction was available in the 1840s, and dime novels were widely distributed from the 1850s onward.

1831   Several wealthy Boston families put up the money to build Mount Auburn Cemetery, the first graveyard designed as a cultural institution.

The first minstrel show was presented by a showman named Thomas Rice.

Nat Turner led some sixty slaves in a revolt in Virginia that left fifty-five men, women, and children dead.

1840s–1850s   Boxing's popularity rose during a time of increasing immigration and violence in poor city neighborhoods. Prizefighting was a brutal sport; boxers fought with bare knuckles and the bout ended only when one of the fighters was unable to continue. In an infamous match, the Englishman Christopher Lilly knocked down his Irish opponent, Thomas McCoy, eighty times. The fight ended with round 119 when McCoy died in his corner.

1845   George Lippard's *Quaker City* sold sixty thousand copies and thirty thousand in each of the next five years. It included fictional hypocrisy, lust, and cruelty among Philadelphia's elite.

1849   A riot and gunfight that took place at the Astor Place Opera House resulted in a loss of twenty lives.

1850   Susan Warner's *The Wide, Wide World* broke all sales records when it appeared in 1850. Harriet Beecher Stowe followed in 1852 with *Uncle Tom's Cabin*, which broke all records set by Warner. In 1854, Maria Cummins's *The Lamplighter* took its place as the third of the monster best-sellers of the early 1850s.

Nathaniel Hawthorne complained about the sentimental novels written by women because they outsold by wide margins his *The Scarlet Letter* and *The House of Seven Gables*, Ralph Waldo Emerson's essays, Henry David Thoreau's *Walden*, Herman Melville's *Moby Dick*, Walt Whitman's *Leaves of Grass*, and other of the "American Renaissance" works of the 1850s.

1860	By this time, 88 percent of southern church members were Methodist, Baptist, Presbyterian, or Disciple of Christ.

GLOSSARY OF IMPORTANT TERMS

anxious bench	The area in a religious revival meeting where the most likely converts were seated.
blood sports	Sporting activities that emphasized bloodiness. The most popular in the early nineteenth century were cockfighting, ratting, dogfights, and various types of violence between animals. They were favored by working-class men of the cities.
"broad" wives	The wives of slave men who lived on other plantations and were visited by their husbands during off hours.
domestic fiction	Books and articles that concentrated on household and domestic life. Often very sentimental, they emphasized the toil and travails of women and children. Usually they had a strong female character who overcame adversity in the end. The greatest appeal of this type of literature was to middle-class women.
middle class	A term and social group that developed in the early nineteenth century. Those who claimed to be middle class were large-city and country merchants, master craftsmen who had turned themselves into manufacturers, and the mass of market-oriented farmers. The social status first developed in New England, and many middle-class values prevalent in areas of the United States were based on New England morality.
minstrel shows	The most popular form of theater among working men of the northern cities. White men in blackface portrayed African Americans in song and dance.
postmillennialism	The belief (held mostly by middle-class evangelists) that Christ's second coming would occur when missionary conversion of the world brought about a thousand years of social perfection. **Premillennialism** assumed that the millennium would arrive with world-destroying violence, followed by a thousand years of Christ's rule on earth. It was assumed that God would end the world in his own time. Most ordinary Baptists, Methodists, and Disciples of Christ followed this belief.
spirituals	Religious songs of slaves that told of their ultimate deliverance from slavery.
Sunday schools	These first appeared in the 1790s to teach working-class children to read and write. By the 1820s and 1830s, they were becoming moral training grounds.

WHO? WHAT? WHERE?

WHO WERE THEY?

Complete each statement below (questions 1–9) by writing the letter preceding the appropriate name in the space provided. Use each answer only once.

 a. Alexander Campbell
 b. Charles Colcock Jones
 c. Charles G. Finney
 d. Denmark Vesey
 e. Nat Turner
 f. Sarah Josepha Hale
 g. Thomas Rice
 h. William Charles McCready
 i. William Miller

_____ 1. Great evangelist of the 1830s who was remarkably successful in organizing the new middle-class culture into a millennium crusade.

_____ 2. Editor of the first mass-circulation magazine for women, *Godey's Lady's Book*.

_____ 3. Rural New York Baptist who concluded that God would destroy the world during the year following March 1843.

_____ 4. One of the founders of the Disciples of Christ.

_____ 5. Trained Shakespearean actor with a restrained style whose performance was the object of an angry mob.

_____ 6. White performer who blacked his face and presented the first minstrel show.

_____ 7. Presbyterian minister who spent much of his career writing manuals on how to preach to slaves.

_____ 8. Free black from Charleston, South Carolina, who hatched an ambitious conspiracy to free slaves in the area.

_____ 9. Baptist lay preacher who led a slave revolt in Southhampton County, Virginia, that killed fifty-five whites.

WHAT WAS IT?

Complete each statement below (questions 1–8) by writing the letter preceding the appropriate response in the space provided. Use each answer only once.

 a. cockfighting
 b. Exodus
 c. families
 d. hunting
 e. minstrel show

f. penny
g. spirituals
h. *Uncle Tom's Cabin*

_____ 1. Most successful of the sentimental novels.

_____ 2. One of the most popular of the blood sports in urban working-class neighborhoods.

_____ 3. Most popular form of theater.

_____ 4. Cost of a daily newspaper.

_____ 5. One of the passionate pursuits among southern men.

_____ 6. Most precious privilege many of the slaves obtained.

_____ 7. Book of the Old Testament appropriated by slaves in their version of Christianity.

_____ 8. Slaves' religious songs that told of their ultimate deliverance.

WHERE WAS IT?

Complete each statement below (questions 1–5) by writing the letter preceding the appropriate response in the space provided. Use each answer only once.

a. Boston, Massachusetts
b. New Orleans, Louisiana
c. Niagara Falls, New York
d. Palmyra, New York
e. Rochester, New York

_____ 1. Location of Charles Finney's greatest revival.

_____ 2. Location of the first cemetery designed to serve as a cultural institution.

_____ 3. Most venerated spot in America.

_____ 4. Place where Joseph Smith received visions from the angel Moroni that led him to the golden plates he translated into The Book of Mormon.

_____ 5. Horse-racing capital of the country and the only southern city that had professional prizefights.

CHARTS, MAPS, AND ILLUSTRATIONS

1. The renowned American landscape artist who painted Niagara Falls in 1857 was
   _____.

2. The time of day when plantation burial ceremonies often were held was
   _____.

3. The leader of the bloodiest of all North American slave revolts was
   _____.

MULTIPLE CHOICE

Circle the letter that best completes each statement.

1. Charles Grandison Finney preached what became the organizing principles of northern middle-class evangelism. He insisted on all of the following except
   a. Individual holiness was to be valued over a permanent and sacred social order.
   b. People would make themselves and the world better by choosing right over wrong. However, they only would choose right after an evangelical conversion experience in which they submitted their rebellious wills to the will of God.
   c. The social order, the troubles of this world, and the spiritual state of individuals were divinely ordained.
   d. God made man a moral free agent.

2. In the old yeoman-artisan republic, the lawgivers and disciplinarians consisted of all the following people except
   a. fathers who owned property.
   b. heads of households.
   c. single female teachers.
   d. men who governed family labor.

3. The new middle-class evangelism resulted in a feminization of domestic life that raised all of the following spiritual possibilities for women and children except
   a. Mothers replaced fathers in main child-rearing responsibility.
   b. Mothers enlisted the doctrines of free agency and individual moral responsibility in raising their children.
   c. Mothers sought to develop the children's conscience and their capacity to love, to teach them to make good moral choices, and to prepare themselves for conversion and a lifetime of Christian service.
   d. Mothers raised their children with fear, not love and reason.

4. After the revivals of the 1820s and 1830s, the emphasis of Sunday schools shifted to
   a. teaching working-class children to read and write by having them copy long passages from the Bible.
   b. expecting children to perform feats of memory by reciting verses of scripture.
   c. preparing children's souls for conversion.
   d. keeping children out of trouble by teaching them to fear God.

5. The top-selling sentimental novels written by women were successful because of all of the following characteristics except
   a. The action took place on the frontier and the heroes were men.
   b. They upheld the new middle-class domesticity and included a story line of spiritual struggle.
   c. They sanctified the middle-class home and the trials and triumphs of Christian women.
   d. The women characters were intelligent, generous persons who grew in strength and independence.

6. In the 1820s and 1830s, educated Americans began to view literature and the arts more favorably for all of the following reasons except
   a. American nationalists began to demand American art that could compete with the art of the despotic Old World.
   b. They associated the fine arts with sensuality, extravagance, and artificiality.
   c. Evangelical Christianity and sentimental culture glorified a romantic cult or feeling that was, within limits, far more receptive to aesthetic experience than Calvinism and the more spartan forms of republicanism had been.
   d. More comfortable and educated Americans fell into a relationship with nature that called out for aesthetic expression.

7. For all their diversity, the churches of the northern plain folk had all the following things in common except
   a. Most trusted outside organizations and religious professionalism, especially the emerging missionary work.
   b. Most shared an evangelical emphasis on individual experience over church authority.
   c. Most favored democratic, local control of religious life.
   d. Most rejected middle-class optimism and reformism, reaffirming God's providence and humankind's duty to accept an imperfect world even while waging war against it.

8. Country Baptists and working-class Methodists mourned their dead, but they were careful not to "murmur" against God for all of the following reasons except
   a. In a world governed by providence, the death of a loved one was considered a test of faith.
   b. Plain folk considered it a privilege to witness a death in the family, for it released the sufferer from the tribulations of this world and sent the deceased to a better place.
   c. In the case of children, parents would be humiliated by a public display of emotion.
   d. Humbler people regarded death as a lesson in the futility of pursuing worldly goals and a lesson in the need to submit to God's will.

9. Which of the following faiths assumed that the millennium would arrive with world-destroying violence, followed by a thousand years of Christ's rule on earth?
   a. Baptists
   b. middle-class evangelists
   c. Methodists
   d. Disciples of Christ

10. Millerites predicted that the world would end on March 23, 1844. When it did not end, those who continued to believe in an end-of-the-world doctrine founded this church in the 1860s.
    a. Seventh-day Adventists
    b. Church of Christ
    c. Church of Jehovah's Witnesses
    d. Church of Jesus Christ of Latter-Day Saints

11. All of the following items were condemned by some of the poorer and more conservative evangelists as a descent into worldliness that almost certainly would provoke God's wrath except
    a. railroads.
    b. banks and the credit system.
    c. subsistence farming.
    d. personal greed.

12. Prizefighting emerged from the same subterranean culture that sustained cockfights and other blood sports. Which of the following statements incorrectly characterizes prizefighting?
    a. It was imported from Australia.
    b. It took place in an enclosed ring.
    c. It called for clear rules, a referee, and a paying audience.
    d. The early fighters were Irish or English immigrants.

13. In the eighteenth and early nineteenth centuries, the only theaters in America were in the
    a. rural Midwest.
    b. small river communities.
    c. large seaport cities.
    d. Appalachian Mountain communities.

14. Those who attended American theater in the eighteenth and early nineteeth centuries were members of the urban elite, and nearly all plays, managers, and actors were
    a. American.
    b. English.
    c. French.
    d. Spanish.

15. The cheap story papers, yellow-backed fiction, and dime novels were distributed throughout the North and West but found their first and largest audience among
    a. city workers.
    b. the educated elite.
    c. rural females.
    d. young children.

16. Which of the following statements incorrectly depicts antebellum white southerners?
    a. They remained localistic and culturally conservative.
    b. Farm and plantation labor and the routines of family life still were conducted within the household.
    c. Prospects for most white southerners remained rooted in inherited land and family help.
    d. They trusted outsiders.

17. Southern revivals continued throughout the antebellum years, but they were no longer the inclusive, ecstatic camp meetings of the past. Instead, southern revivals featured all of the following aspects except
    a. They often were limited to a single denomination.

b. They were held on permanent camp grounds maintained by the churches.

c. They were conducted with less decorum than in the past, and frenzied participants often were led away.

d. They were routine events in the community.

18. Which of the following groups of slaves seldom revolted because their country's environment discouraged such events?
   a. Cuban slaves
   b. Jamaican slaves
   c. American slaves
   d. Brazilian slaves

ESSAY

Description and Explanation (one- to two-paragraph essay)

1. Describe Yankees and the development of middle-class values and culture with some emphasis on the role of religion.

2. Describe how middle-class evangelism encouraged the division of domestic labor and how it affected the role of women and the view of them as mothers.

3. Compare middle-class and common-folk religious views, including their views of providence and the earthly world.

4. Describe the way the theater reflected class divisions.

5. Compare northern and southern views of God and death.

6. Describe the slave family, why it was allowed to develop, and how it was modified to accommodate circumstances.

Discussion and Analysis (class discussion or one- to two-paragraph essay)

1. Discuss how sentimental domestic literature of the period reinforced middle-class domesticity. Contrast it with the way women were portrayed in cheap yellow fiction.

2. Discuss the religious views of plain folk on such things as the market revolution and the changes in the economy, the millennium, and the family organization.

3. Discuss popular culture and entertainment and how they differed between the North and the South. How much of this depended on whether the area was rural or urban?

What If (include an explanation of your position)

1. If you were a member of the plain folk of the North, which of the activities in popular culture would you most enjoy?

2. If you were a slave living in the Deep South, what would the condition of your family's everyday life be?

Crossword Puzzle: Toward an American Culture

ACROSS

1. Famous name in ministry and literature
5. Boxer's fists, 1840s style
7. Most venerated spot in the U.S.
9. Stowe's villain
10. Gullah Jack's homeland
12. What melodramatic heroes acknowledged
13. Cheap place to watch Edwin Forrest
15. Ultimate locus of good to Stowe
18. Omen to Nat Turner
19. Part of *Hale's Magazine*
20. Their architecture was copied by Americans

DOWN

1. Ned of dime novels
2. Charles Grandison Finney for one
3. Millerites destination March 3, 1844
4. Activity for fan of Maria Cummins, Lydia Maria Child, etc.
5. Minstrel show makeup
6. Forte of Elias Hicks, Joseph Smith
8. Character in *Uncle Tom's Cabin*
11. Author of *The Wide, Wide World*
14. The Penny ___ , one cent news
15. Monarch
16. Landscape artist of note
17. Originator of minstrel show

ANSWER KEY

WHO? WHAT? WHERE?

Who Were They?

1. c. Charles G. Finney, p. 356
2. f. Sarah Josepha Hale, p. 359
3. i. William Miller, p. 364
4. a. Alexander Campbell, p. 365
5. h. William Charles McCready, p. 368
6. g. Thomas Rice, p. 369
7. b. Charles Colcock Jones, p. 379
8. d. Denmark Vesey, p. 383
9. e. Nat Turner, p. 383

What Was It?

1. h. *Uncle Tom's Cabin*, p. 359
2. a. cockfighting, p. 366
3. e. minstrel show, p. 369
4. f. penny, p. 370
5. d. hunting, p. 374
6. c. families, p. 377
7. b. Exodus, p. 382
8. g. spirituals, p. 382

Where Was It?

1. e. Rochester, New York, p. 357
2. a. Boston, Massachusetts, p. 360
3. c. Niagara Falls, New York, p. 361
4. d. Palmyra, New York, p. 365
5. b. New Orleans, Louisiana, p. 374

CHARTS, MAPS, AND ILLUSTRATIONS

1. Frederick Edwin Church, p. 362
2. night, p. 382
3. Nat Turner, p. 384

MULTIPLE CHOICE

1. c. (pp. 356–357)
2. c. (p. 357)
3. d. (pp. 357–358)
4. c. (p. 358)
5. a. (p. 359)
6. b. (p. 360)
7. a. (p. 363)
8. c. (p. 363)
9. b. (p. 364)
10. a. (p. 364)
11. c. (p. 365)
12. a. (p. 366)
13. c. (p. 367)
14. b. (p. 368)
15. a. (p. 370)
16. d. (p. 373)
17. c. (p. 375)
18. c. (p. 383)

ESSAY

Description and Explanation

1. pp. 355–357
2. pp. 357–358

3. pp. 362–364

4. pp. 367–369

5. pp. 363–364, 375–376

6. pp. 377–378

Discussion and Analysis

1. pp. 358–360

2. p. 365

3. pp. 365–369, 374

What If

1. pp. 366–370

2. pp. 376–378

Crossword Puzzle

CHAPTER 11

SOCIETY, CULTURE, AND POLITICS, 1820s–1840s

From the 1820s to the 1840s, many important policy questions fell to the states. There, Whigs and Democrats fought out such matters as support for internal improvements, banking, the creation of public school systems, prisons, the care of the insane, and the prohibition of alcohol. The two parties had political cultures with consistent attitudes toward government and politics that were embedded in religion, family, and economic life. The Whigs argued for government support of economic growth and social progress; the Democrats wanted to keep government small and inexpensive. Both appealed to coherent voting groups and proposed coherent programs in every corner of the republic.

Both the Whigs and the Democrats accepted the transition to market society, but they wanted to direct it into different channels. Whigs wanted to use government and the market to make an economically and morally progressive republic. They insisted that economic development, moral progress, and social harmony were linked, and the government should encourage them. Democrats viewed both government and the new market society with suspicion and vowed to allow neither to subvert the equal rights and rough equality of conditions that they considered necessary to republican citizenship. Democrats saw government not as a tool of progress, but rather as a dangerous concentration of power in the hands of imperfect, self-interested men. The only safe course was to limit its power.

Northern Whig evangelists began to envision a world based on Christian love and achieved, not inherited, status. They transformed marriage from rank domination into an unequal partnership, but still a partnership. They also questioned the virulent forms of racism. At the same time, official discrimination against African Americans was on the rise. Educated whites began to think in racist terms. Democratic ideologues pronounced blacks unfit to be citizens of the white man's republic. The insistence that blacks were incapable of citizenship reinforced a white male political dominance. At the same time, a group of uncompromising reformers attacked slavery and patriarchy as national sins. Increasingly, there were differences between the two groups and less rhetoric of compromise and conciliation. The stage was being set for major differences.

LIBERTY, EQUALITY, POWER

Most whites in antebellum America believed in natural differences based on sex and race. God had ordained a fixed social hierarchy in which men exercised power over others. Before 1830, hierarchy based on sex and race seldom was questioned in public, particularly by people in a position to change it. A few began to question the absence of liberty or equality for nonwhites and females. Slavery, and its lack of liberty, was becoming a moral issue to the churchgoing middle class that provided much of the electoral support of the Whig Party. This group helped bring the issue of slavery to public attention and tied it to questions of liberty in the North and power in the South.

The small groups of women reformers fought the double standard and assumed the power to question their own subordinate status with a system of gendered social roles. Some reformers, men and women, called for the radical idea of absolute human equality regardless of gender or race. This view threatened the power of the dominant white male, and the reformers usually knew it. Southern Democrats wanted to protect their position through limiting the power of government over their lives.

OBJECTIVES

After studying this chapter, a student should be able to

1. Analyze the membership of the Whig and Democratic parties in both the North and South.

2. Compare Whigs and Democrats and their views of the government and the economy.

3. Compare the North and South on the various areas of social reform.

4. Trace the growth of the temperance movement.

5. Explore the Democrats' views of racism.

6. Describe the reforms of the Whig evangelicals.

7. Examine the role of women in the reform movement.

CHRONOLOGY

1790s	Physicians and a few clergymen began to attack not only habitual drunkenness but alcohol itself.
1812	For a short time after 1812, Federalist politicians and Congregational clergymen formed "moral societies" in New England that discouraged strong drink. However, their tone and association with old seats of authority doomed them to failure.
1816	The American Colonization Society was founded. It proposed the voluntary and compensated emancipation of slaves and returning them to West Africa.
	The African Methodist Episcopal church was organized in Philadelphia.
1820s	Many states introduced uniform banking laws to replace the unique charters previously granted to individual banks.
	State governments began to build institutions to house orphans, the dependent poor, the insane, and criminals.
	The growing number of white wageworkers began to edge blacks out of their jobs by underselling them, by pressuring employers to discriminate, and by using outright violence.

Middle-class women in the North assumed roles that would have been unthinkable to previous generations. They became models of fashion, diet, and sexual behavior. Their new roles motivated them to join the temperance movement and moral reform societies.

Hierarchy based on sex and race seldom was questioned in public, particularly by persons who were in a position to change it. Additionally, before 1830 only a few whites thought of slavery as a moral question.

1825 State support for church-run charity schools persisted. For example, Catholic, as well as Protestant, schools received such support in New York City until 1825, and in other cities support continued until the 1860s.

1826 The temperance crusade began in earnest when northeastern evangelists founded the American Society for the Promotion of Temperance (soon renamed the American Temperance Society).

1830s The economic boom of the 1830s and the destruction of the national bank created a dramatic expansion in the number of state-chartered banks—from 329 in 1830 to 788 in 1837.

By this time, Whigs and Democrats agreed that providing common schools was a proper function of government.

Robert Wiltse was named by the Democrats to run Sing Sing prison. He used harsh punishments, sparse meals, and forced labor in order to punish prisoners and fund prison expenses.

Whigs made temperance a political issue.

1831 The radical abolitionist paper known as *The Liberator* was first published by William Lloyd Garrison.

The New York Magdalen Society's *First Annual Report* denounced male lust and printed shocking life histories of prostitutes.

1832 The regular army put an end to the age-old liquor ration, and increasing numbers of militia officers stopped supplying their men with whiskey.

1833 The temperance movement spread as members of Congress formed the American Congressional Temperance Society.

The American Anti-Slavery Society was founded.

1834 Women were a cheap source of labor for schools and were utilized for that reason. As a result, the percentage of women among Massachusetts teachers rose from 56 percent in 1834 to 78 percent almost thirty years later.

The first major American race riot broke out in Philadelphia between working-class whites and blacks. It lasted several days and did considerable damage.

| 1835 | The American Anti-Slavery Society launched a "postal campaign," flooding the nation's postal system with abolitionist materials that southerners and most northerners regarded as incendiary. |

1835 — The American Anti-Slavery Society launched a "postal campaign," flooding the nation's postal system with abolitionist materials that southerners and most northerners regarded as incendiary.

1836 — From this time onward, the American Anti-Slavery Society petitioned Congress to abolish slavery and the slave trade in the District of Columbia and to deny the slaveholding Republic of Texas admission to the Union.

1840 — Beginning around this time, women lobbied state legislatures and won significant changes in the laws governing women's rights to property, to the wages of their own labor, and to custody of children in cases of divorce.

1840s — The Washington Temperance Society and other voluntary temperance groups won solid footing in towns, and cities; overall consumption of alcohol per capita dropped from 1.8 to 1.0 gallon annually.

1848 — The first Women's Rights Convention was held at Seneca Falls, New York. It began with a Declaration of Sentiments and Resolutions, based on the Declaration of Independence, that denounced "the repeated injustices and usurpations on the part of man toward woman."

1840s–1850s — German immigrants arrived in the United States and introduced lager beer. This became a wholesome alternative for those who wished to give up spirits without joining the teetotalers.

1850s — Prohibition, which became dominant in the North, got nowhere in the South. While one northern legislature after another passed statewide prohibition, the only slave state to follow was tiny, northern-oriented Delaware.

1860s — Northern children attended school for an average of more than fifty days a year, while white children in the South attended school for an average of ten days annually.

By this time, every slave state except Florida (which had a tiny population) and the Carolinas operated prisons modeled on the Auburn prison system.

GLOSSARY OF IMPORTANT TERMS

Auburn system — The prison system introduced by the state of New York and copied by many other states. Prisoners slept in solitary cells and marched in military formation to meals and workshops. They were forbidden to speak to one another at any time. This system was designed to reform criminals and reduce expenses through the sale of items produced in the workshop.

butternuts — Democrats from the southern river-oriented counties of the Northwest region. The name came from the yellow vegetable dye with which they colored their homespun clothing.

common schools	Tax-supported public schools built by state and local governments.
hard money Democrats	Those who wanted to eliminate paper money and regarded banks as centers of trickery and privilege.
limited liability	A term used to describe the protection of directors and stockholders from debts incurred by their bank. The bank debts were separate from their personal liabilities. Usually, their liability was limited to the amount of capital they had invested.
normal school	State colleges that were established for the training of teachers.
postal campaign	One of the ways the abolitionists used to make the nation confront the slavery question. They flooded the mails, both North and South, with antislavery literature, which many northerners and most southerners considered incendiary.
Safety-Fund Law	This New York state law required banks to pool a fraction of their resources to protect both bankers and small stockholders in case of bank failures.

WHO? WHAT? WHERE?

WHO WERE THEY?

Complete each statement below (questions 1–8) by writing the letter preceding the appropriate name in the space provided. Use each answer only once.

    a. Dorothea Dix
    b. Herman Melville
    c. John Humphrey Noyes
    d. John Van Evrie
    e. Lydia Maria Child
    f. Richard M. Johnson
    g. Sylvester Graham
    h. William H. Seward

_____ 1. Whig governor of New York who supported transportation projects because they broke down neighborhood isolation and hastened the emergence of a market society.

_____ 2. Boston humanitarian who was the leading advocate of humane treatment of the insane.

_____ 3. New York doctor and pamphleteer who declared that Negroes were a different species and that the story of Adam and Eve referred only to whites.

_____ 4. Democrat and writer who wrote a novel about slaves commandeering a sailing ship and its crew.

_____ 5. Vice president under Van Buren who openly kept a mulatto mistress.

_____ 6. Full-time temperance lecturer who also warned of the danger of excess in diet and sex.

_____ 7. Reformer who set up a community based in plural marriages. He also believed that, in a perfect Christian world, there would be no meat eating.

_____ 8. Writer of sentimental fiction and manuals on household economy as well as a leading moral reformer.

WHAT WAS IT?

Complete each statement below (questions 1–11) by writing the letter preceding the appropriate response in the space provided. Use each answer only once.

a. American Colonization Society
b. American Anti-Slavery Society
c. common schools
d. Fifteen Gallon Law
e. German immigrants
f. hard money Democrats
g. Irish immigrants
h. The Killers
i. New York Magdalen Society
j. oysters
k. Washingtonians

_____ 1. Those who wanted to eliminate paper money and regarded banks as centers of trickery and privilege.

_____ 2. Tax-supported public schools built by state and local governments.

_____ 3. This decreed that merchants could sell ardent spirits only in large amounts.

_____ 4. Working-class temperance society members who were nonreligious and welcomed hopeless drunkards.

_____ 5. Group that introduced lager beer to the United States.

_____ 6. Generally a black monopoly in the food business in early-nineteenth-century northern coastal cities.

_____ 7. Group that displaced many of the free blacks in the economic life of the northeastern cities.

_____ 8. Gang of Irish immigrants who attacked a black-owned tavern and gambling hall in Philadelphia.

_____ 9. Organization that proposed the voluntary, gradual, and compensated emancipation of slaves and the repatriation of free blacks to West Africa.

_____ 10. Formed in 1833 by William Lloyd Garrison and other abolitionists, this demanded the immediate emancipation of slaves and full civil and legal rights for blacks.

_____ 11. Society of women reformers who tried to teach prostitutes morality and household skills to prepare them for a new life as domestic servants in middle-class homes.

WHERE WAS IT?

Complete each statement below (questions 1–8) by writing the letter preceding the appropriate response in the space provided. Use each answer only once.

a. Auburn, New York
b. Baltimore, Maryland
c. Maine
d. Massachusetts
e. New York
f. Oneida, New York
g. Philadelphia, Pennsylvania
h. Seneca Falls, New York

_____ 1. Location of the prison whose system was most copied by other states. Prisoners slept in solitary cells and were forbidden to speak to one another.

_____ 2. First state to outlaw public drinking establishments.

_____ 3. Location where the national Washington Temperance Society was formed.

_____ 4. First state to establish legal prohibition.

_____ 5. Haven of thousands of southern black refugees.

_____ 6. Location of a reform community that indulged in plural marriages.

_____ 7. One of the states that passed a major law dealing with women's property rights.

_____ 8. Site of the first Women's Rights Convention in 1848.

CHARTS, MAPS, AND ILLUSTRATIONS

1. One state that continued to inflict public corporal punishment was _____ _____. Why were small children present? _____

2. In return for sobriety and heavy dues, the Sons of Temperance promised its members _____.

3. The scientific text that portrayed white men as Greek gods and black men as apes _____.

MULTIPLE CHOICE

Circle the letter that best completes each statement.

1. Whigs found loyal support in all of the following except
   a. some southern rural areas.
   b. the merchant elite.
   c. new urban commercial classes created in the market revolution.
   d. factory owners and native-born factory workers.

2. Isolationist southern neighborhoods tended to support the
   a. Democrats.
   b. Whigs.
   c. Republicans.
   d. Free-Soilers.

3. Following Andrew Jackson's destruction of the Bank of the United States, state governments took over regulation of all of the following except
   a. banking.
   b. military spending.
   c. credit.
   d. currency.

4. Before tax-supported public schools, most children learned reading, writing, and arithmetic at home or in one of the following places except
   a. poorly staffed town schools.
   b. private schools.
   c. mainstreamed classrooms.
   d. charity schools run by churches or other benevolent organizations.

5. Which one of the following men was not among the Whig reformers who created the most advanced, expensive, and centralized state school systems?
   a. David Walker
   b. Horace Mann
   c. Henry Barnard
   d. Calvin Stowe

6. Normal schools were
   a. colleges of law.
   b. colleges of medicine.
   c. agricultural and mechanical colleges.
   d. state teacher's colleges.

7. Democrats preferred to give power to individual school districts, thus enabling local school committees to do all of the following except
   a. segregate and exclude children of non-Protestant faiths.
   b. determine the curriculum.
   c. establish the length of the school year.
   d. choose teachers and texts according to local needs.

8. Many Catholic parents
   a. refused to send their children to public schools due to the strong vein of Protestant morality found there.
   b. approved of all textbooks used in public schools.
   c. welcomed the King James Bible in public schools.
   d. supported paying taxes to fund public schools.

9. State governments began to build institutions to house orphans, the dependent poor, the insane, and criminals in the
   a. 1770s.
   b. 1790s.
   c. 1820s.
   d. 1860s.

10. Robert Wiltse, during his administration at Sing Sing prison in the 1830s, subjected prisoners to all of the following treatments except
   a. harsh punishments, including flogging and starvation.
   b. forced labor to fund prison expenses.
   c. sparse meals.
   d. disciplinary hearings run by other prisoners.

11. While northern evangelists preached that criminals could be rescued, southern preachers demanded Old Testament vengeance. They argued that the less-expensive measures sanctioned in the Bible were more effective than incarceration. These measures included all of the following except
   a. hanging.
   b. whipping.
   c. time out.
   d. branding.

12. Prohibition, which became dominant in the North, got nowhere in the South. In the 1850s, when one northern legislature after another passed statewide prohibition, the only slave state to follow was tiny, northern-oriented
   a. Maryland.
   b. Delaware.
   c. Kentucky.
   d. Arkansas.

13. The American Temperance Society's manifesto was Lyman Beecher's *Six Sermons on the Nature, Occasions, Signs, Evils, and Remedy of Intemperance* (1826). Which of the following statements incorrectly characterizes Beecher's beliefs?
   a. Beecher declared alcohol a semiaddictive drug and stated that moderate drinkers were not at risk of becoming drunkards.
   b. Beecher presented temperance, like other evangelical reforms, as a contest between self-control and slavery to one's appetites.
   c. Beecher encouraged total abstinence.
   d. Beecher believed middle-class abstainers could help him spread reform through example and coercion.

14. Realizing that voluntary abstinence would not put an end to drunkenness, Whig evangelists drafted coercive, prohibitionist legislation. Which of the following statements incorrectly characterizes this legislation?
   a. It attacked the licenses granting grocery stores and taverns the right to sell liquor by the drink and to permit it to be consumed on the premises.
   b. It gave local authorities the power to cancel the licenses of troublesome establishments.

c. It took away the right to use alcohol in religious services or at home for medicinal purposes.

d. It was the instrument authorities used to outlaw all public drinking places.

15. From the 1820s, white wage earners began replacing blacks in the work place by employing all of the following tactics except
a. underselling them.
b. pressuring employers to discriminate.
c. outright violence.
d. payoffs.

16. As official discrimination increased, African Americans responded by
a. building their own institutions.
b. marching and demonstrating in the streets.
c. employing random acts of violence.
d. none of the above

17. The first major American race riot broke out in 1834 between working-class whites and blacks at a street carnival. It occurred in the city of
a. Philadelphia.
b. New York.
c. Chicago.
d. Charleston.

18. Who was the radical abolitionist and publisher of *The Liberator?*
a. Theodore Parker
b. Wendell Phillips
c. Thomas Wentworth Higginson
d. William Lloyd Garrison

19. Beginning around 1840, women won significant changes in the laws governing women's rights concerning all of the following topics except
a. property.
b. the wages of their own labor.
c. custody of children in cases of divorce.
d. voting.

ESSAY

Description and Explanation (one- to two-paragraph essay)

1. Describe how southern differences in party preference were tied to differences in economic life.

2. Describe the role of states in banking and how politics affected this.

3. Compare Democrats and Whigs on social reforms in the North, such as public schools, prisons, and alcohol.

4. Describe the Whig view of education and morality.

5. Describe the views of foreign immigrants on public schools. Explain why they did not send their children to them.

6. Describe the southern view of social reform and the area's level of participation in it.

7. Describe the rise of opposition to distilled spirits.

8. Describe the relationship between abolitionism and increased interest in women's rights.

Discussion and Analysis (class discussion or one- to two-paragraph essay)

1. Discuss the general membership of the Whig and Democratic parties with comparisons on economic matters, religion, internal improvements, and general geographic areas of strength.

2. Discuss the changes in race relations in the Northeast, including effects on education, politics, levels of violence, and the way whites perceived blacks racially.

What If (include an explanation of your position)

1. If you were a parent in the 1830s and 1840s, would you support public schools? Would it be different if you were in the Northeast or the Southeast?

2. If you were a member of the Washington Temperance Society, what would your views be toward alcohol?

3. If you were a woman in 1848, would you attend the Women's Rights Convention of Seneca Falls, New York?

Crossword Puzzle: Society, Culture, and Politics, 1820s–1840s

ACROSS

1. Graham disciple and future feminist (3 words)
6. Goals for Garrison
8. ___ rum was temperance taboo
12. Women were the ___ source of labor for teaching profession
13. Threesome
14. A ___ school was a teacher's college
15. Winning combo in popular game
16. A ___ school was an early tax-supported public school
17. Sarah and Angelina ___ , feminist antislavery sisters
18. Dietary disaster for Graham
19. New York's model prison

DOWN

1. Feminist falls
2. Reformist Whig governor of New York
3. Melville tale of deception
4. Prohibitionist (2 words)
5. Oberlin's state
7. Opposite of specie (2 words)
9. Whigs insisted that ___ and moral progress were linked
10. Short for New England state
11. Horace Mann was one, so was Dorothea Dix
13. Abolitionist mailings of postal campaign

ANSWER KEY

WHO? WHAT? WHERE?

Who Were They?

1. h. William H. Seward, p. 393
2. a. Dorothea Dix, p. 397
3. d. John Van Evrie, p. 407
4. b. Herman Melville, p. 407
5. f. Richard M. Johnson, p. 411
6. g. Sylvester Graham, p. 413
7. c. John Humphey Noyes, p. 413
8. e. Lydia Maria Child, p. 415

What Was It?

1. f. Hard Money Democrats, p. 392
2. c. common schools, p. 394
3. d. Fifteen Gallon Law, p. 401
4. k. Washingtonians, pp. 401–402
5. e. German immigrants, p. 402
6. j. oysters, p. 404
7. g. Irish immigrants, p. 406
8. h. The Killers, p. 406
9. a. American Colonization Society, p. 407
10. b. American Anti-Slavery Society, p. 409
11. i. New York Magdalen Society, p. 413

Where Was It?

1. a. Auburn, New York, p. 397
2. d. Massachusetts, p. 401
3. b. Baltimore, Maryland, p. 401
4. c. Maine, p. 403
5. g. Philadelphia, Pennsylvania, p. 405
6. f. Oneida, New York, p. 413
7. e. New York, p. 416
8. h. Seneca Falls, New York, p. 416

CHARTS, MAPS, AND ILLUSTRATIONS

1. Delaware; learning a lesson, p. 398
2. death by suicide, p. 399
3. *Types of Mankind*, p. 406

MULTIPLE CHOICE

1. a. (p. 388)
2. a. (p. 390)
3. b. (p. 392)
4. c. (p. 394)
5. a. (p. 394)
6. d. (p. 395)
7. a. (p. 395)
8. a. (p. 396)
9. c. (p. 396)
10. d. (p. 397)
11. c. (p. 398)
12. b. (p. 399)
13. a. (p. 400)
14. c. (pp. 400–401)
15. d. (p. 404)
16. a. (p. 405)
17. a. (p. 406)
18. d. (p. 418)
19. d. (p. 416)

ESSAY

Description and Explanation

1. p. 390
2. pp. 392–393
3. pp. 394–398
4. pp. 394–395, 399–403
5. p. 396
6. pp. 398–399
7. pp. 400–402
8. pp. 415–416

Discussion and Analysis

1. pp. 388–392
2. pp. 403–407

What If

1. pp. 394–396, 398
2. pp. 401–402
3. p. 416

Crossword Puzzle

CHAPTER 12

JACKSONIAN DEMOCRACY

Jacksonian democracy was rooted in two events that occurred in 1819. First, the angry debates over Missouri's admission as a slave state brought the South's commitment to slavery and the North's resentment of southern political power into direct opposition. And second, the American financial collapse, known as the Panic of 1819, was the first failure of the market economy. This failure, combined with the debate regarding slavery in Missouri, created doubt by many that a market revolution was compatible with the Jeffersonian republic. Some politicians were determined to dismantle the limited-government states' rights coalition of northern and southern agrarians that elected Jefferson. By 1828, they formed the Democratic Party with Andrew Jackson at its head.

More completely than any of his rivals, Jackson captured the rhetoric of the revolutionary republic. With his fixation on secrecy, corruption, and intrigue, he transformed both the rhetoric and his own biography into popular melodrama. It was the goal of the Jackson presidency to curtail government involvement in the economy, to end special privileges, and to rescue the republic from the power of money, which was seen as a type of corruption. Jackson attacked the Bank of the United States, which he considered the most dangerously privileged institution in the United States.

The Democratic Party linked popular democracy with the defense of southern slavery. The alliance of the planters of the South and the plain Republicans of the North was revived by Martin Van Buren. The new Democratic Party was committed to a program of states' rights and minimal government but was dependent on votes in both slaveholding and nonslaveholding states. Most southerners thought the surest guarantee of their ability to maintain the institution of slavery was a disciplined Democratic Party that was determined to avoid sectional arguments.

The election of 1840 signaled the completion of the second-party system, the most fully national alignment of parties in American history. William Henry Harrison and Martin Van Buren ran against each other in the election and won nearly equal levels of support in the slave and free states. There was not a single state that the Democrats or Whigs could take for granted. The result was an increased popular interest in politics and one of the highest levels of voter turnout the nation had ever seen. By 1840, American politics took place within a stable, national system with two political parties that debated on questions of economics and the granting of statehood, but that avoided any sectional discussions. This system worked well until it disintegrated on the eve of the Civil War.

LIBERTY, EQUALITY, POWER

Much of the rhetoric and issues of the Jacksonian era encompassed liberty, equality, and power. Jacksonian rhetoric emphasized Jackson as a protector of liberties against special privilege and legislation that unfairly favored certain groups. In some ways, Americans during this period experienced a government with a more limited role. A type of crude equality was emphasized for white men, but, again, it was only for white men.

The removal of Indians clearly demonstrated the power of whites over Native Americans. The passage of tariff acts benefited citizens in the cities and protected commercial food producers at the expense of plantation owners. These tariffs were passed despite the South's efforts to block them. The use of the gag rule revoked the constitutional right of all citizens to petition Congress with grievances.

Jackson decidedly changed the role of the presidency. He emphasized that he was the only government official elected by the entire country. By expanding the veto power of the presidency, he turned the office of the president into a powerful legislative force. Jackson established the president's right to demand loyalty from cabinet members and to appoint and remove them at will. This move was a major extension of presidential power.

OBJECTIVES

After studying this chapter, a student should be able to

1. Compare the elections of 1824 and 1828, noting similarities and differences.

2. Discuss the role of Van Buren in the forming of the early Democratic Party.

3. Examine Jackson as a symbol for his time.

4. Describe the principles of nullification and how it was used by South Carolina.

5. Analyze the role of Jackson in the Bank War.

6. Describe how Jacksonianism answered the question of how to protect the slaveholding South within the Union and how to deal with the market economy.

7. Discuss the development of the second-party system and the role of the election of 1840 in it.

CHRONOLOGY

1803	Jefferson purchased the Louisiana Territory to give future generations of Americans a huge "Empire for Liberty," but the unexplored territory was a vast unknown.
1804	Jefferson sent an expedition under Meriwether Lewis and William Clark to explore the Louisiana Territory. In **September 1806**, Lewis and Clark reached St. Louis with volumes of drawings and notes, along with assurances that the Louisiana Purchase was worth many times its price.
1812	Louisiana, including the important port of New Orleans, entered the Union.
1817–1818	In the Rush-Bagot Treaty of 1817 and the British-American Convention of 1818, Adams helped to pacify the Great Lakes, restore American fishing rights off the Canadian coast, and draw the United States-Canadian boundary west of the Rocky Mountains.

1819	Missouri applied for admission to the Union as a slave state. It was the first new state to be carved out of the Louisiana Purchase.
	The North held the majority in the House of Representatives, and the South controlled a bare majority in the Senate.
	With matters spinning out of control, William Jones resigned the presidency of the Bank of the United States. The new president, Langdon Cheves, rescued the bank from the paper economy created by state-chartered banks, but at the expense of the national money and credit system.
	The depression that followed the Panic of 1819 was the first nationwide failure of the market economy.
	Following Jackson's raid into Florida, the Adams-Onis Treaty procured Florida for the United States and defined America's southwestern border.
1819–1820	After much dispute, the new Congress that convened in the winter passed the legislative package that became known as the Missouri Compromise.
	Many Republicans were calling for a Jeffersonian revival that would limit government power and guarantee southern rights within the Union. Others were determined to reconstruct the limited-government states' rights coalition that had elected Thomas Jefferson.
1821	After having been "betrayed" by members of Monroe's cabinet over his raid into Florida, Jackson retired to his plantation in 1821 to ponder the state of the nation in his "memorandums."
1823	John Quincy Adams wrote what came to be known as the Monroe Doctrine. It declared American opposition to any European attempt at colonization in the New World without denying the right of the United States to annex new territory.
1824	With Republican Party unity broken, there were four sectional candidates for president. None of them received a majority in the election, so the decision went to the House of Representatives.
1825	In **January**, John Quincy Adams accepted what became known as the Corrupt Bargain. The controversy began when Andrew Jackson turned down Henry Clay's offer of support during the election. Clay then went to Adams and made the same offer of support. Adams accepted Clay's support and was elected president by a narrow margin. In return, Adams appointed Clay as his secretary of state.
	Andrew Jackson regarded the intrigues that robbed him of the presidency as the culmination of a long history of corruption that the nation had suffered over the past ten years.
	As early as 1825, it was clear that the election of 1828 would pit John Quincy Adams against Andrew Jackson.

1827   Cherokees in Georgia pressed the land issue by declaring themselves a republic with their own constitution, government, courts, and police. However, after the discovery of gold on their land made it more attractive to white settlers, the Georgia state legislature promptly declared Cherokee law null and void, extended Georgia's authority into Cherokee country, and began surveying the lands for sale.

John C. Calhoun embraced the principle that states had the right to nullify federal laws.

1828   The presidential campaign was an exercise in slander rather than a debate on public issues. Adhering to custom, neither Adams nor Jackson campaigned directly. However, their henchmen viciously personalized the campaign. The presidential election captured the attention of the public and, as a result, voter turnout doubled what it had been four years earlier.

For the South, the Tariff of 1828 was the last straw. It benefited the city and commercial food producers at the expense of plantations, and it demonstrated that the South could do nothing to block the passage of such laws.

In his anonymously published essay *Exposition and Protest*, John C. Calhoun argued that the Constitution was a compact between sovereign states, and that the states, not the federal courts, could decide the constitutionality of federal laws.

1828–1829   Middle-class evangelists petitioned the government to stop movement of the mail on Sundays, but Jackson turned them down.

1829   In **January**, Jackson's wife, Rachel, died. He remained convinced that her declining health and ultimate death stemmed from accusations made by his political enemies. On **March 4**, Jackson delivered his inaugural address, still in mourning for her.

Martin Van Buren, who had mobilized much of the support Jackson gained between 1824 and 1828, became the new secretary of state, which positioned him to succeed Jackson as president.

1830   In the Indian Removal Act, Indians were relocated to federal land west of the Mississippi, where they would be under the authority of the federal government.

The Supreme Court ruled in *Cherokee Nation* v. *Georgia* that the Cherokees could not sue Georgia because they were dependents of the federal government, not the state of Georgia.

1830s   The Sioux were devastated by the spread of smallpox. The disease had moved up the Missouri River periodically from the 1790s onward, but the epidemics of the 1830s annihilated the sedentary peoples of the Missouri.

1832   Jackson asked Congress to reduce the tariff. The resulting tariff act lowered rates on many items but affirmed the principle of protection. South Carolina, with Calhoun's open support, called a state convention that nullified the tariffs of 1828 and 1832.

In *Worcester* v. *Georgia* the Supreme Court declared that Georgia's extension of state law over Cherokee land was unconstitutional.

In **January**, Nicholas Biddle applied to Congress for a recharter of the Bank of the United States.

In **July**, Jackson's Bank Veto Message was sent to Congress. The message combined Jeffersonian truths with appeals to the public's prejudice against the bank.

Presidential campaign issues centered around the Bank of the United States and Jackson's veto. Jackson won reelection over Henry Clay by a landslide.

1833

A compromise tariff lowered rates over the course of several years, gave southern planters the relief they demanded, and maintained moderate protectionism that allowed northern manufacturers time to adjust to the lower rates.

Congress also passed the Force Bill, which authorized the president to use the military against South Carolina.

Isolated South Carolina backed down on nullification.

For the only time in history, the United States paid off its national debt.

1834

It was over deposit removal and related questions of presidential power that opposition to the Jacksonian Democrats united as the Whig Party.

1835

Abolitionists launched a "postal campaign," flooding the North and South with antislavery publications.

When John Marshall died, Jackson rewarded Roger B. Taney with the position of chief justice of the Supreme Court. A loyal Democrat, Taney hated banks as much as Jackson did.

1836

The Deposit Act increased the number of banks receiving federal deposits (thus taking power away from Jackson's "pet banks") and distributed any federal surplus to the states for roads, canals, and schools.

Jackson issued a "specie circular," which provided that speculators could buy large parcels of public land only with silver or gold coins, while settlers could continue to buy farm-sized plots with bank notes. This represented Jackson's last attack on the paper economy.

The Whigs acknowledged that Henry Clay, the leader of their party, could not win a national election. They ran three sectional candidates—Daniel Webster, William Henry Harrison, and Hugh Lawson White—but the strategy failed.

1836–1844	In dealing with antislavery petitions, Congress simply voted at each session from 1836 to 1844 to table them without reading them—acknowledging that they had been received but sidestepping any debate on them. This procedure became known as the gag rule.
1837	President Van Buren barely had taken office when the inflationary boom of the mid-1830s collapsed. The first business failures came in **March** and, by **May**, New York banks were unable to accommodate people who were demanding hard coin for their bank notes.
	Van Buren asked Congress to set up the Independent Treasury, and Congress spent the rest of his time in office arguing about it.
1838	Following his predecessor's policy, President Martin Van Buren sent the army to march the 18,000 remaining Cherokee to Oklahoma. Along this "Trail of Tears," 4,000 of them died of exposure, starvation, and disease.
1840	The Independent Treasury Bill finally was passed, thus completing the Jacksonian separation of bank and state.
	The election between Harrison and Van Buren represented the completion of the second-party system, the most fully national alignment of parties in American history. It was also the high-water mark of voter turnout.

GLOSSARY OF IMPORTANT TERMS

Bucktail Republican	A coalition group in New York state politics that opposed the power of Governor DeWitt Clinton. The name came from the buck's tail worn in the hats of some of the leaders of a New York City political organization. On the national level, they often were considered to be prosouthern. One of the main leaders was Martin Van Buren.
congressional caucus	In the early republic, this was the group of congressmen that traditionally chose the party's presidential candidates. By the 1820s, the American public distrusted the caucus as undemocratic, since it represented only the party currently in power.
Corrupt Bargain	Jackson and his supporters claimed this happened in the election of 1824 when Henry Clay allegedly sold his support during the House vote in the disputed election of John Quincy Adams.
Era of Good Feelings	The era of partyless politics during President James Monroe's administration. It was created by the collapse of the Federalists at the end of the War of 1812.
favorite son	The candidate for president supported by delegates from his home state.
nullification	According to this, the Union was a voluntary compact between sovereign states, states were the ultimate judges of the validity of federal law, and

states could break the compact if they wished. They could nullify it within the border of that state. This process would be called nullification.

patronage Government jobs were given out to the political supporters of the winning party, regardless of ability.

pet banks The term used by the Whigs to refer to carefully selected banks in which Democratic Secretary of the Treasury Roger B. Taney deposited government funds.

spoils system A system by which the victorious political party rewarded its supporters with government jobs.

table a petition or bill The act of removing a petition or bill from consideration without debate.

WHO? WHAT? WHERE?

WHO WERE THEY?

Complete each statement below (questions 1–14) by writing the letter preceding the appropriate name in the space provided. Use each answer only once.

a. Amos Kendall
b. George Troup
c. Henry Clay
d. James Tallmadge, Jr.
e. Jesse Thomas
f. John C. Calhoun
g. John Quincy Adams
h. Langdon Cheves
i. Martin Van Buren
j. Nicholas Biddle
k. Peggy O'Neal Timberlake
l. Rachel Donelson
m. Roger B. Taney
n. Sacajawea

_____ 1. Teenage Shoshone girl who was an indispensable guide and interpreter for the Lewis and Clark expedition.

_____ 2. Congressman from New York who proposed two amendments to the Missouri statehood bill that would have eliminated slavery in Missouri.

_____ 3. Senator from Illinois who proposed the compromise that if Missouri were allowed to be a slave state, the South would agree to outlaw slavery in territories north of the 36° 30′ line.

_____ 4. President of the bank that curtailed credit and demanded that state bank notes received by the bank be redeemed in specie. This was a factor in the Panic of 1819.

_____ 5. Sole candidate for vice president in the election of 1824.

_____ 6. Speaker of the House of Representatives and presidential candidate who had enough support to throw the election of 1824 in the House to either Jackson or Adams.

_____ 7. This person was one of the biggest issues in the election of 1828.

_____ 8. Governor of Georgia who brought Native American lands under state jurisdiction and then turned them over to poor whites through lotteries.

_____ 9. Washington tavernkeeper's daughter who married one of Jackson's cabinet members and closest friends.

_____ 10. Congressman from Massachusetts who was known as "Old Man Eloquent" and one of the leaders in opposing the gag rule.

_____ 11. Postmaster general in Jackson's administration who looked the other way as local postmasters removed abolitionist materials illegally from the mail.

_____ 12. Brilliant, aristocratic president of the Bank of the United States.

_____ 13. Close adviser of Jackson who withdrew government deposits from the bank and was rewarded later with the position of chief justice of the Supreme Court.

_____ 14. President during the deepest, most widespread, and longest economic depression that Americans had ever faced.

WHAT WAS IT?

Complete each statement below (questions 1–10) by writing the letter preceding the appropriate response in the space provided. Use each answer only once.

   a. Adams-Onis Treaty
   b. Civilized Tribes
   c. Corrupt Bargain
   d. *Exposition and Protest*
   e. Independent Treasury
   f. Log Cabin Campaign
   g. "The Millennium of the Minnows"
   h. Monroe Doctrine
   i. monster
   j. post office

_____ 1. Name Jacksonians used to describe the Bank of the United States.

_____ 2. What Jackson claimed happened in the election of 1824 when Clay sold his support to Adams for the office of secretary of state.

_____ 3. Agreement by which the United States acquired Florida and defined its southwestern border with Spain.

_____ 4. This declared American opposition to any European attempt at colonization in the New World.

_____ 5. Largest government department.

_____ 6. What one critic of the Jackson administration called his first cabinet.

_____ 7. Five tribes of Native Americans who remained on their ancestral lands in the old Southwest.

_____ 8. Anonymously published essay in which John C. Calhoun argued that the Constitution was a compact between sovereign states.

_____ 9. Complete divorce of government from the banking system. The federal government would hold and dispense its money without depositing it in banks.

_____ 10. Campaign that portrayed Harrison as a folksy man, as opposed to his luxury-loving opponent.

WHERE WAS IT?

Complete each statement below (questions 1–4) by writing the letter preceding the appropriate response in the space provided. Use each answer only once.

    a. Missouri
    b. New York City
    c. South
    d. South Carolina

_____ 1. First new state to be carved out of the Louisiana Purchase.

_____ 2. Base of Jackson's political support in the election of 1828.

_____ 3. State most opposed to the Tariff of 1828.

_____ 4. Place where most abolitionist materials were published.

CHARTS, MAPS, AND ILLUSTRATIONS

1. The Native American tribe who hosted the Lewis and Clark expedition and was later extinct due not only to smallpox but also the Sioux expansion was _____.

2. In the presidential election of 1836, the two states carried by Hugh Lawson White were _____ and _____.

MULTIPLE CHOICE

Circle the letter that best completes each statement.

1. In 1804, Jefferson sent an expedition to explore the Louisiana Territory under
   a. Robert Y. Hayne and Louis McLane.
   b. William Jones and Langdon Cheves.
   c. Meriwether Lewis and William Clark.
   d. George Rogers Clark and William Gouge.

2. The Sioux were aided in their conquest of other Indian nations by the spread of
   a. smallpox.
   b. white settlers.
   c. famine.
   d. locusts.

3. The origins of the Panic of 1819 included all of the following except
   a. European agriculture was recovering from the Napoleonic Wars, thereby increasing the demand for American foodstuffs.
   b. War and revolution in the New World cut off the supply of precious metals (the base of the international money supply) from the mines of Mexico and Peru.
   c. Debt-ridden European governments hoarded the available specie.
   d. American bankers and businessmen met the situation by expanding credit and issuing bank notes that were mere dreams of real money.

4. In 1816, the Second Bank of the United States was under the presidency of the genial Republican politician
   a. William Gouge.
   b. Henry Clay.
   c. John Branch.
   d. William Jones.

5. Who wrote what came to be known as the Monroe Doctrine?
   a. James Monroe
   b. Martin Van Buren
   c. Andrew Jackson
   d. John Quincy Adams

6. As early as 1825, it was clear that the election of 1828 would pit Adams against Andrew Jackson, and Adams
   a. refused to prepare for the contest.
   b. removed his noisiest enemies from appointive offices.
   c. built up a strong political organization.
   d. was much more active than the Jackson opposition.

7. The new Democratic Party linked popular democracy with
   a. the rise of national banking.
   b. the defense of slavery.
   c. the new market revolution.
   d. the national debt.

8. In the 1828 election, Jackson was successful in the South due to all of the following reasons, except
   a. Southerners had grown wary of an activist government in which they were a minority.
   b. Southerners admired Jackson for supporting the rights of the federal government at the expense of states' rights.

c. Southerners looked to Jackson not only as a military hero, but also as a Tennessee planter.

d. Southerners liked Jackson because he talked about getting back to republican fundamentals.

9. Under the Indian Removal Act of 1830,
   a. Georgia was given authority over Indians within their state.
   b. Indians were declared a sovereign people independent of the federal government.
   c. Georgia's extension of state law over Cherokee land was declared constitutional.
   d. Indians were given the option of relocating to federal land west of the Mississippi.

10. Following his predecessor's policy, President Martin Van Buren sent the army to march the 18,000 remaining Cherokee to Oklahoma. Four thousand of them died of exposure, starvation, and disease along the
    a. Southern Trail.
    b. Santa Fe Trail.
    c. Trail of Tears.
    d. Oregon Trail.

11. Indian removal had all of the following consequences except
    a. It violated Supreme Court decisions.
    b. It weakened Jackson's reputation as an enemy of the rule of law and a friend of local solutions.
    c. It reaffirmed the link between racism and white democracy in the South.
    d. It reaffirmed Jackson's commitment to state sovereignty and limited federal authority.

12. Which of the following events did not lead the whites of South Carolina and Georgia to intensify their distrust of outside authority and to insist on the right to govern their own neighborhoods?
    a. The Boston abolitionist William Lloyd Garrison's declaration of war on slavery
    b. The Tariff of 1832
    c. Nat Turner's slave uprising
    d. The case of *Plessy* v. *Ferguson*

13. Middle-class evangelists went after Jackson in all of the following ways except
    a. They petitioned the government to stop movement of the mail on Sundays—after learning Jackson wanted to keep moral issues out of politics.
    b. They petitioned the government for the humane treatment of the Civilized Tribes.
    c. They had him impeached.
    d. They suspected Jackson of immorality and were appalled by his defense of Peggy Eaton.

14. Jackson's Bank Veto Message, sent to Congress on July 10, 1832, was written by all of the following men except
    a. Amos Kendall.
    b. Francis Preston Blair.
    c. Roger B. Taney.
    d. William Henry Harrison.

15. It was over deposit removal and related questions of presidential power that the opposition to the Jacksonian Democrats united into the
    a. Socialist Party.
    b. Free-Soil Party.
    c. Know-Nothing Party.
    d. Whig Party.

16. The Deposit Act of 1836 resulted in all of the following except
    a. It increased the number of banks receiving federal deposits.
    b. It took power away from Jackson's pet banks.
    c. It secured federal deposits in foreign banks, such as in Switzerland.
    d. It distributed any federal surplus to the states for roads, canals, and schools.

17. Jackson's last attack on the paper economy came in 1836 with the provision that speculators could buy large parcels of public land only with silver or gold coins, while settlers could continue to buy farm-sized plots with bank notes. This was known as a
    a. monopoly.
    b. Federal Reserve Act.
    c. specie circular.
    d. cooperative.

18. In 1836, the Whigs acknowledged that Henry Clay, the leader of their party, could not win a national election. So they ran three sectional candidates:
    a. Daniel Webster, William Henry Harrison, and Hugh Lawson White.
    b. Martin Van Buren, W. P. Mangum, and John Floyd.
    c. William Wirt, James G. Birney, and Zachary Taylor.
    d. Lewis Cass, Franklin Pierce, and John P. Hale.

19. The Whigs, confident they could blame Van Buren for the depression, passed over their best-known leaders to nominate William Henry Harrison as their presidential candidate in 1840. Harrison was an attractive candidate for all of the following reasons except
    a. He was the hero of the battle of Tippecanoe.
    b. He was a westerner whose Virginia origins made him palatable in the South.
    c. He was a proven vote-getter.
    d. He had strong publicized opinions on national issues, with a strong political record to defend.

ESSAY

Description and Explanation (one- to two-paragraph essay)

1. Describe the role of the Bank of the United States in the Panic of 1819 and how both were viewed by the American people.

2. Describe the election of 1824: the candidates, the dispute, and the lasting political effects.

3. Describe the "Petticoat Wars" and explain their significance.

4. Describe Jackson's view of corruption and give some examples of how it affected his political activities.

5. Describe Van Buren's coalition and the members' views of limited government.

6. Describe the rise of presidential power as shown in Jackson's use of the veto and control of his cabinet.

Discussion and Analysis (class discussion or one- to two-paragraph essay)

1. Discuss Jackson's life and career as a melodrama. If it really was a melodrama, why?

2. Discuss Jackson's different views on states' rights as expressed during the Jefferson birthday celebration, the Indian removal issue, and the tariff crisis.

3. Discuss the role of Jackson in the Bank War.

4. Discuss Martin Van Buren's role in developing the Democratic Party, his leadership style and ability, and his political views.

What If (include an explanation of your position)

1. If you were a member of Washington society, would you support or oppose Peggy O'Neal Eaton?

2. If you were living in South Carolina in the early 1830s, what would your position be on nullification?

3. If you were a voter in the 1830s, would you be a Whig or a Democrat? Would it make a difference if you were benefiting from the market economy?

Crossword Puzzle: Jacksonian Democracy

DOWN

1. Target of Tallmadge Amendments
2. Andrew's beloved
3. Removal victims of 1830 law
4. Lewis and Clark's ___ with Mandans lasted all winter
5. "___ in office" was Jacksonian principle
6. Jackson's home town
11. What Marshall couldn't do with his decision in *Worcester* v. *Georgia*
12. Disunion to Jackson
14. Decay
15. Owner of Florida during Jackson's invasion
17. Common word in toasts of Jackson and Calhoun
18. Lighthouse of the ___ was idea of John Quincy Adams
19. Surprise word

ACROSS

1. Whig name for incumbent in 1840 election
7. Does what Calhoun claimed a state could do
8. Old inaugural month
9. Monroe's second term was ___ ___ government
10. Election of 1824 reflected the ___ nature of politics
13. Jackson's feeling for Clay
15. What Cherokees did on the Trail of Tears
16. What Marshall ruled Cherokees couldn't do in 1830
18. Veto
20. Log cabin candidate
21. John Quincy Adams was favorite ___ of New England
22. Type of improvement favored by Henry Clay

ANSWER KEY

WHO? WHAT? WHERE?

Who Were They?

1. n. Sacajawea, pp. 420–421
2. d. James Tallmadge, Jr., p. 421
3. e. Jesse Thomas, p. 422
4. h. Langdon Cheves, p. 423
5. f. John C. Calhoun, p. 424
6. c. Henry Clay, p. 426
7. l. Rachel Donelson, p. 429
8. b. George Troup, p. 434
9. k. Peggy O'Neal Timberlake, p. 438
10. g. John Quincy Adams, p. 440
11. a. Amos Kendall, p. 440
12. j. Nicholas Biddle, p. 442
13. m. Roger B. Taney, p. 443
14. i. Martin Van Buren, p. 448

What Was It?

1. i. monster, p. 423
2. c. Corrupt Bargain, pp. 425–426
3. a. Adams-Onis Treaty, p. 427
4. h. Monroe Doctrine, p. 428
5. j. post office, p. 428
6. g. "The Millennium of the Minnows," p. 431
7. b. Civilized Tribes, p. 434
8. d. *Exposition and Protest*, p. 437
9. e. Independent Treasury, p. 448
10. f. Log Cabin Campaign, p. 449

Where Was It?

1. a. Missouri, p. 421
2. c. South, p. 434
3. d. South Carolina, p. 436
4. b. New York City, p. 440

CHARTS, MAPS, AND ILLUSTRATIONS

1. Mandans, p. 420
2. Tennessee and Georgia, p. 448

MULTIPLE CHOICE

1. c. (p. 420)
2. a. (p. 421)
3. a. (p. 423)
4. d. (p. 423)
5. d. (p. 428)
6. a. (p. 428)
7. b. (p. 428)
8. b. (p. 434)
9. d. (p. 434)
10. c. (p. 436)
11. b. (p. 436)
12. d. (pp. 436–437)
13. c. (p. 440)
14. d. (p. 442)
15. d. (pp. 443–444)
16. c. (p. 445)
17. c. (p. 446)
18. a. (p. 447)
19. d. (p. 448)

ESSAY

Description and Explanation

1. p. 423
2. pp. 424–426
3. pp. 438–439
4. pp. 444–445
5. p. 424
6. pp. 444–445

Discussion and Analysis

1. pp. 426–427
2. pp. 434, 438

3. pp. 441–443
4. pp. 428–429, 432, 434, 438, 439, 447–448

What If

1. pp. 438–439
2. pp. 436–438
3. pp. 441, 443, 445

Crossword Puzzle

Manifest Destiny:
An Empire for Liberty—or Slavery?

The generation of Americans before the Civil War saw the geographical area of the United States quadruple in size during their lifetime. Many Americans took this prodigious growth for granted. They considered it to be their God-given right, or Manifest Destiny, to take over the entire continent of North America. For Americans of European descent, the future was in the West. "Oregon fever" pushed many families along the Oregon Trail to the Pacific coast. In addition, the Mormon exodus to the Great Salt Lake area in search of religious freedom and liberty was under way.

Many Americans had moved to the Mexican province of Texas, but tensions between settlers and the Mexican government were increasing. These conflicts resulted in the Texas Revolution, and the American government was eager to annex the newly independent area. Fear of provoking Mexico and concern about reopening the issue of slavery in the territories delayed the decision until 1845. When Texas finally was annexed in 1845, it led to a war with neighboring Mexico.

After the war with Mexico was concluded successfully, the United States acquired major portions of the territory, intensifying the issue of the expansion of slavery. With the discovery of gold in California and the opening of territory in the Mexican cession, population in the area increased dramatically. Congress was forced to act on the question of slavery. Henry Clay participated in one of the most important debates ever held in the Senate. After a number of basic positions were debated vigorously, the Compromise of 1850 was enacted. Rather than calming the issue, the compromise seemed to ignite even more emotional conflict on slavery. This led to increased bitterness between North and South. In addition, events such as the publishing of *Uncle Tom's Cabin* and attempts by some southern sympathizers to acquire more slave territory heightened tensions in the United States.

LIBERTY, EQUALITY, POWER

In this era of Manifest Destiny, most Americans were debating the issues of slavery, liberty, equality, and power. American expansion into the Southwest reduced or eliminated the equality and power of Native Americans. Many Mexican settlers in the area lost much of their power and seldom were treated with equality. Mormons settled the area around present-day Utah in a quest for religious freedom and individual equality.

Slavery is the most obvious example of unequal treatment between Americans. Southerners saw the issue of slavery and its expansion into new areas as their right to continue their way of life. The Fugitive Slave Law of 1850 gave the federal government extensive powers to force the return of runaway slaves. As northerners watched in horror as this act was used to deny basic freedom to escaped slaves, they viewed it as wrong, despite their reluctance to consider African Americans as equals. This issue of slavery was one of liberty and power in the United States.

OBJECTIVES

After studying this chapter, a student should be able to

1. Describe expansion into the Pacific areas in the 1840s and the views of Manifest Destiny.

2. Describe the differences between the ways men and women looked at moving westward.

3. Explore the role of the slavery controversy in westward expansion, especially involving Texas.

4. Discuss the military aspects of the Mexican War.

5. Explore Polk's role in the Mexican War and his use of politics.

6. Describe the views of different senators during the debates on the Compromise of 1850 and the provisions of the compromise.

7. Explain the controversy over the Fugitive Slave Act and the differences between the way northerners and southerners reacted to it.

8. Describe the purpose and activities of the filibusters during the 1850s.

CHRONOLOGY

1835	There were thirty thousand Americans in Texas, outnumbering Mexicans in the area by six to one.
1836	In **March**, delegates from across Texas assembled at a convention to declare Texas an independent republic and adopt a constitution based on the American model.
	Mexican forces captured the Alamo, a former mission in San Antonio, which was converted to a fort by Texan fighters. All of the 187 defenders of the Alamo were killed, including Davy Crockett and Jim Bowie. "Remember the Alamo!" became a rallying cry for Texans.
1840	Richard Henry Dana's *Two Years before the Mast* was one of many books to entice settlers to California and the Pacific Northwest.
1840s	The "Young America" movement, started by a group of Democratic expansionists, praised Manifest Destiny and considered unbridled expansion evidence of God's generosity to a noble country.
	Horace Greeley urged, "Go West, young man." Americans went west in record numbers to find opportunity and prosperous land.
1841	President John Tyler, states' rights advocate from Virginia, broke with the Whig Party because of its programs for a national bank, higher tariffs, and federal aid for roads and waterways.

1842   In *Prigg* v. *Pennsylvania*, the Supreme Court relieved state officials of any obligation to enforce the return of fugitive slaves who had escaped into free states, declaring this was a federal responsibility.

1844   In **June**, a mob, angered by a publication in support of polygamy, broke into a jail where Mormon leader Joseph Smith was being held and killed him.

1845   In **March**, Congress passed a joint resolution allowing Texas to bypass the territorial stage and become the fifteenth slave state.

1846   In order to provoke a war with Mexico, Polk ordered four thousand soldiers, under the command of General Zachary Taylor, to advance to the Rio Grande in **January**. The United States officially declared war on Mexico in **May**. Taylor defeated the Mexican army south of the Rio Grande. General Stephen W. Kearney captured New Mexico, and various American groups took California.

The "Oregon fever" migration of 1842–1843 was followed in 1846 by the Mormon exodus to a new Zion in the basin of the Great Salt Lake territory.

In June, Polk accepted a compromise treaty to split the Oregon country between the United States and Britain at the forty-ninth parallel.

1847   General-in-Chief Winfield "Old Fuss and Feathers" Scott led an invasion into Mexico's heartland from a beachhead at Veracruz and was able to capture Mexico City by **September**.

In **February**, southern Democrat John C. Calhoun formulated the "southern rights" position. Directly challenging the Wilmot Proviso, Calhoun introduced resolutions in the Senate asserting the right of slave owners to take their human property into any territory.

1848   In **February**, Nicholas Trist signed the Treaty of Guadalupe Hidalgo, ending the war with Mexico. The treaty cut off half of Mexico and increased the size of the United States by one fourth.

Whig candidate Zachary Taylor won the presidential election by a narrow margin against Democrat Lewis Cass and the Free-Soil Party's candidate Martin Van Buren.

Gold was discovered in California and confirmed in Polk's last message to Congress in **December**.

1849   Narciso Lopez, a Venezuelan-born Cuban soldier of fortune, recruited several hundred American adventurers for the first "filibustering" expedition against Cuba.

1850   John C. Calhoun, suffering from consumption, and Zachary Taylor, suffering from gastroenteritis, died.

The most famous congressional debate in American history took place dealing over the territory acquired in the Mexican War. It ended with the Compromise of 1850, which admitted California as free state and organized New Mexico and Utah without restrictions on slavery. It also prohibited the slave trade but not slavery in the District of Columbia. Another part of it, the Fugitive Slave Act of 1850, required that a slave who escaped into a free state must be returned to the owner.

1852   *Uncle Tom's Cabin*, by Harriet Beecher Stowe, became a best-seller. Within a year, it sold three hundred thousand copies and eventually was translated into twenty languages.

1854   Three American diplomats met at Ostend, Belgium, and signed a manifesto declaring that Cuba was necessary to the United States.

1856   The focus of American filibustering shifted from Cuba to Nicaragua, where William Walker, the most remarkable of the *filibusteros*, proclaimed himself president and restored the institution of slavery. He was overthrown in 1857 but made several attempts to recapture Nicaragua. He was executed in Honduras in 1860.

1857   Tensions between the U.S. Army and the Mormons temporarily concluded as Brigham Young, governor of the Utah Territory and the Mormon leader, surrendered his civil authority and made an uneasy peace with the government. However, the Mormon community continued to prosper.

GLOSSARY OF IMPORTANT TERMS

abolitionist   A person who wanted to abolish slavery.

armistice   A temporary stop in fighting. Often in effect before a final peace treaty is signed.

border state   A state in the region between the Deep South and the free states of the North. States, such as Kentucky, often were caught in the debate between proslavery and antislavery groups. Many of the compromises negotiated regarding slaves were initiated in the border states.

caucus   A meeting of members of a political group.

Conscience Whigs   A group of antislavery members of the Whig Party.

dark horse   A candidate nominated at a political convention who had not been a serious contender before the convention. The first dark horse candidate for president was James J. Polk.

doughface   A northern man with southern principles or sympathies.

filibustering   A term used to describe the invasion or attempt to invade various Latin American areas to attempt to add them to the slaveholding regions of the

United States. The word originated from *filibustero*, meaning a freebooter or pirate.

Free-Soiler	A term used to describe people who opposed the expansion of slavery into the territories. It came from the name of a small political party in the election of 1848.
Great American Desert	The treeless area in the plains most Americans considered unsuitable for settlement. It generally was passed over by settlers going to the Pacific coast areas.
joint resolution	An act passed by both houses of Congress with a simple majority rather than the two-thirds majority in the Senate.
lame-duck presidency	The portion of a president's term between the time when his party fails to win an election and the time he officially leaves office.
Manifest Destiny	The belief that the United States was destined to grow from the Atlantic to the Pacific and from the Arctic to the tropics. Providence supposedly intended for Americans to have this area for a great experiment in liberty.
missions	Outposts established by the Spanish along the northern frontier to aid in Christianizing the native peoples. They also were used to exploit their labor.
Old Northwest	The region west of Pennsylvania, north of the Ohio River and east of the Mississippi River.
omnibus bill	Grouping a number of items together in an attempt to get them passed. Often used to enact controversial legislation.
personal liberty laws	Laws enacted by nine northern states to prohibit the use of state facilities, such as jails or law officers, in the recapture of fugitive slaves.
plurality	An election won by less than a majority.
polygamy	The act of having more than one wife.
popular sovereignty	The concept that settlers of each territory would decide for themselves whether to allow slavery.
presidios	Military posts constructed by the Spanish to protect the settlers from hostile Indians. They also were used to keep non-Spanish settlers from the area.
saint	A name used by the Church of Jesus Christ of Latter-Day Saints, or Mormons, to describe a member of their religious group.
tejanos	Spanish-speaking settlers of Texas. The term comes from the Spanish word *Tejas* for Texas.
underground railroad	A small group that helped slaves escape bondage in the South. It took on legendary status and its role was much exaggerated.

Young America movement	A group of young members of the Democratic Party who were interested in territorial expansion in the 1840s.
Zion	A term used by the Mormons to describe their "promised land," where they could prosper and live without persecution.

WHO? WHAT? WHERE?

WHO WERE THEY?

Complete each statement below (questions 1–14) by writing the letter preceding the appropriate name in the space provided. Use each answer only once.

a. Harriet Beecher Stowe
b. Henry Clay
c. James Mason
d. John Tyler
e. Lewis Cass
f. Martin Van Buren
g. Millard Fillmore
h. Narciso Lopez
i. Nicholas Trist
j. Pierre Soulé
k. Richard Henry Dana
l. Stephen W. Kearny
m. William Walker
n. Zachary Taylor

_____ 1. Author of a book on the wonders of California.

_____ 2. President who wanted to annex Texas as part of an attempt to promote southern support for his weak administration.

_____ 3. American general ordered to advance to the Rio Grande by President Polk.

_____ 4. American commander of an army of frontiersmen who went west from Fort Leavenworth to capture Santa Fe and California.

_____ 5. Diplomat who signed the treaty that ended the Mexican War, despite orders recalling him.

_____ 6. Senator originally identified with the idea of popular sovereignty.

_____ 7. Free-Soil candidate for president in 1848.

_____ 8. Nationalist from Kentucky and the most respected member of the Senate.

_____ 9. Conservative president from New York who gave his support to the Compromise of 1850.

_____ 10. Senator from Virginia who sponsored the Fugitive Slave Act.

_____ 11. Author of *Uncle Tom's Cabin*.

_____ 12. Organizer of the first filibustering expedition against Cuba.

_____ 13. Louisiana diplomat who was responsible for the Ostend Manifesto, calling for the acquisition of Cuba.

_____ 14. American who proclaimed himself president of Nicaragua and recruited southerners for an invasion of Central America.

WHAT WAS IT?

Complete each statement below (questions 1–4) by writing the letter preceding the appropriate response in the space provided. Use each answer only once.

    a. "Fifty-four forty or fight"
    b. Nashville Convention
    c. Oregon fever
    d. *Prigg* v. *Pennsylvania*

_____ 1. Wave that swept through the Mississippi Valley, persuading large numbers of farmers to trek two thousand miles to the Pacific coast.

_____ 2. Slogan used by some Americans to demand all of Oregon territory.

_____ 3. Supreme Court decision that relieved state officials of any obligation to enforce the return of fugitive slaves.

_____ 4. Meeting of southerners to organize resistance to northern demands.

WHERE WAS IT?

Complete each statement below (questions 1–8) by writing the letter preceding the appropriate response in the space provided. Use each answer only once.

    a. Alamo
    b. Boston, Massachusetts
    c. California
    d. Cuba
    e. Great Salt Lake
    f. Independence, Missouri
    g. Rio Grande
    h. Veracruz

_____ 1. Town where the Oregon Trail and the trade routes with Santa Fe began.

_____ 2. Basin area that the Mormon exodus regarded as their Zion.

_____ 3. Spanish mission converted to a fort that became a symbol of the Texas Revolution.

——— 4. Location of a coastal fortress conquered by General Winfield Scott in 1847.

——— 5. River designated as the boundary between the United States and Mexico.

——— 6. Territory whose admission to statehood was a major issue in the Compromise of 1850.

——— 7. City where the greatest opposition to the fugitive slave law developed.

——— 8. Spanish territory that the South wanted to convert into slave states.

CHARTS, MAPS, AND ILLUSTRATIONS

1. Examine the map showing the overland trails (p. 458). What river did the Oregon Trail, California Trail, and Mormon Trek begin with? _____

2. In the painting romanticizing westward expansion (p. 452), locate six methods of transportation and communication. _____

3. What was unusual about the picture of General John E. Wool and his staff (p. 465)?
_____

4. The painting of a slave auction (p. 469) hints at one of the ugliest dimensions of the slave trade. What was it? _____

MULTIPLE CHOICE

Circle the letter that best completes each statement.

1. Manifest Destiny refers to
   a. Native American land claims.
   b. unbridled expansion by Americans.
   c. Protestant religious dogma.
   d. United States government regulations on trade.

2. The ranching economy of the nineteenth-century American West was built on
   a. Irish foundations.
   b. Portuguese foundations.
   c. German foundations.
   d. Hispanic foundations.

3. The term *presidio* refers to
   a. a new type of frontier housing.
   b. a new type of longhorn cattle.
   c. a military post.
   d. an Indian reservation.

4. Who succeeded Joseph Smith as Mormon leader?
   a. Timothy Dwight
   b. Joseph Smith, Jr.

    c. Brigham Young

    d. William Miller

5. By the 1830s, problems arose between the United States and Mexico. Which one of the following statements does not accurately portray the situation?

    a. American settlers in Texas never were wanted by the Mexican government.

    b. American settlers in Texas retained their Protestant religion.

    c. American settlers in Texas defied Mexican law abolishing slavery.

    d. American settlers in Texas outnumbered Mexicans six to one by 1835.

6. Mexican forces were commanded by General Antonio Lopez de Santa Anna, while the revolutionary army made up of Texans was commanded by

    a. Davy Crockett.

    b. Jim Bowie.

    c. William Travis.

    d. Sam Houston.

7. The victorious Texans established their new republic and petitioned for annexation to the United States. Annexation was delayed for all of the following reasons except

    a. The republic had not met requirements for annexation.

    b. Some were concerned that annexation would provoke a war with Mexico.

    c. Some feared political ramifications of annexation.

    d. Abolitionists charged that annexation was a proslavery plot.

8. American victory in the Mexican War was due largely to the military expertise of "Old Fuss and Feathers," also known as

    a. Stephen Watts Kearny.

    b. Zachary Taylor.

    c. Winfield Scott.

    d. John C. Frémont.

9. Which one of the following statements concerning the Wilmot Proviso is incorrect?

    a. It framed the national debate over slavery for the next fifteen years.

    b. Discussion of it created a sectional division between Whigs and Democrats.

    c. On August 8, 1846, it was offered by Democratic Congressman James Russell Lowell as an amendment to an army appropriations bill.

    d. It stated that neither slavery nor involuntary servitude would exist in territory gained from the Republic of Mexico.

10. When discussing the Treaty of Guadalupe Hidalgo, signed on February 2, 1848, which of the following statements is incorrect?

    a. The treaty involved paying Mexico $15 million.

    b. The treaty sheared off a small portion of Mexico, approximately one eighth, and did little to increase United States's territory.

    c. American diplomat and negotiator Nicholas Trist refused presidential orders recalling him back to Washington until after the treaty was signed.

    d. Half the opposition to the treaty came from Democrats who wanted more Mexican territory and half from Whigs who wanted none.

11. In February of 1847, which of the following people formulated the "southern rights" position directly challenging the Wilmot Proviso?
    a. James K. Polk
    b. John C. Calhoun
    c. John P. Hale
    d. James Buchanan

12. The concept "popular sovereignty" refers to
    a. a system of government in which many of the means of production and trade are owned by the government.
    b. a period of reduced economic activity, less serious than a depression.
    c. letting settlers of each territory decide for themselves whether to permit slavery.
    d. the greatest number of votes cast for a candidate, but not more than half of the votes cast.

13. During the election of 1848, a new third political party was formed that
    a. nominated Lewis Cass.
    b. nominated Zachary Taylor.
    c. approved of slavery for territories, but not states.
    d. called for no more slave states or territories.

14. Political organization of California came out of necessity, due to a tremendous influx of settlers after the discovery of gold. Which one of the following was not a factor of organization?
    a. Coastal ports had to be regulated for military vessels.
    b. Mining camps needed law and order.
    c. Settlers needed courts, land and water laws, and mail service.
    d. In New Mexico, the sixty thousand former Mexican citizens, now Americans, needed a governmental structure.

15. In 1850, Henry Clay once again hoped to turn a crisis into an opportunity for compromise. One of his proposals stated that
    a. California would be admitted as a slave state.
    b. the Texas boundary dispute would be settled in favor of Texas.
    c. slave trade would continue in the District of Columbia.
    d. Congress had no jurisdiction over the interstate slave trade.

16. Of the following people, which one did not support a strong national fugitive slave law?
    a. Henry Clay
    b. John C. Calhoun
    c. William H. Seward
    d. Daniel Webster

17. The Compromise of 1850 finally was successful due mainly to the efforts of the young Senator
    a. Daniel Webster.
    b. Stephen A. Douglas.

c. Henry Clay.
d. John C. Calhoun.

18. The Compromise of 1850 included all of the following except
    a. the organization of New Mexico and Utah as territories, with some restrictions against slavery.
    b. the admission of California as a free state.
    c. the passage of a new fugitive slave law.
    d. the elimination of slave trade in the District of Columbia and the guarantee of slavery there.

19. Fugitive slaves became an issue because of all the following except
    a. Southern slaveowners demanded more specific regulations.
    b. The Constitution required that escaped slaves be returned but did not specifically state how that should be done.
    c. Officials in free states were not always willing to cooperate.
    d. Professional slave-catchers sometimes went too far—kidnapping free blacks, forging false affidavits to "prove" they were slaves, and selling them south into bondage.

20. The fugitive slave law included all of the following provisions except
    a. It created a federal commissioner to issue warrants for the arrest of fugitives.
    b. Fugitives could give testimony and call witnesses to support their case.
    c. The commissioner was paid five dollars if he let the fugitive go and ten dollars if he returned a fugitive to the owner.
    d. Any citizen who harbored a fugitive or refused to assist marshals could be fined and/or imprisoned.

21. As used during the antebellum period, the term *filibustering* means
    a. the use of private armies to seize territory for the purpose of adding it to the United States.
    b. the practice of dividing an organization into contentious, or self-seeking, groups.
    c. the right of the government to take private property forcibly but with compensation for public purposes.
    d. the right to buy or sell anything to anyone across national borders without regulation or taxes.

22. Between 1849 and 1861, the focus of the slavery-expansion controversy had shifted from
    a. Cuba to Nicaragua to Kansas.
    b. Cuba to California to Nicaragua.
    c. Nicaragua to Cuba to Kansas.
    d. Kansas to California to Cuba.

ESSAY

Description and Explanation (one- to two-paragraph essay)

1. Describe the role of the slavery issue in the annexation of Texas.

2. Describe the different views of progress that were held by the Whigs and the Democrats.

3. Describe the factors that help split the northern Democrats from President Polk.

4. List the provisions of the Compromise of 1850 and explain the role of Stephen A. Douglas in its enactment.

5. Describe the impact of *Uncle Tom's Cabin* on the North and the South and how the sections reacted differently.

6. Describe the role of the filibusters in Cuba and Nicaragua and why some southerners wanted these areas.

Discussion and Analysis (class discussion or one- to two-paragraph essay)

1. Compare the views of Manifest Destiny and westward expansion that might be held by a white American, a Native American, or an Hispanic. What were the differences between males and females?

2. Describe the military campaigns of the Mexican War.

3. Discuss the positions of John C. Calhoun, William H. Seward, and Daniel Webster on slavery and the government as expressed during the debates of 1850.

What If (include an explanation of your position)

1. If you were a woman in the 1840s, would you want to move to Oregon?

2. If you were Henry Clay, would you be pleased or dismayed by the Compromise of 1850?

3. If you were a runaway slave living in Boston, what would be your reaction to the Fugitive Slave Act of 1850?

Crossword Puzzle: Manifest Destiny: An Empire for Liberty—or Slavery?

ACROSS

1. Old Fuss and Feathers
7. West Pointer
9. Career for old Rough and Ready
10. His road to Gettysburg went by way of Mexico
11. Military posts of New Spain
14. Goal of travelers on Santa Fe Trail
15. Conjunction
16. Popular prefix
17. Sailor who sang the praises of old California
19. Faded, dull
20. March 7, 1850, activity for Daniel Webster
21. Douglas, Lincoln compared to Clay, Calhoun, Webster
24. Kansas conflict of 1850s (2 words)
25. Ostend wheeler-dealer
26. Number of states prior to Compromise of 1850

DOWN

1. Congressional nightmare for Calhoun (2 words)
2. Tempting target for William Walker
3. Jumping off point for the Oregon Trail
4. Brigham's saints
5. Underground railroad feature
6. He bent but didn't break at Buena Vista
8. Promotion
12. Pull the plug
13. "Higher law" senator
18. Stowe on slavery
22. He applied what he learned in Mexico against Robert E. Lee
23. Pocket protector for congressional hotheads

ANSWER KEY

WHO? WHAT? WHERE?

Who Were They?

1. k. Richard Henry Dana, p. 455
2. d. John Tyler, p. 462
3. n. Zachary Taylor, p. 465
4. l. Stephen W. Kearny, p. 466
5. i. Nicholas Trist, p. 469
6. e. Lewis Cass, p. 470
7. f. Martin Van Buren, p. 471
8. b. Henry Clay, p. 474
9. g. Millard Fillmore, p. 475
10. c. James Mason, p. 476
11. a. Harriet Beecher Stowe, p. 478
12. h. Narciso Lopez, p. 479
13. j. Pierre Soulé, p. 480
14. m. William Walker, p. 480

What Was It?

1. c. Oregon fever, p. 456
2. a. "Fifty-four forty or fight," p. 464
3. d. *Prigg* v. *Pennsylvania*, p. 473
4. b. Nashville Convention, p. 473

Where Was It?

1. f. Independence, Missouri, p. 457
2. e. Great Salt Lake, p. 460
3. a. Alamo, p. 462
4. h. Veracruz, p. 468
5. g. Rio Grande, p. 469
6. c. California, p. 473

7. b. Boston, p. 477
8. d. Cuba, p. 479

CHARTS, MAPS, AND ILLUSTRATIONS

1. Missouri River, p. 458
2. stagecoach, railroad, telegraph, wagons, horseback, foot, p. 452
3. One of the earliest known military photographs, p. 465
4. Separation of families, p. 469

MULTIPLE CHOICE

1. b. (p. 454)
2. d. (p. 454)
3. c. (p. 455)
4. c. (p. 456)
5. a. (p. 460)
6. d. (p. 462)
7. a. (p. 463)
8. c. (p. 465)
9. c. (p. 468)
10. b. (pp. 469–470)
11. b. (p. 470)
12. c. (p. 470)
13. d. (p. 471)
14. a. (p. 471)
15. d. (p. 474)
16. c. (p. 474)
17. b. (p. 475)
18. a. (p. 475)
19. a. (p. 475)

20. b. (p. 476)

21. a. (p. 479)

22. a. (p. 479)

ESSAY

Description and Explanation

1. pp. 462–463

2. p. 468

3. pp. 468–469

4. p. 475

5. pp. 478–479

6. pp. 479–481

Discussion and Analysis

1. pp. 454–455, 457–459

2. pp. 465–468

3. p. 474

What If

1. pp. 458–459

2. pp. 474–475

3. pp. 476–478

Crossword Puzzle

CHAPTER 14

THE GATHERING TEMPEST, 1853–1860

In the 1850s, the battle over slavery in the territories involved areas that had been designated as free by the Missouri Compromise more than thirty years before. By 1853, settlers had pushed up the Missouri River, and businessmen were talking about a railroad to the Pacific. This led to the congressional act to organize Nebraska as a territory. After heated debate, Congress produced the Kansas-Nebraska Act, which divided the area into two territories, Kansas and Nebraska, and broached the possibility of slavery in them. Reaction to the bill was intense—the northern branch of the Democratic Party lost control of the House of Representatives as a result. The Republican Party was formed and became the largest party in the North by 1856, hastening the destruction of the Whigs as a national party.

In the decade after 1845, the highest proportional volume of immigration in American history took place. A wave of nativism sprang up in reaction to the streams of immigrants flooding some parts of the country. This nativistic mood culminated in the formation of the "Know-Nothing," or American, Party. During the same period, the United States became the second-leading industrial producer in the world as it adapted new technology in business and transportation. Changes in the economy increased the differences between the North and the South. Some diversification took place in the South, but the northern economy was growing much faster.

Gradually, southerners became more involved in defending slavery than in promoting economic growth. During the short-lived but intense Panic of 1857, the South largely escaped the effects of the depression, and this justified their feeling that they possessed a superior economy. Many northerners blamed the South for causing the panic or for blocking measures that would aid in northern development.

Meanwhile, violence erupted in Kansas as a result of questionable election returns. The Supreme Court delivered a decision in the controversial Dred Scott case. Numerous other incidents wounded relations between the North and South. The decade ended with a violent attack on Harpers Ferry by a radical abolitionist, producing noticeably different reactions from the North and South and demonstrating the growing split in the political atmosphere of the United States.

LIBERTY, EQUALITY, POWER

The decade of the 1850s resulted in an entangled relationship between liberty, equality, and power. The growth in nonslave states increased their economic power. The influx of immigrants seeking liberty and economic freedom threatened many native-born Americans, who felt that their political power was being diluted. Nativists felt that the way to control immigrants was by denying them the right to hold office and lengthening the time it took to become a naturalized citizen.

The Supreme Court decision in the Dred Scott case denied African Americans their equal rights under the law by stripping them of citizenship, as well as of the right to sue in courts. Most southern whites believed in equality, as long as one was referring to the "master race," but not in equality for anyone who did not fit into the category of white male. They thought all classes of whites, including nonslaveowners, were equal in their whiteness.

OBJECTIVES

After studying this chapter, a student should be able to

1. Analyze the role of Stephen A. Douglas in the Kansas-Nebraska Act.

2. Describe the death of the Whig Party and the organization of the Republican Party.

3. Discuss the changes in immigration and the rise of nativism as a reaction to immigration.

4. Describe the American system of manufacturing and the advantages of the United States for the development of technology.

5. Compare and contrast the economy, North and South, in the 1850s.

6. Analyze the effects of the Panic of 1857 on relations between the sections.

7. Trace the deterioration in the relationship between the sections as shown in the political changes of the 1850s, the different types of literature published, and various incidents, including the caning of Senator Sumner and the raid on Harpers Ferry.

CHRONOLOGY

1844–1856   Americans enjoyed a significant increase in per capita production and income. The value of exports and imports increased by 200 percent; the tonnage of coal mined by 270 percent; the amount of banking capital, industrial capital, and industrial output by approximately 100 percent; the value of farmland by 100 percent; and the amount of cotton, wheat, and corn harvested by about 70 percent.

1845–1855   Three million immigrants entered the United States—15 percent of the total American population. This was the highest proportional volume of immigration in American history.

1846   James D. B. DeBow, a young champion of economic diversification in the South, founded a New Orleans periodical that came to be known as *DeBow's Review*. On the cover page, this publication proclaimed that "Cotton Is King," and set out to make this slogan a southern reality.

1850   Between 1845 and 1855, cotton prices and production doubled in the South. This time of prosperity encouraged many southerners to call for economic independence from the North.

1850s   The most-discussed issues of state and local government were temperance and schools.

Almost three quarters of public-school educators in New England were women, a trend that spread into the Middle Atlantic states and the Old Northwest.

Economic diversification in the South progressed. Slave states quadrupled their railroad mileage, increased the amount of capital invested in manufacturing by 77 percent, and boosted their output of cotton textiles by 44 percent. However, the North made similar strides, and the slave states' share of the nation's manufacturing capacity actually dropped from 18 to 16 percent during the decade.

The widespread adoption of the recently invented sewing machine lowered per-unit piecework wages of seamstresses, forcing them to turn out more shirts and trousers than before.

1850–1855   The political power of immigrants grew in comparison to that of native-born voters. In Boston, for example, the number of foreign-born voters (mostly Irish) increased by 200 percent, while the number of native-born voters grew by only 14 percent.

1851   Beginning with Maine in 1851, twelve states established prohibition laws over the next four years. Initially, temperance crusaders associated drunkenness and rowdiness with Irish immigrants, which resulted in heightened ethnic tension.

1853   A House bill creating the Nebraska Territory, an area from Indian Territory to the Canadian border, increased tensions and ignited the long debate over slave versus free states.

1854   The American Party, or "Know Nothings," burst onto the political scene. This new faction was the result of a merger between two secret fraternal societies that restricted membership to native-born Protestants. The informal name of "Know Nothings" was derived from the membership pledge of secrecy about the association: If asked, they were to reply, "I know nothing."

As large numbers of settlers poured into Kansas, battle lines were established in the slave versus free-soil debate. In the fall of 1854, 1,700 illegal votes were cast to send a proslavery territorial delegate to Congress.

mid-1850s   The tonnage of freight carried on the East-West rail and water routes was more than double the North-South river tonnage. The growth rate of industrial output in the free states west of Pennsylvania was double that of the Northeast and triple that of the South.

1855   The volume of immigration dropped by more than half and stayed low for the next several years. Accordingly, nativism faded and ethnic tensions eased.

During the **winter** of 1854–1855, more settlers came to Kansas looking for a political fight rather than good land. Approximately five thousand illegal votes were cast to elect a proslavery territorial legislature.

1856

By **January**, there were two territorial governments in Kansas, one officially authorized, but fraudulently elected, and one unauthorized, with majority support. Kansas soon became the leading issue in national politics and a testing ground for the Civil War factions.

In **May**, a minor civil war broke out as armed proslavery Missourians marched on the free-state capital of Lawrence, Kansas. The term "bleeding Kansas" was born.

Senator Charles Sumner of Massachusetts was severely injured by Congressman Preston Brooks of South Carolina on the floor of Congress. This was one of the escalating incidents of violence between the North and the South.

The Republicans became the largest party in the North and the first truly sectional party in American history.

James Buchanan, a Democrat who was left unscathed by the Kansas-Nebraska controversy, since he had been out of the country during that time, was elected president in **November**.

1857

The proslavery legislature, fraudulently elected two years earlier, called for a constitutional convention at Lecompton to prepare Kansas for statehood. In **December**, eligible voters overwhelmingly rejected constitutions, one with no slavery and one with slavery. This split the Democratic Party, and Kansas would not be admitted to statehood for some time.

George Fitzhugh, a Virginia farmer and lawyer, compiled his newspaper writings in *Cannibals All*. This work, and his earlier *Sociology for the South*, promoted slavery as a paternal institution that guaranteed protection of workers. In contrast, Fitzhugh proclaimed free-labor capitalism was exploited by the strong and starved the weak.

Hinton Rowan Helper's *The Impending Crisis of the South* was virtually banned in the South. In his book, Helper, who considered himself a spokesman for the nonslaveholding whites of the South, painted an ominous picture of economic backwardness, caused by slavery, in the South. Along with the writings of Fitzhugh, Helper exacerbated sectional tensions in the **summer** of 1857.

The Panic of 1857, a short-lived but intense depression during the **fall**, intensified sectional hostility, because the South largely escaped the effects of it. This gave false assurance to many southerners, who boasted about their superior economy and labor systems.

Supreme Court Justice Roger B. Taney delivered the majority decision in *Dred Scott* v. *Sanford*, which declared that neither Scott nor any slave was a citizen under the Constitution and, therefore, could not sue. In addition, the Court declared that Congress did not have the power to keep slavery out of a territory because slaves were property and the Constitution protected the right of property.

1858   The central issue of seven debates in Illinois between Abraham Lincoln and Stephen A. Douglas was slavery. These debates turned out to be a dress rehearsal for the presidential election of 1860.

1859   In **October**, John Brown launched an attack on the federal arsenal at Harpers Ferry. The purpose of this attack was to obtain weapons for slaves to lead a revolt in the South. It was thwarted when commanders Robert E. Lee and J.E.B. Stuart captured members of the raiding party. This attempt by Brown set off waves of alarm and suspicion throughout the South.

1860   Free states in the United States made significant strides in education, which resulted in a literacy rate of approximately 95 percent for adults and almost 100 percent for children who had received a few years of schooling. In the South, however, approximately 85 percent of the free population and 10 percent of slaves were literate.

The North had five times more industrial output per capita than the South and three times the railroad capital and mileage per thousand square miles. Almost 80 percent of the North's labor force worked in manufacturing, although farming remained the largest single occupation, at 40 percent of the labor force.

GLOSSARY OF IMPORTANT TERMS

Black Republicans   Those who believed that the Republican Party stood for racial equality. The Democrats used this fear to convince many whites to remain loyal to them.

bona fide   Acting in good faith.

bushwhacking   The act of attacking from a hidden place, usually suddenly.

colonial economy   An economy based on the export of agricultural products and the import of manufactured goods.

demagoguery   The act of appealing to the emotions and prejudices of people, often to get elected to office.

dissenter   A person who disagrees openly with the majority opinion.

evangelical   A term used to describe crusading zeal or enthusiasm, often associated with a religious group.

free labor ideology   The belief that all work in a free society is honorable and that manual labor is degraded when it is equated with slavery or bondage.

guerilla warfare	A type of warfare conducted by irregular units or small groups.
herrenvolk **democracy**	A concept that emphasized the equality of all who belonged to the master race—not all mankind.
interchangeable parts	An industrial technique using machine tools to cut and shape a large number of similar parts that can be fitted together with other parts to make an entire item, such as a gun.
mudsill	The lowest sill of a structure, directly on the ground or foundation. In this chapter, the "structure" is the social scale, and "mudsill" refers to the belief by some whites that slavery formed a mudsill of blacks that kept whites from the bottom of society.
nativism	An attitude that favors the interest of native-born Americans over immigrants.
parochial schools	Schools associated with a church, usually Roman Catholic, but not always. The funding of these became a major political issue in the 1850s.
per capita	A term used to describe income and production and means "per person."
red herring	A term used to describe an issue used to distract voters from more controversial or serious issues.
referendum	The procedure of allowing voters to cast their votes on controversial issues alone. This was expected to settle the slavery issue in Kansas peacefully, but it did not.
religious bigotry	The intolerance of one by another based on religious beliefs or practices.
straddle the fence	Description of a political party that refuses to take a firm stand on a controversial issue. This was fairly common in the years before the Civil War when the parties were uncertain about the opinions of the voters.
temperance	The act of abstaining from the partaking of alcoholic beverages.

WHO? WHAT? WHERE?

WHO WERE THEY?

Complete each statement below (questions 1–12) by writing the letter preceding the appropriate name in the space provided. Use each answer only once.

a. Abraham Lincoln
b. George Fitzhugh
c. Hinton Rowan Helper
d. James D. B. DeBow
e. John Brown
f. John C. Frémont
g. John Hughes

  h. Preston Brooks
  i. Roger B. Taney
  j. Stephen A. Douglas
  k. Samuel Colt
  l. Winfield Scott

_____ 1. Sponsor of the Senate bill organizing Kansas and Nebraska into territories.

_____ 2. Military hero and the last Whig candidate for president.

_____ 3. Catholic archbishop of New York and spokesman for the church.

_____ 4. Congressman from South Carolina who tried to avenge a relative's honor by caning a senator.

_____ 5. First Republican candidate for president and known sometimes as the "Pathfinder of the West."

_____ 6. Supreme Court chief justice who delivered the majority decision in the Dred Scott case.

_____ 7. Inventor of the six-shooter and early user of interchangeable parts.

_____ 8. Journal editor from the South who encouraged greater economic diversification for the area.

_____ 9. Virginia author of two books containing comparisons of free labor, capitalism, and slavery that made slavery seem beneficial.

_____ 10. North Carolina author who considered himself the spokesman of the nonslaveholding South.

_____ 11. Creator of the phrase "a house divided against itself cannot stand."

_____ 12. User of the biblical quote "Without shedding of blood, there is no remission of sin."

WHAT WAS IT?

Complete each statement below (questions 1–7) by writing the letter preceding the appropriate response in the space provided. Use each answer only once.

  a. border ruffians
  b. Black Republicans
  c. free labor ideology
  d. Kansas-Nebraska Act
  e. Know Nothings
  f. Lecompton constitution
  g. "this species of property"

_____ 1. Term that southerners sometimes used to refer to slaves.

_____ 2. Congressional act that propelled Abraham Lincoln back into politics.

_____ 3. Anti-immigrant group whose members were often young, skilled workers.

_____ 4. Bands of Missourians who traveled to Kansas to install a proslavery government.

_____ 5. Group that many voters considered to be racial equalitarians.

_____ 6. Test case for popular sovereignty that was supposed to be settled in a fair election.

_____ 7. Belief that all work in a free society is honorable.

WHERE WAS IT?

Complete each statement below (questions 1–7) by writing the letter preceding the appropriate response in the space provided. Use each answer only once.

  a. Chicago, Illinois
  b. Freeport, Illinois
  c. Harpers Ferry, Virginia
  d. Lynn, Massachusetts
  e. Old Northwest
  f. Pottawatomie Creek
  g. Ripon, Wisconsin

_____ 1. Small town where the name Republican Party first was used.

_____ 2. Location of a murderous attack on a proslavery settlement.

_____ 3. Town used by fifteen rail lines in the 1850s.

_____ 4. Location of a strike of shoemakers that became the largest in the United States up to that time.

_____ 5. Region where such measures as the Homestead Act and land grants to colleges were especially popular.

_____ 6. Town attacked to gain weapons to arm slaves.

_____ 7. Village where the most famous debates in the senatorial election of 1858 took place.

CHARTS, MAPS, AND ILLUSTRATIONS

  1. The location of the first Republican convention was _____.

  2. According to the graph on immigration (p. 488), what were two events in Europe that caused an increase in immigration to the United States? _____ _____ and _____

  3. According to the table on the 1856 election (p. 497), which section of the United States did not give Frémont any electoral votes? _____

  4. On the maps showing railroads in 1850 and 1860 (p. 500), which section had the greatest growth in railroad construction? _____

MULTIPLE CHOICE

Circle the letter that best completes each statement.

1. After California was admitted as a free state, proslavery forces were determined to salvage something from Nebraska. It was in this spirit that a senator from Missouri vowed to see Nebraska "sink in hell" before becoming free soil. He was
   a. David R. Atchison.
   b. John C. Calhoun.
   c. Stephen A. Douglas.
   d. Jefferson Davis.

2. Of the following people, which one exhibited a "care not" attitude and did not have strong convictions concerning slavery?
   a. Stephen A. Douglas
   b. Abraham Lincoln
   c. John C. Calhoun
   d. David R. Atchison

3. During the decade after 1845, three million immigrants entered the United States—15 percent of the total American population in 1845—and most of them were
   a. highly skilled.
   b. Japanese.
   c. Protestant.
   d. Roman Catholic.

4. Immigrants often were not readily accepted due to all of the following factors except
   a. They were resented for possessing highly technical skills and an education.
   b. They spoke a foreign language.
   c. They had alien cultural values.
   d. They were blamed for an increase in crime and poverty in cities.

5. Political power of immigrants grew with their numbers, and most belonged to the
   a. Whig Party.
   b. Democratic Party.
   c. Free-Soil Party.
   d. Republican Party.

6. Two of the hottest issues in state and local politics during the early 1850s were
   a. temperance and schools.
   b. slavery and transportation.
   c. temperance and slavery.
   d. sanitation and schools.

7. The "Know Nothings," formally known as the American Party, can be described as all of the following except
   a. the party resulting from a merger in 1852 of two secret fraternal societies.
   b. limiting membership to native-born Protestants in skilled blue-collar and lower white-collar occupations.

c. instructing members to vote for certain candidates or parties at election time.

d. generally supporting increased taxes for parochial schools and seeking to shorten the naturalization for citizenship.

8. By the mid-1850s, Kansas was a mixture of all of the following except
   a. the normal migration of settlers from adjoining states.
   b. free-soilers and northern settlers migrating for good land.
   c. Missourians who were prepared to vote as many times as necessary to install a pro-slavery government.
   d. Chinese who formerly had worked building railroads and now wanted to become small farmers.

9. The first truly sectional party in American history was
   a. Republican.
   b. Democratic.
   c. Whig.
   d. Know Nothing.

10. All of the following statements describe the election of 1856 except
    a. Republicans denied racial equality and insisted they wanted no slavery in the territories, thus limiting competition from black labor.
    b. Democrats focused on federal aid for internal improvements, including a railroad to California.
    c. James Buchanan owed his election to the South, where he received three fourths of the electoral votes needed for victory.
    d. Fear originating from southern threats of secession caused many ex-Whigs in the North to support Buchanan over Frémont or Fillmore.

11. Dred Scott was
    a. a slave.
    b. an army doctor.
    c. a Supreme Court justice.
    d. a former congressman.

12. The Dred Scott case
    a. began legal proceedings in Kansas.
    b. was a test case of Congress's power to prohibit slavery in the territories.
    c. ultimately was heard by the Supreme Court, which contained a majority of five justices from free states.
    d. affirmed that slaves were not property if they lived in a free territory more than one year.

13. Of the following statements, which one is an incorrect description of events surrounding the Lecompton constitution?
    a. Stephen Douglas regarded the Lecompton constitution as a travesty of popular sovereignty.
    b. It caused a long, bitter fight in Congress, where two dozen northern Democrats defected.

    c. Lecompton was defeated, and both sides accepted a compromise proposal to resubmit the constitution to Kansas voters, who rejected it.

    d. President Buchanan never gave in to southern threats and stood by his promise of a fair referendum.

14. The economy in the 1850s can be described by all of the following except
    a. There was a significant increase in per capita production and income.
    b. There existed an expanding economy in all areas, not including coal mining or farm production.
    c. The value of both exports and imports increased by 200 percent.
    d. There was a widening of the economic distance between rich and poor.

15. By the later 1850s, the United States was the second-leading industrial producer in the world, behind only
    a. Germany.
    b. France.
    c. Britain.
    d. China.

16. Mass production using interchangeable parts resulted in
    a. less expensive and more widely available products.
    b. higher wages for skilled craftsmen.
    c. more elegant and more durable products.
    d. more expensive and rare products.

17. By the 1850s, southern corps provided three fifths of all U.S. exports. Of the following crops, which one supplied more than half of all exports?
    a. sugar
    b. cotton
    c. tobacco
    d. indigo

18. All of the following statements describe labor conditions in the North except
    a. Average per capita income was 10 percent less in the North as compared with the South.
    b. Many people worked sixty or seventy hours a week and earned less than a living wage.
    c. The invention of the sewing machine lowered the wages of seamstresses.
    d. Much employment was seasonal or intermittent, so workers were left without wages for long periods.

19. The short and intense Panic of 1857 was due to a combination of each of the following factors except
    a. American railroads built beyond the capacity of what they could earn and could not service their debts.
    b. American banks made too many risky loans.
    c. International economic events precipitated the Panic.
    d. Unprecedented winter and summer weather hurt farming and ranching industries.

20. The effects of the Panic of 1857 included which one of the following?
    a. The South was unaffected, which led to further beliefs that the South's superior economy was being pulled down by the rest of the country.
    b. The Panic decreased sectional hostilities.
    c. The depression ran its course in twenty-nine months, compared with the previous eight-year depression.
    d. Violence was widespread and three people died in demonstrations.

21. *The Impending Crisis of the South* by Hinton Rowan Helper
    a. was very popular and widely read by southern whites.
    b. was criticized and virtually prohibited in the North.
    c. was based on selective 1850 census statistics, which portrayed a South mired in economic backwardness.
    d. portrayed a South working to improve education and living, economic, and labor conditions for everyone.

22. The Lincoln-Douglas debates focused primarily on the issue of
    a. transportation.
    b. slavery.
    c. the economy.
    d. immigrants.

23. John Brown intended to use the weapons seized at the federal arsenal of Harpers Ferry, Virginia, to
    a. start a slave rebellion in the South.
    b. arm southerners if war broke out.
    c. start a rebellion among the four hundred thousand slaves in Cuba.
    d. arm proslavery terrorists in a planned march on the capital.

ESSAY

Description and Explanation (one- to two-paragraph essay)

1. Describe the role of Stephen A. Douglas, including his possible motives, in enacting the Kansas-Nebraska bill.

2. Describe Lincoln's view of slavery as expressed during the Kansas-Nebraska dispute and in his debates with Douglas.

3. Describe the death of the Whig Party.

4. What did native-born Americans have against immigrants?

5. Compare the majority and dissenting decisions in the Dred Scott case.

6. Explain why nonslaveowners in the South supported slavery.

7. Describe the free labor ideology and its view of the American dream.

Discussion and Analysis (class discussion or one- to two-paragraph essay)

1. Discuss the changing pattern of immigration in the 1840s and 1850s and how immigration and religious bigotry influenced politics.

2. Discuss the growth in the economy in the 1850s and compare the overall economic growth of the slave and free states.

3. Discuss the views southern authors had of the South and of slavery. Include in your discussion an analysis of the argument that slaves in the South lived better than wage-workers in the North. Was this argument believable?

4. Discuss the increasing sectional tension as evidenced in reactions to the Dred Scott decision, the Lecompton constitution, the Panic of 1857, and John Brown's Raid.

What If (include an explanation of your position)

1. If you were an emigrant from Ireland, would you believe that you and your lifestyle were welcome in all parts of the United States?

2. If you were a witness to John Brown's execution, would you be impressed by his behavior?

3. If you were a small farmer living in the South in the 1850s, would you support the pro-slavery arguments of many of the leaders of your region?

Crossword Puzzle: The Gathering Tempest, 1853–1860

DOWN

1. Helper on southern crisis
2. Crystal Palace event
3. Brown's action at Harpers Ferry
4. Election of 1856 had three
5. Little Giant's rival
9. Republican freebie for a farmer
11. Mr. Whitney
12. Hammond to Calhoun
16. End of the line for Brown
17. Two wheeler
18. Popular cookie
19. Home for a wage slave according to "king cotton"
22. Public relations

ACROSS

1. Seward on free v. slave state conflict
6. Exploring epithet for Frémont
7. Taney to Scott
8. Workplace for a woman
10. What Lincoln predicted "house" would cease to be
13. 51 in Roman numerals
14. Change the Constitution
15. A "Know Nothing" was one
17. Lecompton document
20. Crimean event
21. They refused to be crushed by the Dred Scott decision
23. Tempest

ANSWER KEY

WHO? WHAT? WHERE?

Who Were They?

1. j. Stephen A. Douglas, p. 484
2. l. Winfield Scott, p. 487
3. g. John Hughes, p. 489
4. h. Preston Brooks, p. 495
5. f. John C. Frémont, p. 496
6. i. Roger B. Taney, p. 498
7. k. Samuel Colt, p. 503
8. d. James D. B. DeBow, p. 504
9. b. George Fitzhugh, p. 505
10. c. Hinton Rowan Helper, p. 511
11. a. Abraham Lincoln, p. 514
12. e. John Brown, p. 515

What Was It?

1. g. "this species of property," p. 484
2. d. Kansas-Nebraska Act, p. 484
3. e. Know Nothings, p. 491
4. a. border ruffians, p. 493
5. b. Black Republicans, p. 497
6. f. Lecompton constitution, p. 499
7. c. free labor ideology, p. 510

Where Was It?

1. g. Ripon, Wisconsin, p. 487
2. f. Pottawatomie Creek, p. 495
3. a. Chicago, Illinois, p. 501
4. d. Lynn, Massachusetts, p. 509
5. e. Old Northwest, p. 510

6. c. Harpers Ferry, Virginia, p. 515
7. b. Freeport, Illinois, p. 514

CHARTS, MAPS, AND ILLUSTRATIONS

1. Pittsburgh, Pennsylvania, p. 487
2. potato famine in Ireland and revolution in Germany, p. 488
3. slave states, p. 496
4. Midwest, p. 500

MULTIPLE CHOICE

1. a. (p. 484)
2. a. (p. 485)
3. d. (p. 488)
4. a. (pp. 488–489)
5. b. (p. 489)
6. a. (p. 490)
7. d. (pp. 490–491)
8. d. (p. 493)
9. a. (p. 496)
10. b. (p. 496)
11. a. (p. 498)
12. b. (p. 498)
13. d. (p. 499)
14. b. (p. 502)
15. c. (p. 502)
16. a. (pp. 502–503)
17. b. (p. 504)
18. a. (p. 508)
19. d. (p. 508)
20. a. (pp. 508–510)

21. c. (p. 511)

22. b. (p. 514)

23. a. (p. 515)

ESSAY

Description and Explanation

1. pp. 484–485

2. pp. 485–486

3. pp. 487–488

4. pp. 488–489

5. p. 498

6. p. 512

7. pp. 510–511

Discussion and Analysis

1. pp. 488–491

2. pp. 501–502, 503–505

3. pp. 505, 508, 511

4. pp. 498, 499, 509–510, 517

What If

1. pp. 498–501

2. pp. 515–517

3. p. 512

Crossword Puzzle

CHAPTER 15

SECESSION AND CIVIL WAR, 1860–1862

As 1860 began, only a few national institutions remained in the country. One of these was the Democratic Party, but it divided into northern and southern camps over the issue of slavery in the territories. By the fall of 1860, there were four candidates for president in one of the most important elections in American history. When Abraham Lincoln and the Republicans won the election, many southerners believed that it meant an end to their control of their own political destiny and a threat to the existence of slavery. Lincoln's victory provided the shock that southern secessionists needed. South Carolina seceded in December 1860, followed quickly by six other Deep South states. Delegates from the seven states met in Montgomery, Alabama, and organized the Confederate States of America.

By early 1861, attention focused on Charleston Bay, where Fort Sumter refused to surrender to the Confederates. By the time Lincoln took office, a decision had to be made about the fort. After much thought and pressure from all sides, Lincoln decided to send in unarmed ships with supplies. The Confederate government ordered the fort taken before the supplies arrived. When Lincoln declared an insurrection in the South and called on the states for men, four of the eight remaining slave states joined the Confederacy.

The economic balance sheet of war favored the Union, with its larger population, industrial capacity, registered shipping, railroad mileage, and taxable wealth. Southerners emphasized that their martial qualities were better, with a higher percentage of southerners trained for the military. They also had the advantage of being in control of their territory, and fighting on the defensive gave them early morale benefits. The Confederates failed to manage their overseas diplomacy well and did not receive vital help and support from Great Britain.

The early campaigns centered around the Virginia area, especially after the Confederate capital moved to Richmond. The battle of Manassas in 1861 bred overconfidence in the South and awakened northerners to the real dangers of the war. In other areas, the Union fared better—capturing New Orleans, Fort Henry, Fort Donelson, and Nashville. Shiloh, the Seven Days' battles, the second Bull Run, and the Shenandoah Valley campaigns made it obvious that defeating the South would not be easy. By early fall 1862, Robert E. Lee's Army of Northern Virginia had begun an offensive by invading Maryland. Many issues, such as foreign recognition and control of the national government, awaited the outcome of this invasion.

LIBERTY, EQUALITY, POWER

For much of the period since the Revolution, the national government had been controlled by the South. Many southerners saw the election of Lincoln as a loss of power over their destiny. Southerners considered secession to be one of their rights and liberties. Northerners thought the southerners were rebelling to protect only slavery, not liberty. While both sides mobilized their armies and marshaled their resources, it became clear that this war would be determined by the side with more power. Most of the issues of the day, such as liberty, equality, and power for various groups, rested on what happened on the battlefield. By the middle of 1862, it was not certain which side had more military power.

OBJECTIVES

After studying this chapter, a student should be able to

1. Analyze and compare the candidates and parties in the election of 1860.

2. Compare and contrast the advantages and disadvantages of the Confederacy and the Union at the beginning of the war.

3. Describe modern forms of transportation and communications and their effects on logistics.

4. Explain Confederate and Union means of financing the war.

5. Discuss Great Britain and the Civil War, as well as the role of cotton in foreign diplomacy.

6. Describe the role that sea power and control of the rivers had for the Union.

7. Describe the war in the West in 1861 and 1862 and the Confederate counteroffensive in 1862.

CHRONOLOGY

1860   At the Democratic national convention in Charleston, South Carolina, some southern delegates insisted on a federal slave code for the territories. Instead, the 1856 platform that endorsed popular sovereignty was reaffirmed by a slim majority. A short time later, a second meeting was held in Baltimore. Southerners walked out in large numbers, organized the Southern Rights Democratic Party, and nominated a candidate for president. A group of former Whigs formed the Constitutional Union Party and nominated a candidate. The Republicans drew up a platform that appealed to many groups in the North and was attractive especially to young people. The party nominated Abraham Lincoln and entered the campaign as a united front.

In the **November** presidential election, Lincoln won every free state; most southern whites voted for Breckinridge; Bell won the conservative upper-South states and Douglas carried one state.

Abraham Lincoln's presidential victory provided the proverbial last straw for many southerners. Using the theory of secession as grounds, South Carolina voted unanimously to withdraw from its "compact" on **December 20**.

South Carolina demanded evacuation of Fort Moultrie and, on **December 26**, Major Robert Anderson moved his men to a stronger fortification.

Senator John J. Crittenden of Kentucky proposed a series of amendments that clearly favored the southern political position and slavery but found little support.

1861

Star of the West, an unarmed merchant ship carrying two hundred soldiers for Fort Sumter, was driven away by South Carolina artillery on **January 9**.

Six state conventions followed the example of South Carolina and voted to leave the Union. These states were Mississippi, Florida, Alabama, Georgia, Louisiana, and Texas. In **February**, delegates from the seceding states met in Montgomery, Alabama, to form the Confederate States of America.

Jefferson Davis and Alexander Stephens were elected provisional president and vice president for the Confederate States of America. They were used to present an image of moderation and respectability to the eight upper-South states still in the Union.

Sectional tension and a crumbling Union marred Lincoln's inauguration on **March 4**. In his inaugural address, he tried to demonstrate his peaceful intentions. The next day, the new president received dispatches informing him that provisions for Fort Sumter soon would be exhausted. After many sleepless nights, he decided to send in unarmed ships with supplies. This shifted responsibility of advocating war or peace to the Confederacy.

The Confederacy opened fire on Fort Sumter before the supplies arrived. This officially set off the Civil War or "War between the States" on **April 12**.

The first blood of the war was shed in Maryland when a mob attacked part of a Massachusetts regiment traveling through Baltimore on its way to Washington on **April 19**. The same day, Lincoln imposed a blockade of Confederate ports to shut off imports of material from abroad and exports of cotton—a source of substantial income for southern states.

Recognizing the militia was limited by law to ninety days' service, Lincoln issued a call on **May 3** for three-year volunteers to deal with the "insurrection." Afterwards, Virginia, Arkansas, Tennessee, and North Carolina seceded and joined the Confederacy.

Although small by Civil War standards, the battle of Manassas (or Bull Run, as northerners called it) in **July** boosted southern morale and gave the Confederacy the false impression that it was to be a brief war.

The Confederacy adopted a foreign policy known as "King Cotton diplomacy." Hoping to compel the British to intervene, southerners kept the 1861 cotton crop at home. By the next year, Britain had a surplus of cotton and it was more difficult for the South to export, due to the blockade.

Anticipating a short war, the Confederate Congress authorized unlimited issue of treasury notes. By the end of the year, the Confederacy had an inflation rate of 12 percent a month. Just prior to the war's end, the Confederate dollar was worth one U.S. cent.

In **summer** and **fall** elections, Unionists gained control of the Kentucky and Maryland legislatures. Kentucky Confederates reacted by forming a state government in exile.

Winfield Scott stepped down as general-in-chief and George B. McClellan took his place. Captain Charles Wilkes of the U.S.S. *San Jacinto* stopped the British mail steamer *Trent* and arrested James Mason and John Slidell, southern envoys to Britain and France. The British and American popular press stirred up war fever, but good sense prevailed on both sides. The Lincoln administration released the two Confederates with the explanation that Wilkes had acted without instructions.

1862

During the war, the infantry rifle was the most deadly weapon. From 1862 on, most weapons were "rifled" to impart a spin to the bullet, permitting greater accuracy and rapid loading and firing.

Unable to build a major navy, the Confederacy obtained the commerce raiders *Florida* and *Alabama* from a British shipyard.

The Union government raised a small amount (13 percent) of its revenue by printing treasury notes. The Legal Tender Act, passed in **February**, authorizing these "greenbacks" was the origin of modern paper money in the United States.

On **March 8**, the ironclad C.S.S. *Virginia*, usually known as the *Merrimack*, successfully attacked the blockade squadron at Hampton Roads. It has been considered the worst day in the history of the U.S. Navy until the Pearl Harbor attack in 1941. The U.S.S. *Monitor*, the Union ironclad, attacked the *Virginia* on March 9. The battle was a draw, but the ironclads launched a new age in naval history.

In the first two years of the war, most soldiers on both sides were volunteers. In mobilizing for the war, the Confederacy passed a conscription law in **April**. Almost a year later, the Union introduced its form of conscription. Most recruits from both sides continued to be volunteers.

In the battle of Shiloh, Grant snatched victory from the jaws of defeat. However, his reputation suffered because of heavy Union casualties. Soon after this, naval commander David G. Farragut captured New Orleans for the Union.

After Joseph Johnston was wounded at the battle of Seven Pines, Confederate President Jefferson Davis named Robert E. Lee to replace him.

During the **summer** and **fall**, Tennessean Nathan Bedford Forrest and Kentuckian John Hunt Morgan staged repeated raids in which they burned bridges, blew up tunnels, tore up tracks, and captured supply depots and Union garrisons.

In the second battle of Bull Run in **August**, Lee took advantage of the bickering among factions in Washington and the ill will between McClellan and John Pope to inflict another defeat on the Union army.

1863

The Confederate Congress tried to stem runaway inflation by passing an unpopular law that taxed income, consumer purchases, and business transactions, and included a "tax in kind" on farm crops.

The Union Congress modernized the American monetary system with the National Banking Act. This act authorized the chartering of national banks and attempted to replace state bank notes with a more uniform national currency.

In **March**, almost a year after the South's conscription law was passed, the Union followed suit. However, even after conscription laws in the North and South were implemented, most recruits continued to be volunteers.

1865

Congress imposed a tax of 10 percent on state bank notes, thereby taxing them out of existence.

GLOSSARY OF IMPORTANT TERMS

battery
A field artillery unit consisting normally of four or six cannons that were carried by horse-drawn vehicles known as **caissons**. This type of unit consisted of 155 men and 72 horses at the beginning of the Civil War.

blockade
The closing of a country's harbors by enemy ships to prevent trade and commerce, especially to prevent traffic in military supplies.

blockade runner
A ship designed to run through a blockade.

bushwhackers
Confederate guerilla raiders especially active in Missouri. **Jayhawkers** were the Union version of the same type of people. Both groups did a tremendous amount of damage with raids, arson, ambush, and murder.

close-order assault
Attacking with little space between men. In the face of modern weapons used during the Civil War, such fighting produced a high casualty rate.

conscription
A term used during the Civil War that referred to forcing men to serve in the military. The Confederates first introduced conscription in 1862 and the Union followed suit one year later. In the twentieth century, Americans use the term **draft** instead.

fire-eaters
Southerners who were eager, enthusiastic supporters of southern rights and later of secession.

gun turret
A low structure, often round, on a ship that moved horizontally and contained mounted guns.

legal tender
Any type of money that the government requires everyone to accept at face value.

logistics	Military activity relating to such things as the transporting, supplying, and quartering of troops and their equipment.
military organization	A company equaled one hundred men. Ten infantry companies were a **regiment.** Four or more regiments organized as a **brigade.** Three or more brigades formed a **division.** Two or more divisions formed a **corps.** Two or more corps organized together were known as **armies.** Usually disease, casualties, and desertions cut down the numbers in these units considerably.
Minié ball	A cone-shaped lead bullet whose base expanded upon firing.
morale	The general feeling of the people toward such events as a war. Good morale greatly enhances an ability to fight or sacrifice for a cause.
rifled	Process of cutting spiral grooves in a gun's barrel to impart a spin to the bullet. Perfected in the 1850s, it produced greater accuracy and longer range.
secession	The act of a state withdrawing from the Union. South Carolina was the first state to attempt to do this in 1860.
specie	Metal money or coins, usually made of gold or silver.
treasury notes	Paper money used by the Union to help finance the Civil War. One type of treasury note was known as a **greenback** because of its color.
Unionists	Southerners who remained loyal to the Union during the Civil War.

WHO? WHAT? WHERE?

WHO WERE THEY?

Complete each statement below (questions 1–17) by writing the letter preceding the appropriate name in the space provided. Use each answer only once.

a. Charles Francis Adams
b. Charles Wilkes
c. Claude Minié
d. David G. Farragut
e. George B. McClellan
f. Jefferson Davis
g. John C. Breckinridge
h. John J. Crittenden
i. Joseph E. Johnston
j. Nathaniel Lyon
k. Pierre G. T. Beauregard
l. Robert Anderson
m. Robert E. Lee
n. Ulysses S. Grant

o. William L. Yancey
p. William H. Seward
q. Winfield Scott

_____ 1. Leader of the southern delegates who withdrew from the 1860 Democratic convention.

_____ 2. Southern Democratic candidate for president in 1860.

_____ 3. Leading Republican who was considered too controversial for the presidential nomination in 1860.

_____ 4. Senator who sponsored a series of compromises to protect slavery in the territories.

_____ 5. President of the Confederacy.

_____ 6. Union commander of Fort Sumter.

_____ 7. Confederate commander of southern troops in Charleston Bay in the spring of 1861.

_____ 8. Union commander of Missouri who originally drove the Confederates out of the state and later was killed defending it.

_____ 9. Inventor of the cone-shaped lead bullet.

_____ 10. Effective American minister to Britain during the Civil War.

_____ 11. Commander of the *San Jacinto*, which stopped the British mail steamer *Trent*.

_____ 12. General-in-chief of the U.S. Army when the Civil War started and developer of the Anaconda Plan.

_____ 13. Union naval commander who captured New Orleans.

_____ 14. Union general whose experiences in life made him willing to take risks and helped him to win the first big Union victory.

_____ 15. Confederate commander at Shiloh and the highest-ranking officer killed in the Civil War.

_____ 16. Commander of the Army of Northern Virginia.

_____ 17. Organizer of the Army of the Potomac who was known sometimes as the "Young Napoleon."

WHAT WAS IT?

Complete each statement below (questions 1–5) by writing the letter preceding the appropriate response in the space provided. Use each answer only once.

a. *Alabama*
b. *Virginia*
c. Constitutional Union Party
d. cotton famine
e. National Banking Act

_____ 1. Conservative coalition of former southern and northern Whigs that nominated a candidate for president in 1860.

_____ 2. Congressional act that modernized the American monetary system.

_____ 3. Result of the technique of deliberately withholding cotton from the British market in hope of encouraging recognition.

_____ 4. Most feared of the commerce raiders built in British shipyards.

_____ 5. First ironclad ship to see action.

WHERE WAS IT?

Complete each statement below (questions 1–12) by writing the letter preceding the appropriate response in the space provided. Use each answer only once.

    a. Charleston, South Carolina
    b. Fort Henry
    c. Fort Sumter
    d. Glorieta Pass
    e. Hampton Roads
    f. Manassas
    g. Missouri
    h. Montgomery, Alabama
    i. Nashville, Tennessee
    j. New Orleans, Louisiana
    k. Richmond, Virginia
    l. West Virginia

_____ 1. Worst possible place for a national convention.

_____ 2. Firing on this installation opened the Civil War.

_____ 3. City where the Confederate States of America was organized.

_____ 4. State that suffered most from the civil war within the Civil War.

_____ 5. Fifth border state that was produced by the war and entered the Union in 1863.

_____ 6. Battle where the Confederates were forced to withdraw from the Southwest.

_____ 7. Location of the first battle between ironclad ships.

_____ 8. Permanent capital of the Confederate government.

_____ 9. Battle where the feared rebel yell first was heard.

_____ 10. Confederacy's largest city and principal port.

_____ 11. First Confederate state capital to fall to the Union military.

_____ 12. Fort controlling access to the Tennessee River.

CHARTS, MAPS, AND ILLUSTRATIONS

1. How many votes did Lincoln receive in slave states in the election of 1860? _____

2. Describe the connection between the order in which states seceded and the percentage of the population who were slaves. _____

   _____

3. The organization of young Republicans who roused political enthusiasm by marching in huge torch-light parades in 1860 was _____.

4. The plant that served as a centerpiece of South Carolina's secession banner was

   _____.

   The location from which South Carolina soldiers fired on Fort Sumter was

   _____.

5. Give the names of the two railroads that crossed in northeast Mississippi and made Shiloh and Corinth so important militarily. _____
   and _____

MULTIPLE CHOICE

Circle the letter that best completes each statement.

1. Of the following 1860 presidential candidates, which one is paired incorrectly with a political party?
   a. Stephen A. Douglas—Democratic Party (northern)
   b. John C. Breckinridge—Southern Rights Democratic Party
   c. John Bell—Constitutional Union Party
   d. Abraham Lincoln—Democratic Party

2. South Carolina seceded on December 20, 1860, on the rationale that
   a. any state, by the act of its own convention, could withdraw from its "compact" with other states, since the states never gave away their fundamental underlying sovereignty.
   b. when each state ratified the Constitution and joined the Union, it gave away individual sovereignty.
   c. northern abolitionists were determined to tear away at the South's way of life until it was destroyed.
   d. from 1789 to 1860, southern slaveholders held the presidency two thirds of the time, and now Lincoln, a northerner, would seek to stifle the South's economy.

3. Six states to secede after South Carolina were
   a. Mississippi, Alabama, Illinois, Maryland, Georgia, Florida.
   b. Mississippi, Florida, Alabama, Georgia, Louisiana, Texas.
   c. Texas, Missouri, Georgia, Maryland, Alabama, Mississippi.
   d. Louisiana, Texas, Kentucky, Florida, Maryland, Virginia.

4. The Crittenden Compromise contained a series of proposed constitutional amendments. Which one of the following was not part of the compromise?
   a. to guarantee slavery in the states and provide federal regulation for interstate slave trade
   b. to prohibit Congress from abolishing slavery in the District of Columbia or on any federal property
   c. to compensate slaveholders who were prevented from recovering fugitive slaves
   d. to protect slavery south of latitude 36°30′ in all present and future territories

5. Lincoln's inaugural address was meant to
   a. publicly shame those states that had seceded and hopefully to prevent more states from leaving the Union.
   b. reassert his pledge to bring slavery to an end throughout all parts of the United States.
   c. keep the upper South in the Union while cooling emotions in the lower South, hoping that loyalty to the Union would reassert itself.
   d. cool tensions by officially turning over federal property within the borders of states that had seceded.

6. April 12, 1861, at Fort Sumter marked the beginning of the Civil War after
   a. the Confederacy opened fire on the fort.
   b. the fort's commander, Major Robert Anderson, opened fire on Confederate troops.
   c. Lincoln surrendered the fort to Confederate troops.
   d. half of the fort's personnel died of starvation.

7. After the events of Fort Sumter, an additional four states joined the Confederacy. They were
   a. Texas, Tennessee, Louisiana, and Virginia.
   b. Virginia, Arkansas, Tennessee, and North Carolina.
   c. Louisiana, Kentucky, Tennessee, and North Carolina.
   d. Kentucky, Virginia, Arkansas, and Texas.

8. Three slave states that were sharply divided by the war and did not secede were
   a. Kentucky, Delaware, and Tennessee.
   b. Delaware, Texas, and Maryland.
   c. Missouri, Kentucky, and Maryland.
   d. Florida, Missouri, and Kentucky.

9. Guerilla attacks often were staged by Confederate "bushwhackers" and Unionist
   a. "jayhawkers."
   b. "flappers."
   c. "redcoats."
   d. "scalawags."

10. One important advantage for the South was
    a. morale.
    b. manpower.
    c. industry.
    d. transportation.

11. In the tradition of the citizen militia company, officers and sometimes field officers (colonels and majors) were
    a. appointed by the governor.
    b. elected by generals.
    c. elected by soldiers.
    d. appointed by generals.

12. In both the Union and Confederate armies, combat casualties were higher among
    a. privates.
    b. officers.
    c. those with military experience.
    d. those without military experience.

13. During the war, the most lethal weapon, causing 80 to 90 percent of combat casualties, was the
    a. infantry rifle.
    b. sword.
    c. cannon.
    d. hand pistol.

14. The Civil War is often called the world's first "modern" war because of the role played by all of the following except
    a. railroads.
    b. cannons.
    c. telegraph.
    d. steam-powered ships.

15. Of the four methods of paying for a war—taxation, personal loans, foreign loans, and treasury notes—which is the most inflationary?
    a. taxation
    b. personal loans
    c. foreign loans
    d. treasury notes

16. At the end of 1861, the Confederacy was experiencing an inflation rate of 12 percent a month; by early 1863, it took eight dollars to buy what one dollar had bought two years earlier; just before the war's end, the Confederate dollar was worth
    a. one U.S. cent.
    b. ten U.S. cents.
    c. fifteen U.S. cents.
    d. twenty-five U.S. cents.

17. U.S. paper money originated during the Civil War and was known as
    a. blue backs.
    b. Union rounds.
    c. greenbacks.
    d. Confederate rounds.

18. The National Banking Act of 1863 authorized
    a. the chartering of state banks.
    b. the chartering of national banks.
    c. the issuing of bank notes up to 100 percent of the value of the U.S. bonds they held.
    d. the issuing of bank notes up to 50 percent of the value of the U.S. bonds they held.

19. The Confederacy's "King Cotton diplomacy" was unsuccessful, due to all of the following reasons except
    a. Bumper crops in 1859 and 1860 created a surplus of raw cotton in British warehouses and delayed the "cotton famine" until 1862.
    b. The Confederacy missed its chance, while the blockade still was weak, to ship out its cotton and store it abroad, where it could be used as collateral for loans to purchase war materials.
    c. King Cotton diplomacy contradicted Confederate foreign policy objective: to persuade the British and French governments to refuse to recognize the legality of the blockade.
    d. Refusing to be manipulated by the Confederacy, Britain developed its own cotton supply.

20. The battle of Bull Run in 1861 also was known by southerners as the battle of
    a. Manassas.
    b. Stonewall.
    c. Little Creek.
    d. Shenandoah.

21. In November 1862, Lincoln removed George B. McClellan from his command due to all of the following reasons except that McClellan
    a. was a perfectionist in a profession where nothing ever could be perfect, and his army was perpetually never quite ready to move.
    b. was afraid to take risks and he never learned that no victory can be won without risking defeat.
    c. consistently overestimated the strength of enemy forces facing him.
    d. took action without waiting for orders or permission from superiors.

22. Fort Henry and Fort Donelson were taken successfully by Union forces under the command of
    a. Ulysses S. Grant.
    b. Albert S. Johnston.
    c. Pierre G. T. Beauregard.
    d. Henry W. Hallack.

23. The battle of Shiloh was named after a
    a. fort.
    b. church.
    c. river.
    d. general.

24. After General Joseph E. Johnston was wounded, Jefferson Davis replaced him with
   a. Robert E. Lee.
   b. Edwin M. Stanton.
   c. Ulysses S. Grant.
   d. Pierre G. T. Beauregard.

ESSAY

Description and Explanation (one- to two-paragraph essay)

1. Describe the Doctrine of Secession and the northern and southern views of it.

2. Describe the Crittenden Compromise and why it failed.

3. Describe the good and bad aspects of using citizen soldiers, not professionals, in the Civil War.

4. Compare Union and Confederate financing of the Civil War.

5. Discuss what went wrong with Confederate diplomacy.

6. Describe the effects of Manassas on both the North and South.

7. Compare the personal characteristics and strengths of Generals Grant and Lee.

Discussion and Analysis (class discussion or one- to two-paragraph essay)

1. Discuss the four parties in the election of 1860, including the candidates, major issues, anything the parties and candidates had in common, and anything that was different from one party to another.

2. Discuss the balance sheet of war, including a comparison of the Union and Confederacy in population, military manpower, economic resources, military backgrounds, morale, and advantages of a defensive position.

What If (include an explanation of your position)

1. If you were a southerner in 1860, would you have supported secession? Would it make a difference if you lived in Mississippi or Missouri?

2. If you were President Lincoln, would you have sent the supplies to Fort Sumter?

3. If you were a high ranking British official, would you support the Confederacy or prefer neutrality?

Crossword Puzzle: Secession and Civil War, 1860–1862

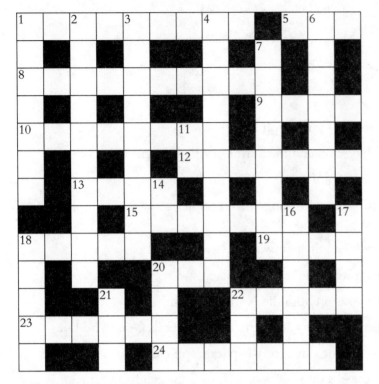

ACROSS

1. Confederate cavalry commander (2 words)
5. Johnny ___ was nickname of a Confederate soldier
8. Site of 1860 Democratic convention
9. Shiloh outcome
10. Fall behind on the march
12. Artillery attack
13. 1/28 of an ounce
15. Innovative ironclad
18. Brigade, division, ___
19. Winslow's service
20. A wound here cost Albert S. Johnston his life
22. Slidell's cellmate
23. Parts of a political platform
24. Mine to Farragut

DOWN

1. Sly one in the Shenandoah
2. Present at Sumter, Bull Run, Shiloh
3. E-mail of 1860s
4. Motion for McClellan on the Peninsula
6. Voluntary ___ of cotton hurt the South
7. Sumter's commander
11. Weight abbreviation
14. Short for a border state
16. Recruited, as in ___ a regiment
17. Union casualty at Wilson's Creek
18. "Tax in kind" allowed officials to seize ___
20. What Pope did at Second Bull Run
21. Number of terms for Confederate president
22. Strategic aid

ANSWER KEY

WHO? WHAT? WHERE?
Who Were They?

1. o. William L. Yancey, p. 520
2. g. John C. Breckinridge, p. 521
3. p. William H. Seward, p. 521
4. h. John J. Crittenden, p. 526
5. f. Jefferson Davis, p. 527
6. l. Robert Anderson, p. 529
7. k. Pierre G. T. Beauregard, p. 530
8. j. Nathaniel Lyon, p. 533
9. c. Claude Minié, p. 539
10. a. Charles Francis Adams, p. 543
11. b. Charles Wilkes, p. 544
12. q. Winfield Scott, p. 546
13. d. David G. Farragut, p. 548
14. n. Ulysses S. Grant, p. 549
15. i. Joseph E. Johnston, p. 551
16. m. Robert E. Lee, p. 553
17. e. George B. McClellan, p. 553

What Was It?

1. c. Constitutional Union Party, p. 521
2. e. National Banking Act, p. 541
3. d. cotton famine, p. 542
4. a. *Alabama*, p. 544
5. b. *Virginia*, p. 544

Where Was It?

1. a. Charleston, South Carolina, p. 519
2. c. Fort Sumter, p. 530
3. h. Montgomery, Alabama, p. 527
4. g. Missouri, p. 534
5. l. West Virginia, p. 534
6. d. Glorieta Pass, p. 534
7. e. Hampton Roads, p. 544
8. k. Richmond, Virginia, p. 546
9. f. Manassas, p. 546
10. j. New Orleans, Louisiana, p. 548
11. i. Nashville, Tennessee, p. 551
12. b. Fort Henry, p. 549

CHARTS, MAPS, AND ILLUSTRATIONS

1. none, p. 523
2. The higher the percentage, the earlier they seceded, p. 533
3. Wide-Awakes, p. 522
4. Palmetto tree, p. 525; Fort Moultrie, p. 549
5. Memphis & Charleston, Mobile & Ohio, p. 549

MULTIPLE CHOICE

1. d. (pp. 520–522)
2. a. (p. 524)
3. b. (p. 525)
4. a. (p. 526)
5. c. (p. 529)
6. a. (p. 530)
7. b. (p. 531)
8. c. (p. 533)
9. a. (p. 533)
10. a. (p. 536)
11. c. (p. 538)

12. b. (p. 539)

13. a. (p. 539)

14. b. (p. 539)

15. d. (p. 541)

16. a. (p. 541)

17. c. (p. 541)

18. b. (p. 541)

19. d. (p. 542)

20. a. (p. 546)

21. d. (p. 548)

22. a. (p. 551)

23. b. (p. 551)

24. a. (p. 553)

3. pp. 537–538

4. p. 541

5. pp. 542–543

6. pp. 546–548

7. pp. 549, 551, 553

Discussion and Analysis

1. pp. 519–522

2. pp. 535–541

What If

1. pp. 524–525, 530–531, 533

2. pp. 528–529

3. p. 542

ESSAY

Description and Explanation

1. pp. 524–525

2. pp. 526–527

Crossword Puzzle

CHAPTER 16

A NEW BIRTH OF FREEDOM, 1862–1865

By mid-1862, the war had become a "total war," requiring the mobilization and/or destruction of any resources that might bring victory or inflict defeat. Although the issue of slavery was divisive in Union areas, especially the border states, any attack on slavery would be an attack on the Confederacy and its major labor source. As the war wore on, moving against the South and its institutions became more appealing to a variety of people. Slavery became a moral, political, and diplomatic issue.

Ultimately, the outcome of the issue of slavery depended on the military situation. After the battle of Antietam, the single bloodiest day in American history, Lincoln decided to issue his preliminary emancipation proclamation. Although it was derived from his power as commander-in-chief to confiscate enemy property and could do nothing to liberate slaves under Confederate control, it essentially made the northern soldiers an army of liberation. If the North won the war, slavery would die.

At first, it was not certain that this was possible. The winter of 1862–1863 was a time of Union defeats at Fredericksburg, Vicksburg, and Stones River. The Peace Democrats were vocal in their opposition. The institution of the draft intensified social unrest in both the North and the South and, at times, produced violence. It was also a time of increased opportunities for women in employment and service as volunteers. African Americans were allowed to demonstrate their effectiveness and courage in the war effort.

Meanwhile, the war went through major campaigns at Chancellorsville, Gettysburg, Vicksburg, Chattanooga, the Wilderness, Atlanta, and the Shenandoah Valley. Increasingly, the Confederacy was losing more men and supplies than could be replaced. The southern home front collapsed, while the Union's continued to grow stronger. General U.S. Grant assumed command of the Army of the Potomac. Sherman blazed through Georgia and the Carolinas, emphasizing the reality of total war. Finally, in the spring of 1865, the last railroad into Richmond was destroyed, and the Confederacy was forced to abandon its capital. On April 9, 1865, Lee surrendered his starving, meager army to Grant's Union forces at Appomattox. Several small groups surrendered over the next few weeks. The tragedy of the American Civil War ended with another tragedy—the fatal shooting of President Lincoln at Ford's Theater. Thus, the war was over and slavery was abolished, but the shape of the new nation to come was yet to be determined.

LIBERTY, EQUALITY, POWER

The Civil War was a preeminent battle over liberty, equality, and power. The majority of southerners owned no slaves, and the official war aim was liberty, not slavery. To southerners, this meant the liberty of whites to own blacks, the ultimate failure of equality and demonstration of power. President Lincoln expressed his use of power as commander-in-chief to issue the Emancipation Proclamation. The suspension of the writ of *habeas corpus* produced more questions about the use or abuse of power during war. The introduction of the draft, with exemptions for the supervision of slaves or a commutation fee, produced the controversy of whether the war was a war of equality or a rich man's war and a poor man's fight.

The important contributions of women and African Americans elevated their position in society. The greatest change with the war came from the Emancipation Proclamation and later the Thirteenth Amendment, which abolished slavery forever in the United States. While this abolition did not settle the issues of equality or power, it did increase the liberty of a significant group of Americans. The Civil War also transferred political power from the South to the North and its economy and ideology. With the end of the fighting, more attention could be placed on the issue of equality.

OBJECTIVES

After studying this chapter, a student should be able to

1. Discuss slavery as an issue in the Civil War.

2. Describe why the Emancipation Proclamation was issued and analyze what its provisions meant.

3. Describe the Antietam campaign and the effects of it.

4. Analyze the statement that it was a "rich man's war and a poor man's fight."

5. Evaluate the role of women and African Americans in the war.

6. Trace the Union victories from the last half of 1863 to 1865.

7. Describe the final months of military action.

CHRONOLOGY

1861	Congress passed a resolution in **July**, declaring that northern war aims included no intention of "overthrowing or interfering with the rights or established institutions of the States"—meaning slavery—but intended only "to defend and maintain the supremacy of the Constitution and preserve the Union."
	Congress passed a confiscation act that authorized the seizure of all property, including slaves, that was being used for military purposes by the Confederates. Major General John C. Frémont, commander of the Union forces in Missouri, issued an order freeing the slaves of all Confederate sympathizers in the state. Because of a strong backlash, Lincoln revoked Frémont's orders in August.
1862	The blueprint for modern America was laid as Congress passed the Homestead Act, the Morrill Land-Grant Act, and the Pacific Railroad Act.
	The Confederacy enacted a draft that made all white men (with certain occupational exemptions) aged eighteen to thirty-five subject to conscription.

As a result of Lincoln's pressure, Congress passed a resolution in the spring offering federal compensation to states that voluntarily abolished slavery.

Lincoln's proposal for compensated emancipation was declined by a vote of twenty to nine by border state congressmen in **July**.

In **August**, Peace Democrats provoked antidraft riots in some localities. Federal response was to arrest rioters and antiwar activists under the president's suspension of the writ of *habeas corpus*.

Almost as many soldiers were killed in combat at the battle of Antietam as had been killed in the Revolutionary War. This Union victory gave Lincoln an occasion to issue his preliminary emancipation proclamation in **September**.

Ulysses S. Grant embarked on a two-pronged drive against Vicksburg in **November**.

The three-day battle of Stones River concluded in **December**, resulting in a Union victory. Because of devastating casualties, both sides were crippled for months.

1863

Lincoln signed the final Emancipation Proclamation as "a fit and necessary war measure" in **January**.

In **March**, Congress decreed that all male citizens aged twenty to forty-five must register for the draft, but married men over thirty-five would not be called to service.

Food supplies in the South were essentially exhausted, and bread riots broke out in several places in the **spring**.

The battle of Chancellorsville resulted in a Confederate victory, which Lee turned into a strategic offensive by invading the North in **May**.

The worst draft riot took place in **July** in New York City, where huge mobs demolished draft offices, lynched several blacks, and destroyed huge areas of the city in four days of looting and burning.

The three-day Gettysburg campaign in **July** was the greatest battle in American history. It ended with "Pickett's Charge," where less than half the men returned unwounded to their own lines. After this confrontation, the Confederates would never again have a large enough army to threaten the North.

On **July 4**, Vicksburg surrendered to Grant and on **July 9**, Port Hudson fell. The northern forces now controlled the entire length of the Mississippi River.

Also in **July**, the 54th Massachusetts Infantry, the first black regiment raised in the North, led an assault on Fort Wagner in South Carolina. The high casualties endured convinced many whites that black men who fought deserved more respect. The next year, Congress mandated equal pay for African American soldiers.

In **September**, the South abandoned Chattanooga. This cut the only direct Confederate east-west rail link. The South counterattacked at Chickamauga and drove the Union back into Chattanooga. This was followed by a Union victory at Lookout Mountain in **November**.

1864

From **May** through **June**, Union and Confederate armies under Grant and Lee maneuvered and fought in Virginia at the Wilderness, Spotsylvania, Cold Harbor, and Petersburg. After this, Grant and the Union army settled down for a lengthy siege of Petersburg.

John Bell Hood counterattacked Union forces under Sherman in the Atlanta campaign in **July**.

In **August**, George B. McClellan received the nomination for president from the Democratic Party. His platform called for immediate termination of the war.

Union troops marched into the industrial and rail city of Atlanta in **September** after Hood was forced to abandon defense of the city in order to save his army. Philip Sheridan's Union army ended Confederate control of the Shenandoah Valley with its valuable farm land.

Sherman's troops began the 280-mile "march to the sea" from Atlanta to Savannah in **November**, destroying everything in their path.

Lincoln was elected over George B. McClellan by an electoral vote of 212 to 21. Seventy-eight percent of the army vote went to Lincoln compared with 54 percent of the civilian vote.

In **November** and **December**, General Hood and his southern army invaded Tennessee, but the campaign was a disaster for the Confederates with bloody fighting at Nashville and Franklin.

1865

In **January**, a combination of Union naval and land forces put an end to blockade running into Wilmington, North Carolina, and prevented supplies from the Carolinas from reaching the Confederate army in Virginia.

In his second inaugural address, Lincoln stated in **March** that the war would not end until the Confederate armies surrendered.

Desperate for manpower, the Confederate Congress passed a bill in **March** to organize black regiments. The war ended before any such units could be established.

General Philip Sheridan's cavalry cut the last railroad into Petersburg, the rail center for Richmond, on **April 1**. The next day, Grant attacked all along the line and forced Lee to abandon both Petersburg and Richmond.

The Confederate army set fire to the military supplies remaining in the city and did more damage to the city than any Union armies had done. Sheridan's cavalry cut off Lee's starving army at Appomattox on **April 8**. Surrender formalities were completed between Generals Lee and Grant the following day.

President Lincoln was shot in the head by John Wilkes Booth at Ford's Theater on **April 14**. He died early the next day.

On **June 23**, the last Confederate army surrendered.

The Thirteenth Amendment became part of the Constitution in **December**. This abolished slavery everywhere in the United States.

GLOSSARY OF IMPORTANT TERMS

AWOL	A military term for men absent without leave.
bounty jumpers	Men who enlisted in the Union army to collect the bounties offered by some districts to fill military quotas. These men would enlist and then desert as soon as they got their money. Then they often enlisted again under a new name in a different place.
commutation fee	A $300 fee that could be paid by a drafted man to exempt him from the current draft call.
compensated emancipation	The idea that the federal government would offer compensation or money to states that voluntarily abolished slavery. Lincoln tried to introduce it in the border states on several occasions, but it was rejected.
contraband of war	The term used to describe slaves who came within the Union lines. It first was used by General Benjamin Butler in the James River area in 1861.
copperheads	A term used by some Republicans to describe Peace Democrats. It implied that they were traitors to the Union. Peace Democrats thought that the war was a failure and should be abandoned.
martial law	Government by military force rather than by citizens. It was used most often in emergency situations.
total war	The military condition requiring the total mobilization of a country's population and materials or the total destruction of the opponent's resources in order to bring victory or inflict defeat. The Civil War was the first American experience of total war.
Twenty Negro Law	The portion of the Confederate conscription law that exempted from the draft one white man on every plantation owning twenty or more slaves. The law's purpose was to exempt overseers or owners, which would ensure discipline over the slaves and keep up production. It was regarded as discrimination by nonslaveholding families.

WHO? WHAT? WHERE?

WHO WERE THEY?

Complete each statement below (questions 1–14) by writing the letter preceding the appropriate name in the space provided. Use each answer only once.

a. Abraham Lincoln
b. Benjamin Butler
c. Clara Barton
d. Clement L. Vallandigham
e. Elizabeth Blackwell
f. George B. McClellan
g. George H. Thomas
h. Horace Greeley
i. James Longstreet
j. Montgomery Blair
k. Philip Sheridan
l. Robert G. Shaw
m. William T. Sherman
n. Wilmer McLean

_____ 1. Union general who first refused to return runaway slaves who came to the Union lines.

_____ 2. He described an emancipation proclamation as "a military necessity, absolutely essential to the preservation of the Union."

_____ 3. Member of Lincoln's cabinet who did not agree with the president's emancipation ideas.

_____ 4. Union commander against Lee's invasion of Maryland. He was removed for being too slow.

_____ 5. Congressman from Ohio who was the best known Peace Democrat.

_____ 6. Most famous wartime nurse and later founder of the American Red Cross.

_____ 7. First American woman to earn an M.D.

_____ 8. General Lee's principal subordinate and 1st Corps commander in 1863.

_____ 9. Union general from Virginia known as the "Rock of Chickamauga."

_____ 10. Colonel of the first African American regiment raised in the North.

_____ 11. Editor of the *New York Tribune* who became involved in abortive peace negotiations.

_____ 12. Author of the quote "I can make the march, and make Georgia howl!"

_____ 13. Union commander whose cavalry cut off Lee's march at Appomattox.

_____ 14. Owner of the house where Lee and his remaining Confederate army officially surrendered to Grant and the Union army.

WHAT WAS IT?

Complete each statement below (questions 1–9) by writing the letter preceding the appropriate response in the space provided. Use each answer only once.

    a. compensated emancipation
    b. contraband
    c. copperhead
    d. Ford's Theater
    e. Morrill Land-Grant Act
    f. trenches
    g. Twenty Negro Law
    h. U.S. Sanitary Commission
    i. writ of *habeas corpus*

_____ 1. Slaves who came within Union lines.

_____ 2. Idea that the federal government would pay states that voluntarily abolished slavery. It was offered to the border states, but they all rejected it.

_____ 3. Order issued by a judge to law enforcement officers requiring them to bring an arrested person before the court to be charged with a crime so that the accused can have a fair trial.

_____ 4. Term used by Republicans to describe Peace Democrats as traitors.

_____ 5. Exemption to the Confederate draft law to ensure discipline over slaves and keep up production.

_____ 6. Congressional act that gave states public land to fund the establishment of colleges.

_____ 7. Most powerful voluntary association of the Civil War.

_____ 8. Technique that gave the defense an enormous advantage and made frontal assaults almost suicidal.

_____ 9. Building where a president was fatally shot.

WHERE WAS IT?

Complete each statement below (questions 1–12) by writing the letter preceding the appropriate response in the space provided. Use each answer only once.

    a. Andersonville, Georgia
    b. Antietam, Maryland
    c. Chancellorsville, Virginia
    d. Fort Pillow, Tennessee
    e. Frederick, Maryland
    f. Gettysburg, Pennsylvania
    g. Harpers Ferry, Virginia
    h. New York City, New York
    i. Petersburg, Virginia

> j. Richmond, Virginia
> k. Vicksburg, Mississippi
> l. Wilmington, North Carolina

_____ 1. Garrison town that lay across the Confederate supply line. It surrendered to Stonewall Jackson in 1863.

_____ 2. Site of the single bloodiest day in American history.

_____ 3. Location near a field where Union soldiers found a copy of Lee's deployment orders for his 1862 offensive.

_____ 4. Confederate city on the Mississippi River that allowed the South to maintain transportation lines between East and West.

_____ 5. City where a mob of over a thousand looted several shops before the militia, commandeered by Jefferson Davis, suppressed the riot.

_____ 6. Site of the worst riot associated with the northern draft law.

_____ 7. Riskiest operation of General Lee's career and a brilliant victory.

_____ 8. Agricultural and college town and the location of the greatest battle in the Civil War.

_____ 9. Industrial city and transportation center twenty miles south of Richmond where several rail lines come together.

_____ 10. Union garrison north of Memphis where scores of black and some white prisoners were slaughtered by a Confederate cavalry.

_____ 11. Confederate stockade of twenty-six acres that became notorious as the worst prisoner-of-war camp.

_____ 12. Last southern city accessible to blockade runners.

CHARTS, MAPS, AND ILLUSTRATIONS

1. Did the largest number of men in the Civil War die in prison, of disease, or from being mortally wounded in combat? _____

2. In what year did the Confederate army have the largest number of men enrolled? _____

3. One of the most successful female spies was _____.

4. How did the Confederates dispose of the dead at Andersonville? _____

5. Explain the absence of trees in the trench warfare area. _____

MULTIPLE CHOICE

Circle the letter that best completes each statement.

1. On August 30, 1861, Major General John C. Frémont issued an order freeing the slaves of all Confederate sympathizers in
   a. Missouri.
   b. Kentucky.
   c. Virginia.
   d. Indiana.

2. Lincoln's decision to issue an emancipation proclamation was based on all of the following factors except
   a. a growing demand from his own party for bolder action.
   b. a rising sentiment in the army to "take off the kid gloves" when dealing with "traitors."
   c. his own sentiment regarding slavery.
   d. pressure from Democrats and border-state Unionists who supported a war against slavery.

3. By 1862, all of the following courses of action were being considered by Lincoln except
   a. no armistice, but peace negotiations.
   b. to keep fighting in the hope that, after a few more Union victories, rebels would lay down their weapons and the Union could be restored.
   c. to officially recognize the Confederacy as a separate country.
   d. to deploy a total war in order to mobilize all northern resources and to destroy all the resources of the South—including slavery.

4. The single bloodiest day in American history, with 23,000 casualties, occurred during the battle of Antietam, which is known by Confederates as the battle of
   a. Sharpsburg.
   b. Potomac.
   c. South Mountain.
   d. Bull Run.

5. All of the following statements are tied correctly to the Emancipation Proclamation except
   a. The proclamation exempted the border states, plus Tennessee and those portions of Louisiana and Virginia that were already under Union occupation.
   b. The proclamation helped liberate slaves in areas under Confederate control.
   c. The proclamation turned the war into a northern fight for freedom as well as a fight for the Union.
   d. Lincoln's authority derived from his powers as commander-in-chief.

6. By the spring of 1863, it was increasingly difficult for the southern economy to produce weapons and dietary staples due to all of the following reasons except
   a. enemy occupation of some of the South's prime agricultural areas.
   b. the escape of slaves to Union lines.

    c. the deterioration of southern railroads and priority given to army shipments.

    d. catastrophic rains in the summer of 1862.

7. People who enlisted in the army for an initial stipend, deserted after being paid, and enlisted again under another name elsewhere in order to get more money were called
    a. bounty jumpers.
    b. rogues.
    c. bluecoats.
    d. magnates.

8. Both the Union and Confederate armies were made up of
    a. men from the upper crust of society, which amounted to 10 percent of the population.
    b. men from all strata of society in proportion to their percentage of the population.
    c. men from the lower and middle classes, which represented 45 percent of the population.
    d. slaves and former slaves, which represented 30 percent of the population.

9. Those who escaped the draft by departing secretly to the woods, the territories, or Canada were mostly
    a. poor.
    b. wealthy.
    c. middle class.
    d. former slaves.

10. The Homestead Act, passed in 1862, granted a farmer
    a. 20 acres for every two children.
    b. 160 acres of land after he had made improvements and lived on it for five years.
    c. 50 acres per dozen head of cattle.
    d. 100 acres of land after he had lived on it for one year.

11. The Pacific Railroad Act
    a. granted money to railroad companies to build a transcontinental railroad from Charleston to San Francisco.
    b. granted land to railroad companies to build a transcontinental railroad from Omaha to San Francisco.
    c. granted land and loans to railroad companies to build a transcontinental railroad from Omaha to Sacramento.
    d. granted land, loans, and materials to railroad companies to build a transcontinental railroad from Houston to Seattle.

12. The war accelerated the entry of women into all of the following occupations except
    a. teaching.
    b. bookkeeping.
    c. factory work.
    d. army clerking.

13. "Pickett's Charge" was part of the
    a. Gettysburg campaign.
    b. Vicksburg campaign.
    c. Sharpsburg campaign.
    d. Atlanta campaign.

14. All of the following statements are true of the 1862 black Union regiments except
    a. They served as labor battalions, supply troops, and garrison forces.
    b. They were paid less than white soldiers.
    c. Their officers were white.
    d. They served as front-line combat troops.

15. The Thirteenth Amendment to the Constitution
    a. abolished slavery.
    b. protects free speech.
    c. forbids unreasonable search and seizure.
    d. deals with naturalization.

16. At the crossroads of Spotsylvania Courthouse, Confederates fought, using the tactic of
    a. encircle and converge.
    b. creating an elaborate network of trenches.
    c. using the cavalry to distract the enemy while the main army charges.
    d. advancing thirty paces, retreating five paces, and holding the position.

17. The battlefield victory that had a strong impact on northern voters in the election of 1864 was the capture of
    a. Richmond.
    b. Atlanta.
    c. New Orleans.
    d. Vicksburg.

18. By 1864, prisons on both sides became death camps due to all of the following except
    a. exposure of northern prisoners to the heat of a Deep South summer and southern prisoners to the cold of a northern winter.
    b. inadequate medical facilities and rations.
    c. overcrowding, poor nutrition, and contaminated water.
    d. the use of gas chambers.

19. On April 14, 1865, Lincoln was fatally shot at Ford's Theater by
    a. John Wilkes Booth.
    b. Edwin Booth.
    c. Benedict Arnold.
    d. an unknown assassin.

ESSAY

Description and Explanation (one- to two-paragraph essay)

1. Describe the Confederate difficulties involved in the Maryland invasion.

2. Describe the weaknesses and problems of the Confederate economy by 1863.

3. Describe the effects of the Civil War on the role of women.

4. Describe how the military situation affected the election of 1864.

5. Describe the Gettysburg campaign.

Discussion and Analysis (class discussion or one- to two-paragraph essay)

1. Discuss the changing views that turned northern opinions about the Civil War into a war against slavery. Why did Lincoln finally decide on the move against slavery? What were the three possible courses of action, and what was the legal basis for his power?

2. Discuss the draft laws and how they intensified social unrest and turned this unrest in the direction of class conflict. Was it neither a rich man's war nor a poor man's fight?

3. Describe the effects of using African American soldiers both at the time of the Civil War and over the longer term. How did using these soldiers affect the prisoner-of-war issue?

4. After studying Chapters 15 and 16, describe which Union or Confederate commander you would prefer to have served under. Why did you select this leader? What battle would you consider to be the most important?

What If (include an explanation of your position)

1. If you were president of the United States would you make the same decision that Lincoln did about slavery?

2. If you were of military age during the Civil War, would you volunteer for military service or be drafted? Would it be different if you were a Confederate or Union supporter, poor or wealthy?

3. If you were an African American living in South Carolina in 1865, describe your view of the Civil War and its possible effects on your life.

Crossword Puzzle: A New Birth of Freedom, 1862–1865

ACROSS

1. Gettysburg grove of second day
7. Lee's men once in Maryland
8. Phony deserters was one of the ___ in Bragg's bag
9. Part of Lee's army
10. Vicksburg victor
12. Target for Sheridan in the Shenandoah
14. Illumination for Stonewall's last ride
15. Vallandigham's state
16. Pricey preservative in Confederacy
18. What soldiers did with hardtack
19. Fought over farm land near 1 across
20. Group subject to conscription
21. Omaha–Sacramento links
22. Confederate general who raided outskirts of Washington, D.C., in 1864

DOWN

1. Yankee at Andersonville (3 words)
2. Three words from Lincoln's second inaugural address
3. Exempted ones from Confederate conscription
4. Salmon P. Chase's concern was what the war was ___
5. Shoot-out at Sharpsburg, September 1862
6. Lincoln on Rosecrans after Chickamauga: "Like a ___ head" (4 words)
11. Border states answer to gradual emancipation
13. What Lincoln felt toward no southerner according to second inaugural address
17. Former U.S. president elected to Confederate Congress
20. Lee on Pickett's Charge: "___ fault"

ANSWER KEY

WHO? WHAT? WHERE?

Who Were They?

1. b. Benjamin Butler, p. 561
2. a. Abraham Lincoln, p. 562
3. j. Montgomery Blair, p. 562
4. f. George B. McClellan, pp. 563–564
5. d. Clement L. Vallandigham, p. 567
6. c. Clara Barton, p. 570
7. e. Elizabeth Blackwell, p. 571
8. i. James Longstreet, p. 575
9. g. George H. Thomas, p. 578
10. l. Robert G. Shaw, p. 580
11. h. Horace Greeley, p. 587
12. m. William T. Sherman, p. 590
13. k. Philip Sheridan, p. 593
14. n. Wilmer McLean, p. 593

What Was It?

1. b. contraband, p. 561
2. a. compensated emancipation, p. 561
3. i. writ of *habeas corpus*, p. 562
4. c. copperhead, p. 562
5. g. Twenty Negro Law, p. 568
6. f. Morrill Land-Grant Act, p. 570
7. h. U.S. Sanitary Commission, p. 571
8. d. trenches, p. 585
9. e. Ford's Theater, p. 594

Where Was It?

1. g. Harpers Ferry, Virginia, p. 563
2. b. Antietam, Maryland, p. 564
3. e. Frederick, Maryland, pp. 563–564
4. k. Vicksburg, Mississippi, p. 577
5. j. Richmond, Virginia, p. 568
6. h. New York City, New York, p. 569
7. c. Chancellorsville, Virginia, p. 573
8. f. Gettysburg, Pennsylvania, p. 574
9. i. Petersburg, Virginia, p. 585
10. d. Fort Pillow, Tennessee, p. 588
11. a. Andersonville, Georgia, p. 588
12. l. Wilmington, North Carolina, p. 592

CHARTS, MAPS, AND ILLUSTRATIONS

1. disease, p. 594
2. 1864, p. 594
3. Rose O'Neal Greenhow, p. 572
4. buried them in long trenches, p. 588
5. They were cut down to provide firewood and create open fields of fire, p. 585

MULTIPLE CHOICE

1. a. (p. 561)
2. d. (p. 561)
3. c. (p. 562)
4. a. (p. 564)
5. b. (pp. 564–565)
6. d. (p. 567)
7. a. (p. 569)
8. b. (p. 570)
9. a. (p. 570)
10. b. (p. 570)
11. c. (p. 570)

12. d. (p. 570)

13. a. (p. 576)

14. d. (p. 579)

15. a. (p. 583)

16. b. (p. 585)

17. d. (p. 589)

18. d. (p. 588)

19. a. (p. 594)

ESSAY

Description and Explanation

1. pp. 563–564

2. pp. 567–568

Crossword Puzzle

3. pp. 570–572

4. pp. 589–590

5. pp. 574–576

Discussion and Analysis

1. pp. 561–562

2. pp. 568–570

3. pp. 579–580, 587–588

4. Chapters 15 and 16 *passim*

What If

1. pp. 561–562

2. pp. 566–571

3. Chapter 16 *passim*

CHAPTER 17

RECONSTRUCTION, 1863–1877

Reconstruction was a traumatic period of transition for many Americans. Concerns focused on the identity of the newly reconstructed union and the roles of the various groups in it. Significant controversy surrounded which branch of the government, the presidency or Congress, would control Reconstruction and the new union. Each president of the period, Abraham Lincoln, Andrew Johnson, and Ulysses S. Grant, handled the issues differently. Their actions, along with their respective struggles with members of Congress, had lasting effect.

Another controversy surrounded the rights of former slaves, now freedpeople, and the role of their former owners in the postwar South. National discussions about African Americans focused on race in both the former Confederate and former Union areas. These discussions often ended in violence or confusion, ultimately leading to the drafting and ratification of constitutional amendments that defined citizenship and its rights. State governments could not abridge the rights of citizens without due process; and African Americans legally were entitled to vote in all states. In practice, however, they often were intimidated and lacked the financial resources to maintain their new position successfully.

Gradually, the public shifted its attention to other controversial issues, including civil service reform, currency, labor unrest, and corrupt elections. Reconstruction ended as a result of the disputed election of 1876, during which a compromise was reached. Rutherford B. Hayes was inaugurated as president and acted quickly to remove federal troops from the South, leaving white southerners in control of the former Confederate states. In other parts of the country, most people reacted with indifference. They wanted to move on to other matters, leaving behind the issues of Reconstruction and race. African Americans were left without a protector, and they gradually lost most of the rights they gained during Reconstruction.

LIBERTY, EQUALITY, POWER

Power is often the critical variable in determining which contending group gets what, and it is often necessary to ensure liberty and equality. This is reflected in the Reconstruction era, with systems of patronage, including the spoils system. To provide conditions for the liberty and equality of former slaves to thrive, for example, the federal government had to assert new powers to combat Black Codes and bulldozing. The powers the federal government adopted ranged from martial law to constitutional amendments (the Thirteenth, Fourteenth, and Fifteenth Amendments) to the creation of the Freedmen's Bureau.

Though Reconstruction was a qualified success, the idea of the strong state as a guarantor of liberty and equality lived on, as we shall see, in the social movements of farmers, workers, feminists, and minorities, and in the politics of liberal reform (Populism, Progressivism, the New Deal, the Great Society) from the 1890s through the 1960s.

OBJECTIVES

After studying this chapter, a student should be able to

1. Compare presidential Reconstruction under Lincoln and Johnson with congressional Reconstruction.

2. Describe life and labor in the South after the Civil War for whites and African Americans.

3. Discuss the purposes, provisions, and results of the three Reconstruction amendments to the Constitution.

4. Analyze the Grant administration.

5. Examine Reconstruction in the South from both the southern and northern points of view.

6. Describe the election of 1876 and compromise of 1877.

CHRONOLOGY

1862–1863   Lincoln advocated that freedpeople immigrate to all-black countries, such as Haiti, where they could advance their lives without experiencing the prejudice of whites.

1863   Lincoln issued his Proclamation of Amnesty and Reconstruction in **December**, which offered a presidential pardon to most southern whites who took an oath of allegiance to the United States.

1864   Union troops controlled considerable portions of the Confederate states of Louisiana, Arkansas, and Tennessee.

Both houses of Congress approved the Wade-Davis Reconstruction bill in **July**. This bill levied such strict loyalty requirements on southern whites that few of them could take the required oath. Lincoln vetoed it.

Andrew Johnson of Tennessee was nominated as Lincoln's running mate to procure support from War Democrats and border-state Unionists.

1865   General William T. Sherman issued a military order in **January** setting aside thousands of acres of abandoned plantation land in Georgia and South Carolina for settlement by freed slaves. However, President Johnson's Amnesty Proclamation restored most of the property to pardoned ex-Confederates.

In **March**, Congress established the Freedmen's Bureau to supervise relations between former slaves and owners. The bureau established posts throughout the South to oversee wage contracts and to circulate food rations.

Lincoln was assassinated by John Wilkes Booth in **April**, and Andrew Johnson succeeded him as the seventeenth president of the United States.

In **May**, President Johnson issued two proclamations that exposed his intentions of excluding both blacks and upper-class whites from the Reconstruction process and establishing yeomen whites as the backbone of the new South.

Republicans began public criticism of President Johnson's special pardons, which restored property and political rights to 13,500 ex-Confederates.

Individual southern states enacted Black Codes.

1866   Congress passed two laws to protect the economic and civil rights of freedpeople, but Johnson vetoed the laws.

In **February**, Johnson denounced Republican leaders as traitors who did not want to restore the Union except on terms that would degrade white southerners.

Congress passed the Freedmen's Bureau and Civil Rights bills, with more than a two-thirds majority in both houses, over the president's vetoes.

The Fourteenth Amendment was proposed.

1867   Congress enacted two laws, over Johnson's vetoes, directing new procedures for the full restoration of the former Confederate states. These acts divided the southern states into five military districts, ordered army officers to register voters for the election of delegates to the new constitutional conventions, and enfranchised males twenty-one and older (including blacks) to vote in those elections.

President Johnson tried to stop the Reconstruction process by placing Democrats in command of southern districts, interpreting the acts contrary to the intention of Congress, and encouraging southern whites to use tactics to defer the registration of voters and the election of convention delegates.

1868   Johnson ensured his impeachment in **February** by removing from office Secretary of War Edwin M. Stanton, who had operated the War Department in support of the congressional Reconstruction policy. This removal appeared to violate the Tenure of Office Act.

In **May**, Republican senators fell one vote short of the necessary two-thirds majority required to remove Johnson. Several moderate Republicans were apprehensive that such a precedent might tip the balance of powers.

The Ku Klux Klan made its initial political appearance during the 1868 elections.

1870   Missionary societies concentrated heavily on making higher education accessible to African Americans.

The Fifteenth Amendment was ratified, which prohibited states from denying individuals the right to vote on the basis of race, color, or previous condition of servitude.

1870–1871	Congress enacted three laws intended to enforce the Fourteenth and Fifteenth Amendments. These laws made interference with voting rights a federal offense.
1871	Secretary of State Hamilton Fish negotiated the Treaty of Washington, which settled the Alabama Claims and the status of Canada.
1873	A Wall Street panic plunged the economy into a five-year depression.
1874	Democrats made large gains in congressional elections, winning a majority in the House of Representatives for the first time in eighteen years.
1875	The Mississippi Plan, using economic pressure, threats, and violence to influence elections, was introduced.
	Congress passed a civil rights act banning racial discrimination in public transportation and accommodations. In 1883 the Supreme Court declared the act to be unconstitutional.
1876	The Supreme Court ruled that parts of the 1870–1871 laws for enforcement of the Fourteenth and Fifteenth Amendments were unconstitutional because the federal government could not prosecute individuals.
	As a reaction to widespread corruption, both Democrats and Republicans selected reform governors as their candidates for president. There were extensive economic coercion, threats, and violence. The very close elections produced disputed returns in three states and caused questions about which party won the presidency.
1877	The electoral commission issued its ruling regarding the 1876 disputed election results and declared Rutherford B. Hayes president in **February**.
	Hayes was inaugurated as president peacefully in **March** as a result of a compromise between northern Republicans and some southern Democrats.
	In **April**, the withdrawal of federal troops constituted both a symbolic and actual end of the twelve-year postwar era known as Reconstruction.

GLOSSARY OF IMPORTANT TERMS

amnesty	A general pardon granted to a large group of people.
appellate jurisdiction	A court with the power to hear appeals and review decisions of other courts.
Black Codes	Laws passed by southern states that defined the rights of former slaves and addressed black-white relationships. In general, these laws excluded blacks from juries and the ballot box and generally discriminated on racial grounds.
bulldozing	Using force to keep African Americans from voting.

carpetbaggers	A term that referred to northerners who settled in the South during Reconstruction.
Credit Mobilier	The construction company for the Union Pacific Railroad. It gave shares of stock to some congressmen in return for favors.
Era of Good Stealings	A term used to describe the explosion of corruption in the years after the Civil War.
felony	A major crime.
Fenian Brotherhood	An Irish-American secret society that believed an invasion of Canada would help bring independence to Ireland.
filibuster	Congressional delaying tactic involving lengthy speeches that prevent legislation from being enacted.
forty acres and a mule	The dream of many former slaves that they would receive free land from the confiscated property of ex-Confederates. Only a few areas gave them land. Most ex-Confederates got their plantations back through general amnesty programs, or they received a special pardon from President Johnson.
franchise	The right to vote. **Enfranchise**: To give or allow a group the right to vote. **Disfranchise**: To take away the right to vote.
Freedmen's Bureau	A federal agency created in 1865 to supervise newly freed people. It oversaw relations between whites and blacks in the South, issued food rations, and supervised labor contracts.
habeas corpus	The right of an individual to obtain a legal document as protection against illegal imprisonment.
impeach	To charge government officeholders with misconduct in office. In the case of the president, the House of Representatives brings the charges; the Senate serves much like a jury, and the members of the Supreme Court preside. The removal (impeachment) of a president requires a two-thirds vote by the Senate.
levee	An earthen dike or mound, usually along the banks of rivers, used to prevent flooding.
martial law	Government by a military force rather than by civilians. Most often, it was used in emergency situations.
monopoly	An individual or company having exclusive control of a service or item sold in the marketplace or having enough control to establish the price of the item.
patronage	Government jobs given out by political figures to their supporters, regardless of ability.
quasi slavery	A position that resembled slavery. Some northerners thought the Black Codes created a type of quasi slavery.

rolling stock	Locomotives, freight cars, and other types of wheeled equipment owned by railroads.
scalawags	Term used by southern Democrats to describe southern whites who worked with the Republicans.
share wages	The payment of workers' wages with a share of the crop rather than with cash.
sharecropping	Working land in return for a share of the crops produced instead of paying cash rent. Shortage of currency in the South made sharecropping a frequent form of land tenure. African American families preferred it because it eliminated the labor gangs used in the days of slavery.
southern yeoman	A farmer who owned relatively little land and few or no slaves.
spoils system	A system by which the victorious political party rewarded its supporters with government jobs.
union leagues	Organizations that informed African American voters of, and mobilized them to, support the Republican Party.
universal male suffrage	A system that allows all adult males to vote without regard to property, religious, or race qualifications or limitations.
vagrant	A person who wanders from place to place and has no occupation or visible means of support.

WHO? WHAT? WHERE?

WHO WERE THEY?

Complete each statement below (questions 1–12) by writing the letter preceding the appropriate name in the space provided. Use each answer only once.

a. Adelbert Ames
b. Alexander H. Stephens
c. Charles Sumner
d. David Key
e. Edwin M. Stanton
f. George W. Curtis
g. Hamilton Fish
h. Jay Cooke
i. Nathan Bedford Forrest
j. Thaddeus Stevens
k. Thomas Nast
l. Samuel J. Tilden

_____ 1. Congressman from Pennsylvania and leader of the Radical Republicans.

_____ 2. One of the principal exponents of the Radical Republicans in the Senate and a leading advocate of civil rights for blacks.

_____ 3. Secretary of war, under whose leadership the War Department supported congressional Reconstruction. He was removed from office by President Johnson.

_____ 4. High-ranking Confederate general who became an official in the Ku Klux Klan.

_____ 5. Important reformer who was appointed by President Grant to head a civil service commission.

_____ 6. Secretary of state under President Grant who negotiated with Britain to end the Alabama Claims dispute.

_____ 7. Prominent political cartoonist who could influence national elections with his incisive cartoons.

_____ 8. Leader of the banking firm that helped finance the Civil War and the building of the Northern Pacific Railroad.

_____ 9. Reconstruction governor of Mississippi who asked for federal troops to control the violence in his state and was refused by Grant for political reasons.

_____ 10. Vice president of the Confederacy who was elected to Congress in Georgia during the first days of Reconstruction.

_____ 11. Democratic governor of New York who was the unsuccessful candidate for president in the disputed election of 1876.

_____ 12. Ex-Confederate from Tennessee who became postmaster general as part of the Compromise of 1877.

WHAT WAS IT?

Complete each statement below (questions 1–10) by writing the letter preceding the appropriate response in the space provided. Use each answer only once.

a. American Equal Rights Association
b. Civil Rights Cases
c. Fifteenth Amendment
d. Fourteenth Amendment
e. Mississippi Plan
f. Proclamation of Amnesty
g. Reconstruction Acts of 1867
h. spoils system
i. Tenure of Office Act
j. Thirteenth Amendment

_____ 1. Bill passed over presidential veto that required the consent of the Senate before removing officeholders approved by the Senate. President Johnson was accused of violating this act.

_____ 2. Prohibited states from denying the right to vote on the grounds of race, color, or previous condition of servitude.

_____ 3. Organization working for both black and woman suffrage.

_____ 4. Bill that divided the ten southern states into five military districts, directed army officers to register voters, enfranchised males of both races who were over age twenty-one, and disfranchised certain ex-Confederates.

_____ 5. Gave United States citizenship to all native-born or naturalized persons and prohibited states from depriving any person of life, liberty, or property without due process.

_____ 6. This document offered a presidential pardon to southern whites, with a few exceptions, who took an oath of allegiance to the United States and accepted the abolition of slavery.

_____ 7. Combination of economic pressure and physical intimidation (from the threat of violence to actual violence) to force black and white supporters of the Republican Party in southern states to vote Democratic or stay away from the polls.

_____ 8. Glue that kept the party faithful together when a party was out of office.

_____ 9. Decision by the Supreme Court that declared the civil rights law of 1875 unconstitutional because the Fourteenth Amendment applied only to states and not to individuals.

_____ 10. Abolished slavery everywhere in the United States.

WHERE WAS IT?

Complete each statement below (questions 1–7) by writing the letter preceding the appropriate response in the space provided. Use each answer only once.

   a. Florida
   b. Hamburg
   c. Louisiana
   d. Memphis
   e. Promontory Point
   f. South Carolina
   g. Tennessee

_____ 1. One of the states with disputed returns in the 1876 presidential election.

_____ 2. City where race riots took place during Reconstruction.

_____ 3. First ex-Confederate state readmitted to the Union.

_____ 4. Place where the Union Pacific and Central Pacific railroads met to form the first transcontinental railroad.

_____ 5. First area to reorganize under Lincoln's moderate plan for Reconstruction.

_____ 6. Only state where African Americans made up the majority of elective officials.

_____ 7. Small village where a battle took place between a black militia unit and white southerners.

CHARTS, MAPS, AND ILLUSTRATIONS

1. According to the map on the Hayes-Tilden election (p. 625), from which former slave states did disputed election returns come in 1876? _____

2. One state in the military district commanded by General Philip Sheridan was _____.

3. One of the illustrations shows the desperate poverty of the South after the Civil War. Which illustration was it and how does it indicate this poverty? _____

4. The generic name for the secret groups that terrorized the southern countryside was the _____. Part of their purpose was _____ _____.

MULTIPLE CHOICE

Circle the letter that best completes each statement.

1. Some northerners wanted more advances over slavery than just the recognition of freedom and a minimal provision for education. They were known as
   a. scalawags.
   b. Radical Republicans.
   c. free-thinkers.
   d. Whigs.

2. All of Lincoln's expectations for the reconstructed government in Louisiana were not realized because of all of the following except
   a. The new government would not grant literate blacks the right to vote.
   b. The new government would not grant black Union soldiers the right to vote.
   c. The new government authorized planters to enforce restrictive labor policies on black plantation workers.
   d. The new government provided a school system for blacks.

3. The Wade-Davis reconstruction bill of 1864
   a. liberated blacks—a policy that commanded a majority of Republicans.
   b. was supported by Lincoln in every aspect.
   c. was passed in the House of Representatives, but not in the Senate.
   d. imposed such strict loyalty requirements on southern whites that few were able to take the required oath.

4. To attract the votes of War Democrats and border-state Unionists in 1864, Republicans adopted the name
   a. Whig Party.
   b. Reconstruction Party.
   c. Union Party.
   d. Representative Party.

5. All of the following statements are true of Andrew Johnson except
   a. He denounced planters as "stuck-up aristocrats."
   b. He became a self-appointed spokesman for southern yeomen.
   c. He was a Democratic senator from a Confederate state who refused to support the Confederacy.
   d. His background of upper-class privileges assured him of political success.

6. Political ambitions motivated President Andrew Johnson to
   a. issue special presidential pardons for ex-Confederates, which restored their property and political rights.
   b. establish new state constitutions that prohibited ex-Confederates from holding state offices.
   c. establish new policies excluding ex-Confederates from holding national offices, such as congressional seats.
   d. issue special presidential pardons for ex-Confederates that restored all their property but not their political rights.

7. The Black Codes of 1865 did all of the following except
   a. exclude blacks from juries, voting, and testifying in court.
   b. ensure blacks were not punished more severely than whites were for crimes.
   c. ban interracial marriages and provide for the apprenticing to whites of black youths who did not have adequate parental support.
   d. exclude blacks from leasing land and, in some states, define unemployed blacks as vagrants who could be hired out to planters.

8. All but one of the following conditions describe the postwar South:
   a. Its landscape was marked by burned-out plantations, fields overgrown with weeds, and railroads without tracks.
   b. Half its livestock and most of its other tangible assets, except the land, had been destroyed.
   c. Many people, both whites and blacks, literally did not know from where their next meal would come.
   d. An increase in the numbers of marshals and other officials was necessary to prevent a collapse of law and order.

9. The Freedmen's Bureau did all of the following except
   a. establish posts throughout the North.
   b. supervise and enforce free-labor wage contracts between landowners and freedpeople.
   c. become the principal agency for overseeing relations between former slaves and former owners.
   d. issue food rations to 150,000 people daily, one third of whom were white, during 1865.

10. The Fourteenth Amendment did all of the following except
    a. define all native-born or naturalized persons as American citizens and prohibit states from denying them their rights as citizens.

    b. increase the number of congressional seats and electoral votes for each state by 2 percent.

    c. disqualify a number of ex-Confederates from holding federal or state offices.

    d. empower Congress to enforce the Fourteenth Amendment by appropriate legislation.

11. Never had a president and Congress been so bitterly at odds as in 1867 when Johnson put every roadblock he could in the way of the Reconstruction process. President Johnson took all of the following actions except to

    a. remove several Republican generals from command of southern military districts and appoint Democrats in their place.

    b. have his attorney general issue a ruling that interpreted the Reconstruction acts narrowly, and thereby force a special session of Congress to pass a supplementary act in July 1867.

    c. encourage southern whites to engage in obstructive tactics to delay the registration of voters and the election of convention delegates.

    d. encourage the Democratic Party to accept black leaders into the party with the hope that this would increase black support for the upcoming election.

12. The underlying cause of Andrew Jackson's impeachment trial was

    a. his defiance of the will of Congress on Reconstruction.

    b. his secret dealings with foreign governments, which some interpreted as treason.

    c. his public behavior, refusal to be held accountable to the American people, and rumors of bribery.

    d. his severe punishment of ex-Confederate military officers, government officers, and government officials.

13. The purpose of the Fifteenth Amendment was

    a. to grant Congress the power to lay and collect taxes on income.

    b. to extend suffrage to women.

    c. to prevent any further revocation of black suffrage by reconstructed states and to extend equal suffrage to the border states and to the North.

    d. to prohibit the manufacture, sale, or transportation of intoxicating liquors.

14. The radical wing of the suffragists opposed the Fifteenth Amendment because

    a. it required all voters to be literate.

    b. it failed to ban discrimination on the grounds of sex as well as race.

    c. it allowed all southern men to vote.

    d. it allowed all veterans to vote.

15. The increase of corruption during the period after the Civil War was due in part to all of the following factors except

    a. an increase in bureaucracy during the war, which created new opportunities for unethical individuals.

    b. the decrease of government contracts during the war.

    c. a relaxation of tensions and standards following the intense sacrifices of the war years.

    d. rapid postwar economic growth, which encouraged greed and get-rich-quick schemes.

16. Ulysses S. Grant
    a. openly supported Johnson's Reconstruction policy.
    b. was a great success as president, owing to his political experience.
    c. was a great military leader, who, by 1866, commanded greater authority and prestige than anyone else in the country.
    d. worked to cultivate supporters in the area of foreign policy.

17. "Scalawags" was a term given to individuals who participated in Reconstruction and were from the
    a. South.
    b. East.
    c. West.
    d. North.

18. The Wall Street Panic of 1873 was caused by the widespread actions of men such as Civil War financier
    a. Horace Greeley.
    b. Jonathan Gibbs.
    c. Orpheus C. Kerr.
    d. Jay Cooke.

19. During the Mississippi election of 1875, the Republican majority of 30,000 changed to the Democratic majority of 30,000. This outcome was the result of all but which of the following:
    a. economic pressures, social ostracism, and persuasive threats, which convinced the 10 to 15 percent of white voters who still called themselves Republicans to switch their allegiance to the Democratic Party.
    b. intimidation of black voters, who represented a 55 percent majority.
    c. the use of economic coercion and violence to keep black voters away from the polls.
    d. widespread bribery to entice black voters to join the Democratic Party.

20. In 1876, the term "bulldozing" came to describe Democratic techniques of intimidation. It meant to
    a. intimidate white Republican voters into voting Democratic.
    b. bribe black voters to support Democratic candidates.
    c. trample black voters or keep them away from the polls.
    d. burn down the homes of Republican candidates.

21. All of the following were part of the Compromise of 1877 except
    a. federal appropriations to rebuild war-destroyed levees.
    b. a guarantee of voting rights for all males in the South.
    c. the appointment of a southerner to the cabinet.
    d. the removal of federal troops from two southern states.

ESSAY

Description and Explanation (one- to two-paragraph essay)

1. Explain the difference between moderate and radical views on African Americans' voting.
2. Describe the destruction of the South during the Civil War.
3. Explain why President Johnson was not removed from office.
4. Explain the role of violence in the election of 1868.
5. Explain why there was so much corruption in the postwar decades.
6. Describe the African American experience in holding office.
7. List and explain the motives of northerners who moved to the South.
8. Which presidential candidate should have won the election of 1876? Explain why.

Discussion and Analysis (class discussion or one- to two-paragraph essay)

1. Compare the Reconstruction policies of Presidents Lincoln and Johnson, and analyze the possibility that either of their respective sets of policies might have been successful.
2. Study the provisions of the Fourteenth Amendment carefully. Discuss which provisions are operative at the end of the twentieth century and why this amendment is considered so important in American history. Develop at least one example of how you might use or benefit from it.

What If (include an explanation of your position)

1. If you were either an ex-Union soldier, a white southerner, or an African American living in the South, how would you view the events of the Reconstruction period?
2. If you were a senator during the impeachment trial of President Johnson, would you vote guilty or not guilty?

Crossword Puzzle: Reconstruction, 1863–1877

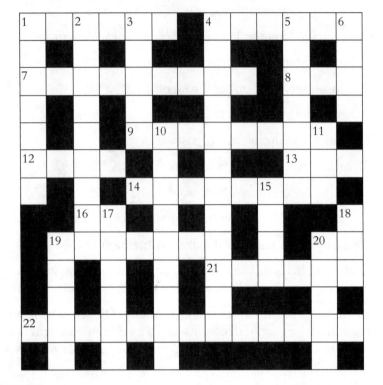

DOWN

1. What Andrew Johnson wanted to make odious
2. The 1876 presidential election returns from this state were disputed
3. Civil service reformers advocated this as a way of finding competent government workers
4. Patronage program entrenched in government since Jacksonian era
5. Arbitrators awarded $15.5 million to the U.S. in _____ claims
6. Ku Klux Klan to freedpeople
10. Trademark luggage of northerners who moved to the South
11. Implement of those carrying out the Mississippi Plan
15. Illumination for KKK
17. _____ Mobilier was a scandal involving construction of Union Pacific Railroad
18. Sharecropper's tool
19. Compromise of 1877 was the _____ act of Reconstruction
20. This vice was satirized by Twain and Warner in *The Gilded Age*

ACROSS

1. "Winner" who lost election of 1876
4. Jury at Johnson's impeachment trial
7. Reconstruction constitutions provided for this for both races in the South
8. Baba or Muhammad
9. White southern Republican
12. Home of Hayes
13. Wet dust

14. Immigrant turned Fenian
16. Short for reconstructed state
19. Sharecroppers and others
20. Ben Wade's plea to Johnson
21. 1866 act of Congress didn't provide this for Edwin M. Stanton
22. Thaddeus Stevens was a _____ _____ (2 words) of the House of Representatives

ANSWER KEY

WHO? WHAT? WHERE?

Who Were They?

1. j.   Thaddeus Stevens, p. 599
2. c.   Charles Sumner, p. 599
3. e.   Edwin M. Stanton, p. 609
4. i.   Nathan Bedford Forrest, p. 612
5. f.   George W. Curtis, p. 613
6. g.   Hamilton Fish, p. 614
7. k.   Thomas Nast, pp. 618–619
8. h.   Jay Cooke, p. 619
9. a.   Adelbert Ames, p. 621
10. b.   Alexander H. Stephens, p. 602
11. l.   Samuel J. Tilden, p. 623
12. d.   David Key, p. 626

What Was It?

1. i.   Tenure of Office Act, p. 609
2. c.   Fifteenth Amendment, p. 611
3. a.   American Equal Rights Association, p. 611
4. g.   Reconstruction Acts of 1867, p. 607
5. d.   Fourteenth Amendment, pp. 606–607
6. f.   Proclamation of Amnesty, p. 600
7. e.   Mississippi Plan, p. 620
8. h.   spoils system, p. 613
9. b.   *Civil Rights Court Cases*, p. 623
10. j.   Thirteenth Amendment, p. 602

Where Was It?

1. a.   Florida, p. 624
2. d.   Memphis, p. 607
3. g.   Tennessee, p. 607
4. e.   Promontory Point, p. 619
5. c.   Louisiana, p. 598
6. f.   South Carolina, p. 615
7. b.   Hamburg, p. 624

CHARTS, MAPS, AND ILLUSTRATIONS

1. Louisiana, South Carolina, and Florida, p. 625
2. Louisiana or Texas, p. 614
3. the lack of a work animal, p. 604
4. Ku Klux Klan; control of the black population, p. 618

MULTIPLE CHOICE

1. b.   (p. 599)
2. d.   (pp. 599–600)
3. d.   (p. 600)
4. c.   (p. 600)
5. d.   (p. 600)
6. a.   (p. 602)
7. b.   (p. 602)
8. d.   (p. 603)
9. a.   (p. 603)
10. b.   (pp. 606–607)
11. d.   (p. 608)
12. a.   (p. 609)
13. c.   (p. 611)
14. b.   (p. 611)
15. b.   (p. 613)
16. c.   (p. 611)
17. a.   (p. 616)

18. d. (p. 619)

19. d. (pp. 621–622)

20. c. (p. 624)

21. b. (pp. 625–626)

ESSAY

Description and Explanation

1. pp. 597–598

2. pp. 603–604

3. p. 609

4. pp. 611–612

5. p. 613

6. p. 615

7. p. 616

8. pp. 624–625

Discussion and Analysis

1. pp. 598–602

2. p. 606

What If

1. Chapter 17 *passim*

2. p. 609

Crossword Puzzle